The Place and the Writer

Research in Creative Writing

Series Editors:

Janelle Adsit *(Humboldt State University*, USA)
Conchitina Cruz *(University of the Philippines)*
James Ryan *(University of Wisconsin-Madison*, USA)

Showcasing the most innovative research and field-defining scholarship surrounding Creative Writing Studies, Research in Creative Writing strives to discuss and demonstrate the best practices for creative writing pedagogy both inside and out of the academy. Scholarship published in the series wrestles with the core issues at the heart of the field including critical issues surrounding the practice of creative writing; multilingualism and diverse approaches to creative production; representation and the politics of aesthetics; intersectionality and addressing interlocking oppressions in and through creative writing; and the impact of teaching established lore. Responsive to emerging exigencies in the field and open to interdisciplinary and diverse contexts for creative writing, this series is designed to advance the field and push the boundaries of Creative Writing Studies. This series benefits from the guidance of and collaboration with the Creative Writing Studies Organization (https://creativewritingstudies.com/).

Editorial board members:
Ching-In Chen *(University of Washington Bothell, USA)*
Farid Matuk *(University of Arizona, USA)*

Forthcoming titles

Craft Consciousness and Artistic Practice in Creative Writing, Benjamin Ristow
A-Z of Creative Writing Methods, edited by Francesca Rendle Short, Julienne Van Loon, David Carlin, Peta Murray, Stayci Taylor and Deborah Wardle

Related titles

Beyond Craft, Steve Westbrook and James Ryan
Imaginative Teaching, edited by Amy Ash, Michael Dean Clark and Chris Drew

The Place and the Writer

International Intersections of Teacher Lore and Creative Writing Pedagogy

Edited by Marshall Moore and Sam Meekings

BLOOMSBURY ACADEMIC
LONDON • NEW YORK • OXFORD • NEW DELHI • SYDNEY

BLOOMSBURY ACADEMIC
Bloomsbury Publishing Plc
50 Bedford Square, London, WC1B 3DP, UK
1385 Broadway, New York, NY 10018, USA
29 Earlsfort Terrace, Dublin 2, Ireland

BLOOMSBURY, BLOOMSBURY ACADEMIC and the Diana logo are trademarks of
Bloomsbury Publishing Plc

First published in Great Britain 2021
Paperback editon published 2022

Cover design: Eleanor Rose

A catalogue record for this book is available from the British Library.

A catalog record for this book is available from the Library of Congress.

ISBN: HB: 978-1-3501-2715-9
         PB: 978-1-3502-1391-3
         ePDF: 978-1-3501-2716-6
         eBook: 978-1-3501-2717-3

Series: Research in Creative Writing

Typeset by RefineCatch Limited, Bungay, Suffolk

To find out more about our authors and books visit www.bloomsbury.com
and sign up for our newsletters.

Contents

Series Preface

Creative Writing Studies (CWS) is a field that exists at the interstices of creative writing, aesthetics, fine arts, composition, rhetoric, creativity studies, critical ethnic and queer studies, and literary studies and in countries around the world is regularly housed in departments and programs such as Liberal Arts, Cultural Studies, Creative Practice, Writing Studies, and Language. While there are few courses and programs that take the name "Creative Writing Studies" explicitly, the field is practiced whenever creative writing pedagogy, aesthetic theory for writers, craft-criticism, fictocriticism are studied deliberately.

Research in Creative Writing is a new series from Bloomsbury Academic designed to advance the academic field of Creative Writing Studies by publishing field-defining scholarly manuscripts. The series wrestles with the core issues of Creative Writing Studies: What is creative writing? What insights are currently emerging at the intersection of creative writing teaching and practice? What is the relation between the practices of creative writing and the practices of social justice? How does technology influence and inform creative writing practice? What kinds of creative writing happen inside the academy, and what sort of knowledge and ways of thinking do these practices produce? What kinds of creative writing happen outside the academy, and what meaning do these practices have for their participants?

Books in this series will explore all of these questions and more in an effort to build the research conversation that accompanies creative production.

Preface

Marshall Moore and Sam Meekings

Falmouth University, UK and Northwestern University in Qatar

As one might expect from the title, Paul Engle's landmark essay "The Writer and the Place," a meditation on the origins of the Iowa Writers' Workshop, proposes that the school's serene location in the American heartland has an inspiring, enlightening effect upon the students fortunate enough to be accepted to the program. This is not merely to do with the benign atmosphere created by mellow Iowa prairies and the lazy, muddy river running through them. Something greater is at work here: Engle's hypothetical young writer should find that Iowa offers—along with bracing criticism—an alternative to the hubbub of Hollywood and the noise of New York. Freed from big-city distractions, the young writer will have ample time and space to reflect upon their work. Also on offer is community, and Engle suggests this is one of the Workshop's greatest benefits: the company of other young writers with similar dreams, aspirations, and levels of talent creates a unique environment in which the work and the writer may flourish. However, it is the idea of *place* that propels Engle's thoughts on Iowa's mystique. There is an ineffable combination of solitude and down-home American goodness to be found there, he asserts. A creative singularity. Or an exceptionalism, if we are to view the matter through the lens of today's geopolitics.

While one can today read Engle's essay and appreciate the passion he felt for the program he helped establish and the bucolic location it occupies, a contemporary scholar-practitioner might raise an eyebrow at his assertion that "[w]e do not have that intense concentration of talent in one city, as certainly exists in Paris, London, or Rome, where writers either know each other or know a good deal about each other" (1961: 5). At least in the English-speaking world, New York must surely rival London in terms of literary output. Other North American cities boast respectable literary communities as well: Los Angeles and Toronto, among many others, come readily to mind. Yet what remains unquestioned in the essay is the supposition—the article of lore, as it were, or perhaps the myth—that a location offering a combination of beauty, stillness, and cultural virtue is a writer's nirvana. In such a setting, Engle suggests, writerly reflection will lead to the process of self-discovery from which inspired creative ideas will flow.

As expatriate scholars and practitioners, our combined experience both confirms and confronts these notions of place. Marshall Moore is from the American South, a region with a strong literary tradition of its own, distinct from that of the country as a whole. Growing up in semi-rural eastern North Carolina, he was keenly aware of the difference that accompanies Southern identity in the United States. However, it took him moving to California for that regional identity to assert itself. Moving out of the country several years later, first to South Korea and then to Hong Kong, he found that the regional distinction mattered somewhat less than it had before. Overseas, he was simply American. Meanwhile, Sam Meekings is from the south coast of England, yet it was only when he moved abroad, living and working first in China and then the Middle East, that he began to notice the peculiarities and idiosyncrasies of English and British identity and how these had manifested in his educational experiences. In short, both our international experiences led us to consider the complicated relationship between practice and place.

The implications of this complex relationship, especially where lore and pedagogy are concerned, were not lost on Paul Engle when he set up the Iowa Writers' Workshop. If practice is to some extent dependent on its context, then place can also be used to bend practice to local aims. It is not for nothing that Engle has been called "the creative writing cold warrior par excellence," for as well as raising funds for the Workshop by claiming that it fought communism, Engle "recruited foreign students from around the world, brought them to Iowa City … and sent them home persuaded (he hoped and claimed) that the American way of life trumped the Soviet. His model for the workshop relegated the strident individualism of aspiring writers to the classroom while framing the workshop as a whole as a quiescent entity crucial to liberal democratic capitalistic America" (Bennett 2015: 11). Using creative writing programs for such an overtly political and ideological goal is clearly problematic for a number of reasons; and yet the workshop model still survives—indeed thrives—across the globe. Part of the impetus of this volume was therefore to examine how writers and instructors have grappled with this complicated legacy, and how they have adapted the structures and lores of the workshop model to accommodate a range of diverse perspectives and varied local contexts in contemporary creative writing classrooms. This project therefore began life as a response to Engle, encapsulated in an urgent questioning of how the relationship between lore and place has evolved in the years since "The Writer and the Place" appeared.

It was probably inevitable that questions surrounding the complex relationship between practice and place that led to this book would emerge. One line of inquiry has its origins in Ross Gibson's review of the tenth-anniversary edition of *Can Creative Writing Really Be Taught* (Vanderslice and Manery, eds.). Gibson frames the pesky question that has hovered around creative writing pedagogy since its early days—no doubt helped along by the Iowa motto that writing cannot be taught but that talent can be cultivated—as a strictly American concern. "Written by US authors ... *for* an assumed-universal US reader, *Can Creative Writing Really Be Taught?* accepts that 'the lore' is the norm and that it really matters," Gibson argues (2018). He goes on to point out that Australians are less susceptible than Americans to glorifying the sovereignty of the creative self. Down Under, tall poppies are the first to be cut. "This proportionate disregard of 'the lore' is the norm for teachers and students in the UK, Australia, New Zealand, Hong Kong, South Africa, Singapore, and Canada too, to name just some of the *Anglophone* pedagogical domains," Gibson goes on to say (2018). What then might those other lores look like? How and to what extent might cultural beliefs around writers in general manifest in writing classrooms?

In the thirty years since Kimberlé Crenshaw wrote the seminal texts on the theorization of intersectionality, the concept has encouraged both scholars and instructors to reconsider their positionality and privilege within writing classrooms. Crenshaw theorized that identification is a process, while identity is an encounter, an event; as the feminist scholar Jasbir Puar notes, "The theory of intersectionality argues that all identities are lived and experienced as intersectional ... and that all subjects are intersectional whether or not they recognize themselves as such" (2011: 2). This has key implications for creative writing classrooms. An understanding that social categorizations such as gender, race, or class are interconnected and thereby create overlapping systems of privilege or disadvantage is essential in any contemporary pedagogy. Indeed, intersectionality as a framework can and must help instructors in understanding that every student writer is necessarily affected by a number of discriminations and disadvantages, while taking into account the fact that students' overlapping identities and experiences contribute to the prejudices, experiences, and power imbalances they face.

Creative writing lore and pedagogy have not always been quick enough to respond to the historical imbalances that intersectional theory hopes to redress. As recently as 2014, Junot Díaz sparked an international discussion with his "MFA vs POC" article in *The New Yorker*, in which he described the workshop, that foundational lynchpin of creative writing lore, as fundamentally "too white," since it too often simply reproduces the dominant culture's ideas and assumptions about race and gender: "Simply put: I was a person of color in a workshop whose theory of reality did not include my most fundamental experiences as a person of color—that did not in other words include me" (2014). The widespread responses to his piece confirmed he was not alone: questions abounded over whether the literary canon used as models within writing classrooms might too narrowly conform to the cliché of dead white males; whether strictures against writing on particular subjects or using particular demotics might be rooted in preserving traditional positions of privilege; and whether different points of views and perspectives are given their due weight and respect. Lynn Domina has suggested that "classrooms today are places of marginalization" whose practices can lead to "anger at your exclusion from a culture by white people or by wealthy people or by men or by heterosexuals, who are all your classmates and/or your teacher" (1994: 33). It is precisely these kinds of experiences that the contributors to this volume are seeking to challenge in their examination of lore and pedagogy, as recounted in the forthcoming chapters. We are proud that this work therefore fits in with one of the main purposes of Bloomsbury's new series, namely to encourage inclusion and the decentering of historically dominant views and voices in creative writing.

This decentering also necessitates questioning the way in which we engage with concepts such as intersectionality. It is important to be aware of the fact that intersectionality emerged from an American context, where its new way of considering identity and privilege encouraged minority voices to question, subvert, and propose alternative perspectives to the dominant and majority narratives. However, as some of our chapters demonstrate, in more ethnically and culturally homogeneous societies such as Finland, Iceland, and South Korea, other ways of questioning dominant narratives (for example, by re-evaluating canons, pedagogies, and writing practices) have gained greater traction and local relevance. It is therefore important to note that such concepts are themselves tied to historical and geographical contexts, and thus the standard US-centric definitions of intersectionality are not always applicable or applied in other countries or academic settings. With that caveat given, it is nonetheless fundamental to consider the intersectional aspects of place in relation to the writer, especially now that creative writing programs are run by an increasing number of international universities. The relationship is necessarily a complex one, since the very concept of place is bound up with many of the structural elements of intersectional marginalization. Indeed, Rosalie Morales Kearns has suggested that many aspects of the creative writing workshop such as the gag rule are "a distinctly raced practice—specifically a Euro-American practice" (2009:

794), and so one question this volume considers is how creative writing programs and instructors must necessarily adapt to different locations, demographics, places, and experiences.

Moving beyond a Euro-American approach to creative writing education necessitates an interrogation of the connections between teaching practices and issues of cultural awareness and privilege. By examining such aspects of pedagogy and lore, this volume aims to contribute to these important areas of discussion. After all, many aspects of lore and pedagogy are deeply interconnected with issues of race, gender, class, sexuality, and ability. Topics such as appropriation, the "canon," voice and authenticity, among others, are fundamentally intertwined with questions of power imbalances and potential marginalization. These offer opportunities for reflection and analysis, as well as new challenges that any instructor should be prepared to undertake. As Janelle Adsit notes, "The creative writing class has a responsibility to take into account the effects of the cultural productions that we teach—those written by our students and those assigned on our syllabi" (2017: 308). It is precisely this responsibility that this volume examines and considers.

The chapters in this volume perform this responsibility through the analysis and dismantling of traditional hierarchies, as well as by re-evaluating positions of privilege and power. For instance, Hanna Sieja-Skrzypulec demonstrates how in Poland the deconstruction of pedagogical hierarchies, such as between mentor and mentee, in new programs has led to particularly localized form of practice, while a similar dismantling of teacher-student hierarchies in Lania Knight's chapter on her experimentation with integrating local cultural habits and extra-curricular social spaces into learning shows a comparable evolution of specifically situated practice as well as inspiring vital questions about cultural assumptions of privilege. Prioritizing diverse student identities is at the heart of many of these chapters, from Holly Thompson writing about how ESL creative writing in Japan enables students to probe their own identity and relationship to the world, to Maria Taylor explaining how reflective writing as a pedagogical tool can be utilized as a platform for students to reflect on and address their influences, such as class, gender, race, and ethnicity, and explore how these are unique to their own writing identities. In Finland, Nora Ekström demonstrates how writing programs respond to local lore in terms of writing guides and thus create conversations that interrogate ideology and national identity, while in Brazil Bernardo Bueno notes how the re-evaluation of local literary forms, in this case myths, legends, traditions, and folklore, can democratize genre and diversity in student choice. It is clear then that intersectionality manifests differently in these various places, and yet each share a focus on the work being done to decenter traditional versions of lore and to prioritize local identities and practices.

If intersectionality thus presents us with a key means of framing this discussion, we would be remiss not to point out that there are also a couple of limitations to our approach. Geography was arguably the most important of these. Certain parts of the world—the Kachruvian "inner circle" Anglosphere countries, Europe, and East Asia—are better represented here than others. Our only Latin American contributor is from Brazil, for example, and the final lineup lacks chapters from the Subcontinent and Southeast Asia, both regions whose colonial histories mean that English is widely used. Ultimately, any such lacunae are down to pragmatic matters: prospective contributors from Singapore, Malaysia, and the Philippines had to drop out for various reasons; invitations to scholars in India, Pakistan, the UAE, and elsewhere went unanswered and may not have been received at all; after our lineup had been more or less finalized, we learned of other programs in other countries, including Sweden, Norway, France, Russia, Israel, and Iran. Language, of course, presented challenges in our search. And in the end, the contracted length of the book dictated how many chapters we could include.

A quick glance at the table of contents might suggest a preponderance of Western expatriate academics, which may appear to be another limitation, at least initially. Both of this volume's editors fit that description, certainly, as do Shea, Disney, and Thompson. However, we contend that the politically loaded nature of the word "expatriate" is problematic, suggesting as it does a status of privileged white transience and seemingly foreclosing the possibility or intent of immigration. It implies choice when others do not have it and is particularly fraught for Americans, suggesting as it does a rejection of patriotism (McCormick 1997). Two of our UK-based contributors could also be termed expatriates: Knight is American; Maria Taylor is a Cypriot. To challenge the political connotations of "expatriates" a bit: any or all of the aforementioned contributors may also be viewed as *immigrants* in the countries/territories where we presently reside. From an academic standpoint, this discussion of expatriate status is essential because the term raises concerns about authenticity and colonialism. However, focusing on authenticity to the exclusion of all else prioritizes the identity of the scholar over the subject matter, suggesting an unwillingness or inability to engage with the culture; yet as can be seen in these chapters, that is precisely the opposite of what has been done. Colonialism is arguably a more relevant discussion, implying as it does an imposition by outside actors and an ensuing process of reclamation rather than an importation and adaptation by cultural insiders, a point discussed herein by Disney and Shea.

Indeed, the issue of colonialism and authenticity brings us back to the towering figure of Paul Engle and the long shadow of the Iowa Writers' Workshop. Conchitina Cruz has noted how one key program in the Philippines which follows the American workshop model utilizes "pedagogy [which] perpetuates colonialist and classist ideas about language and literary production, which are camouflaged, if not naturalized, in the name of person bonds and the service of craft" (2017: 7). This idea of craft and practice being used as a means to spread colonialist ideologies and hierarchical strictures across the globe is one our volume seeks to fight against through highlighting acts of resistance to a colonial hegemony through local and intersectional engagements. The dangers of attempting to import an American model across the world are clear, and the issues surrounding engaging with national and international models of scholarship and practice are raised by a number of the writers in this volume, whether "native," "immigrant," or "expatriate." In some senses, then, a re-engagement with and re-evaluation of national practices (such as the writing guide culture of Finland, or embedded ESL pedagogy in Japan) is part of the process of decolonizing creative writing classrooms around the world through emphasizing the situatedness of practice and the local contexts of lore in which unique and diverse bodies of students and their writing might thrive in a variety of different ways. The chapters that follow demonstrate that the global picture of contemporary creative writing programs and practices is far more complex, nuanced, and diverse than any colonial legacy might suggest. The global conversation around this topic which this volume hopes to both manifest and facilitate, depends both on prioritizing local contexts and their relationality.

In terms of order, Stephanie Vanderslice's chapter opens the book because it is nothing short of an intervention in existing creative writing scholarship. In the aforementioned *Can It Really Be Taught?*, and a decade later in the retitled second edition, Vanderslice, Ritter, and the contributors tackled the set of questions that inspired this volume: how much of creative writing pedagogy is based on teacher lore, and what strategies might we employ in order to base our classroom practices on empirical research and less on the mythologies that exist around writing? In this chapter, Vanderslice draws new distinctions between teacher lore and the mythology that surrounds writing that have perhaps been tacitly understood but have not previously been articulated in the scholarship, and this represents a profound shift in this ongoing debate.

Furthering these distinctions, one group of chapters may be viewed as discussing the challenges and peculiarities of forging a new, unique, and localized context for creative writing in (semi)isolation: in Brazil, Greece, Iceland, Finland, and Poland. Creative writing programs in these locations often find themselves caught between international lore (often in the form of the influence of the US writing workshop as an overarching model) and specific national myths and preconceptions surrounding writers and writing. Each of these chapters demonstrates that as courses grow and evolve in these locations, scholars, writers, and academics are forced to negotiate between the local and the global, and come to define themselves against what might be seen as "Western" notions of writing. The burgeoning variety of creative writing courses in these countries can thus be broadly defined as creating new solutions to the mythologies that have grown up around writing by adapting to local cultural contexts.

Another group, stretching from China and Japan to the UK and US, furthers the discussion of teaching lore by speaking to the ways in which the interpersonal and pastoral issues inherent in teaching creative writing extend beyond classroom and workshop models. These chapters answer such questions as what does it mean, for instance, to learn to write creatively in a second language, or what it might mean to engage with students' creativity in new environments, and how that might impact preconceived notions about lore? The critical analysis of issues of teacher lore thus entail a re-evaluation of how we consider and demarcate both the boundaries and borders of the subject, and our teaching of it.

Finally, a number of our chapters, from South Africa, Korea, Australia, Hong Kong, and the UK, consider the role of lore in terms of the various intersections of language, culture, and place within creative writing classrooms. The critical and creative traditions that inform our notions of writing and genre within specific locations are thus reframed as central considerations rather than fringe concerns.

Our working hypothesis when we conceived of this book was that different cultures might have different mythologies around the creative practice of writing, and these would manifest in some form or another in pedagogy. At the time, we had not yet seen the lore/mythology distinction articulated, and now that Vanderslice has done so, our perspective has shifted. When we look at these chapters in dialog with each other, something rather different emerges: rather than being beholden to mythology, creative writing pedagogy around the world appears to exhibit a robustness and flexibility in its attempts to separate skill and superstition. Teacher lore may not necessarily be a negative force within creative writing pedagogy, but rather the cumulative shared experience of instructors and practitioners. Teacher lore can be a springboard for experimentation and a passed baton that encourages continual adaptation and tweaking in individual and specific contexts, rather than something which proscribes, limits, or negates. Although academic creative writing has its challenges, particularly in countries and territories where there are only a very few programs, the issues are more to do with its newness as a discipline than with contamination by mythology. The fact that creative writing teachers continue to seek their own culturally appropriate ways to adapt existing pedagogical models would seem to bear this assertion out. As Vanderslice notes so presciently: "The future of creative writing is a moving target. If we hope to give our students the tools to succeed and sustain themselves as writers beyond the university, as professors and researchers, we must continually move with it" (2016: 604). In short, what unites this diverse range of voices and approaches to the issue of lore, then, is in highlighting the various possibilities inherent in the adaptation and adaptability of classroom models for a variety of cultures and needs.

References

Adsit, J. (2017), "The Writer and Meta-Knowledge about Writing: Threshold Concepts in Creative Writing," *New Writing: The International Journal for the Practice and Theory of Creative Writing*, 14 (3), 308.

Bennett, E. (2015). *Workshops of Empire: Stegner, Engle, and American Creative Writing during the Cold War*, Iowa City: University of Iowa Press.

Crenshaw, K. (1989), "Demarginalizing the Intersection of Race and Sex: A Black Feminist Critique of Antidiscrimination Doctrine, Feminist Theory and Antiracist Politics," *The University of Chicago Legal Forum Volume: Feminism in the Law: Theory, Practice and Criticism*, 149.

Cruz, C. (2017), "The (Mis)Education of the Filipino Writer: The Tiempo Age and Institutionalized Creative Writing in the Philippines," *Kritika Kultura*, 28.

Díaz, J. (April 30, 2014). "MFA vs POC," *The New Yorker*.

Domina, L. (1994) "The Body of My Work is Not Just a Metaphor," in W. Bishop and H. Ostrom (ed.), *Colors of a Different Horse: Rethinking Creative Writing Theory and Pedagogy*, Urbana, IL, NCTE, 33.

Engle, P. ([1961] 1999), "The Writer and the Place," in R. Dana (ed.), *A Community of Writers: Paul Engle and the Iowa Writers' Workshop*, Iowa City: University of Iowa Press.

Gibson, R. (2018), "Unloreful," *TEXT*, April: 22 (1). Available online: http://www. textjournal.com.au/april18/gibson_rev.htm (accessed December 10, 2019).

Kearns, R. M. (2009), "Voice of Authority: Theorizing Creative Writing Pedagogy," *College Composition and Communication*, 60:4, 794.

McCormick, J. (1997), "Patriots, Expatriates, and Scoundrels," *The Sewanee Review*, Summer: 105 (3): 341–55.

Puar, J. (2011), "I Would Rather Be a Cyborg Than a Goddess: Intersectionality, Assemblage, and Affective Politics," *European Institute for Progressive Cultural Policies*, 2.

Vanderslice, S. (2016), "Beyond the Tipping Point: Creative Writing Comes of Age," *College English*, 78:2, 602–13.

Foreword: The Kinship in Creative Writing

Graeme Harper
Oakland University

Consuming the Literary

A wonderful strain of contemporary consumer theory was born from Colin Campbell's 1987 book *The Romantic Ethic and the Spirit of Modern Consumerism*. Campbell's argument is that our modern consumer culture began in the eighteenth century when the English middle class began to read novels. According to Campbell, we modern consumers, discovering the pleasure of reading novels, soon became enthusiastic devotees of hedonism, of emotionalism, and of creative self-expression. From the eighteenth century on, individuals were considered to be able to shape their life experiences in ways not previously acknowledged, taking into account positive human feeling not simply practical need and pressing utility. Pleasure in the consumption of novels led to the pursuit of pleasure in the consumption of other goods and services, so Campbell's argument goes. Foundationally, it was through the joys of consuming imaginative literature that today's modern consumer emerged.

At first glance, a comparative examination of creative writing lore in higher education seems equally bound up in our enthusiasm for consuming the literary. In other words, the literary marketplace of one nation or another defines the loral conditions of teaching and learning creative writing, and our individual course and program successes (and failures) reflect local abilities to more or less tap into the contemporary consumer enthusiasm for consuming literature (and more broadly, creative works in a wide variety of media). In fact, our kinship in and through teaching and learning creative writing is less mercantile than this, more visceral, less a case of vending and more a case of consociating, connecting, and sharing. "Lore" can mean "traditions" and it can refer to "knowledge"—the two ideas are not identical.

Quite naturally, when faced with questions about what to teach, and about how to teach, we human beings turn to the nature of the things that we do, that we think, and that we believe. It is plainly so because, in taking on the role of passing on knowledge, often between generations, and frequently for the purposes of developing societally significant understanding or skills relevant to our culture or to an economy, we confront the types and range of knowledge that any act of teaching and learning might entail, and the ways in which selected knowledge might best be conveyed to others.

Educational traditions do of course influence us in this process of selection and delivery of knowledge (and lore, as we all know, can be defined as the types and styles of knowledge)—whether those are related to the development of disciplinary paradigms, determined and persisting over time, or to the wider culture (such things, for example, as the role of its older members as mentors and guides, or of one or other gender, or to the societal status of educators). Institutional contexts play their role too, lore being impacted upon by politics, the economy, their singular status comparative to other institutions, and the real or perceived status of particular disciplines within those institutions—the early twenty-first-century focus on science, technology, engineering and math (STEM) subjects is a clear example of this. However, in spite of all that, in essence we individually, and as any disciplinary-specific group, draw on what we do, on what we think, and on what we believe to determine what and how we teach. So it is with the teaching and learning of creative writing.

Creative Writing Institutionally

D. G. Myers (1996), Mark McGurl (2009), and Michelene Wandor (2008), among a relatively small number of others, offer histories of creative writing in higher education—the first two concerning the USA and the latter concerning Great Britain. Their analyses provide an excellent starting point for a consideration of institutional stories. They are not—and largely don't claim to be—a history of actual creative writing teaching and learning practices, though they do reflect upon lore (meaning here, the appearance and operation of traditions).

Similarly, immersing ourselves in the records of the birth and evolution of the Association of Writers and Writing Programs (AWP) in the USA and the National Association of Writers in Education (NAWE) in Britain provides evidence of why and how writers banded together, as educators, as artists at work largely in education. Here we find something of the group motivations, the challenges that brought those into being, the ways such professional associations have sought to be the voice of writers in colleges and schools, to support common goals around academic standing, resourcing, even around recognition of writing practice as a contributor to what is considered the worthy outputs of educational institutions. Likewise in the case of the Australasian Association of Writers and Writing Programs (AAWP) in Australia and New Zealand and, more recently, the Canadian Creative Writers and Writing Programs (CCWWP) in Canada and the European Association of Creative Writing Programmes (EACWP) in continental Europe.

Together with the histories of a few other national or regional organizations, institutional histories and organizational records provide a roadmap of the creation and formalization of creative writing lore as tradition and its influencing of formal education. Education, that is, that results in accepted "qualifications" and the development and, ultimately, official confirmation (by the awarding of a degree) of a range of largely disciplinary skills, in this case in the field of creative writing. What we value about literature and what we value about creative writing have often been connected in and through such formal educational lore. They have been connected in the sense that our valuing of literature culturally and commercially have gone hand-in-hand, regardless of the distain for popular culture seen in certain periods of education—whereby higher education, of all the levels of education, primarily touted high cultural forms—meaning only certain types of literature were found in college courses. This was the associating of higher learning with what was considered discerning taste, with advanced understanding, and with superior values, separating what happened in academe from the less salubrious tastes and activities of the "uneducated masses" beyond it. So the story goes! Popularity, therefore, was not a good measure of worth. The role of the university was to show and tout what was *truly* worthy, regardless of popularity—in that sense, against the uneducated, unaware, or simply brutish measures that might exist beyond academe.

The connections made in this regard include the role of the university as a patron of the arts—supporting what is not supported by the market beyond. Similarly, here in academe art forms such as poetry could (and can) be practiced and appreciated, even if those beyond academe do not have the education that encourages them to buy works of poetry. Paradoxically, because the results of writers' work is valued both in its material form and in its dream form (as Campbell notes, the imagination is key) even when popular culture was unpopular in higher education, *any* creative act (creative writing included) has been bound to the transcendence perceived to be offered in our highest human forms of education. Creativity has thus been seen as essential to the foundation and evolution of quality education and though academe's critical professorial voices, over time, have lamented that the imagination was weak or ill—founded or unsophisticated in the production of popular works, the human imagination has nevertheless been touted, first and foremost.

We have also seen what we value in literature and what we value in creative writing connected in education through a direct appreciation and promotion of individual authorship. In part, this appreciation is a simple celebration of human creativity. An author is perceived as an example of the inventive capacity of *all* humankind. Authoring also deals in encoded knowledge, the production and distribution of disciplinary knowledge, most often through an agreed process of professional review that validates such knowledge. This encoded knowledge is often domain knowledge, so that the language, the style of delivery, and the avenues of distribution confirm a contribution to a particular area of learning and of know-how. Touting of authorship in this regard means assessment and rating of such knowledge additionally within the broader realm of general human knowledge. Politically and economically, domains of knowledge compete for resources in academe. Additionally, such domain knowledge is often also assessed in a particular institution, to determine the career progression (or denial of that progression) of individual contributors to the field. In many cases, governments also take an active role in assessing both encoded and domain knowledge, allocating public funds to institutions, departments of study, and even directly to individuals based on assessments of the quality and extent of such knowledge.

Formal higher education in creative writing deals in approved and accepted qualifications, insisting on both domain knowledge (institutions tending to be administratively divided based on such domain or disciplinary groupings) as well as encoded knowledge (meaning knowledge that is published and distributed, reviewed by experts in an area, and ultimately supporting the importance of authorship).

At first, considering a comparative history of creative writing lore in academe therefore appears to suggest national and institutional preferences, and at times vast differences between one nation's creative writing higher education and that happening in another. Of course, by this the reference is to lore as tradition, not necessarily lore as human knowledge (as noted, the two classifications are not identical). The connection made between literature and creative writing is nevertheless common—this is both for perceived domain knowledge reasons explored here, and because authorship is fundamental to assessing the quality of encoded knowledge (the kind of knowledge higher education most claims to deliver). This short example from Mark McGurl's *The Program Era: Postwar*

Fiction and the Rise of Creative Writing (2009) is indicative of how we go about comparing creative writing education around the world through such an institutional or organizational lens:

> ...the university stepped forward in the postwar period both to facilitate and to buffer the writer's relation to the culture industry and the market culture more broadly. (15)

Astutely here, McGurl interprets a moment in US institutional history. He rightly points to higher education as part of the culture industry, and he soon after makes a decidedly Campbellian reference to the novel as "an experiential commodity," providing "quasi-touristic imaginary experiences" (15). And McGurl notes, as might any historian of the culture industry—for example, of an industry event such as the world's largest book fair, the Frankfurt Book Fair (FBM)—that "the market is everywhere relevant to the story I will tell" (15).

In all this, McGurl is of course not really presenting a history of creative writing teaching and learning on campus, nor of creative writing lore, as such (meaning here "a body of knowledge") despite his book's subtitle. This becomes even more evident when, in the pages that follow, he says that "writing well is by all accounts very hard work" (17)—this perhaps tongue in cheek or empathetic, given his book is, indeed, well written. He later concludes a chapter entitled "The Hidden Injuries of Craft," referring to "literary minimalism" by saying:

> minimalism has the ironic advantage of revealing the systematicity of creativity in the Program Era in its starkest form. In doing [literary minimalism] lays bare the recruitment of that creativity to the inhuman ends of the economic order we serve. (320)

Perhaps so, when viewed from the point of view of the products emerging from the programs to which McGurl refers. However, creative writing is far more than its products—and creative writers, and those who teach creative writing, know that well.

McGurl's is the story of a period of literary enculturation in the US and of the US culture industry in which education is part. It is largely a holistic study, methodologically speaking, systemic and structural in focus. But his is not about the actions of creative writing or the approaches of creative writers or the ways creative writers share their knowledge with others. Institutional and organizational histories of creative writing are exactly that. They are frequently embedded with individual stories (of the "founding program director," "the award-winning poet," the time a particular writer was "in residence" or "gave a reading"), as befits the history of a human endeavor individual creativity is seen to be representative of the creativity of humankind. But these histories do not reveal much about creative writing or about creative writing teaching and learning. They actually do not much claim that they will. They are situated in the creation, declaration, and representation of lore as tradition not lore as practices borne in an exchange of individual experiences and viewpoints, as most often occurs in the reality of creative writing teaching and learning. Lore as human exchange, human proximity, is the foundation of kinship, and in creative writing teaching and learning that kinship transcends lore as tradition.

The Kinship in Creative Writing

If you have not already visited, it is instructive when first arriving at the FBM, which can trace its roots back to a meeting of booksellers in that city in the fifteenth century, to take a moment to consider what is taking place in front of you: the explorations of available sales territories, exchanges of ownership, licensing, mapping-out of rights, design discussions around the selection of images and fonts. FBM defines difference as essential in order that the products of writers can be traded effectively. Similar yet different is the sweet spot here. It is unvarnished rather than cynical to note this is the same sweet spot that also assists the sale of automobiles and condos—even if at FBM marketability is more directly based on a promise of "dreams and the pleasurable dramas" to be "enjoyed in imagination" (Campbell, 1987: 90).

The same can be said for trading in creative writing courses in higher education. Creative writing lore is presented in terms of domain knowledge and encoded knowledge. That is, what identifiable field of study it is, who is teaching it, and how those teaching it are qualified to do so. The romance here is the romance of becoming a successful creative writer—for some students, at least. Using and exploring our imaginations is also part of this consumption. Transcendence is the attraction, the transcending of the ordinary, the permission to meld feeling with thinking. A love of the end products creative writing is part of this too—students, as well as faculty, sharing an interest in novels, or poetry or plays or films or computer games, virtual reality, music and so on. Courses and programs differentiate from each other by touting that they are similar but different; identifiably about creative writing, while distinctively imbued with the input of individual authors, recognized cultural producers, and their recognizable cultural products.

In the end, it is in considering the establishing and marketing of higher education in creative writing that it becomes clearest to us that our real kinship as creative writing teachers and learners is entirely understandable, but that it is not much about what it appears to be about at first glance. It is not much about lore as tradition, but rather lore as knowledge and knowledge that is in conditions of personal, embodied and yet often anagogic exchange. There are also more similarities between us, and what we do, than national institutional or organizational histories have suggested. More than global literary marketplaces might ever be expected to portray; or that we could ever ask them to portray, because literary marketplaces are not really focused on creative writing.

The kinship we have, as a disciplinary-specific group, through what we do, what we think, and what we believe, is manifest in shared common individual practices. It can be celebrated in these as they connect those who teach, and those who teach with those who are learning creative writing. Our shared creative writing lives offer these ideals, globally. This is, in the sense of our knowledge (both individual and communal) our most significant lore:

Practice defines why we are teaching and learning. Even those creative writing programs that have structured critical elements concerned with the study of periods of literary history, with cultural conditions or with linguistic meaning involve creative writing practice. Formal creative writing study frequently being included in the domains of literature or language study, it is often practice that differentiates it from other parts of those knowledge domains, its course content, the primary personal focus of those teaching it, and the expected outcomes of the teaching and learning of it.

Informed choice is key to what we do. A great many of our undergraduate programs begin with exposure to the writing of a range of genre, sometimes offering initial choice; but often, at very least, requiring some engagement with a range. As a student progresses, a narrowing of choice is made possible; and, most programs conclude with an ethos of informed choice defining a student's final project.

Individualism is at the core. While we often exchange ideas about the mainstream, and encourage recognition of what is identifiably of a particular genre or purpose or cultural or even political position, we celebrate and encourage the individual writer and individual writing because intellectual capacity and imagination capacity are seen to be founded on openness to the influence of the self.

Evolution, while not necessarily the point of assessment, is almost always the point of teaching and learning in creative writing. Institutional necessities intrude, the logistics of semesters concluding, or degrees having a certain length, but creative writing tends to be taught and learnt an essentially evolutionary, points reached on a journey of indeterminate length. These assessment points often reflect only what the formalization of education requires not what either teacher or learner experiences or, quite often, desires.

Association comes to the fore in creative writing education, because even though creative writing is most often an individual practice we tend to encourage ideals of exchange. Creative writing workshops are explicit in doing this, within their groups. Suggesting creative writing is a form of communication—which is a common way of speaking about it—requires communication between one another. Creative writing as either art or craft entails a recognition of techniques that rely on shared group understanding. Particular forms, particular techniques, even particular topics are associated with certain periods of literary history, certain cultures, certain genre.

Modeling is the underlying reason for the study of completed work by other writers. While it might be this is presented as the study of particular texts, the exchange between teacher and learner is more likely based in a sense of admiration of the finished result that harks back to how it might have come about. The bridge-making here, while not entirely removing the critical study of the text in itself, is between the teacher's practice, the student's practice, and the contribution to that practice that any textual model might provide.

Unobservable work is nevertheless legitimate work. So we often suggest in creative writing education. In some fields, whether work is undertaken in a lab or in a community, in a classroom or in place of work, unless action is observable, its status is reduced. But creative writing is universally taught as a practice empowered by our human imaginations; and, while observation and verification is not irrelevant (some courses might ask for a diary of a project, or an exegetical component that explores the practice or a reflective essay on a project), it is accepted, globally, that work that takes place in and through the imagination is entirely valid.

Kinetics defines creative writing education, the movement between elements, whether those elements are the actions of creative writing, learning and learnt techniques, the making and the disseminating, communicating with others, the experiences that inform your writing, the structural historical or contextual classes that add to understanding, the sense of progression, whereby what you teach or learn is considered to be part of a continuum.

Our kinship in creative writing—as teachers and learners—is defined and informed by these primary loreal elements. These elements are universal, and—though they are nuanced and influenced nationally, regionally, and institutionally by lore as tradition they live day-to-day in how we exchange our values and beliefs in creative writing, person to person.

We can consider creative writing education from the point of view of the literary market place, and see both producer and product celebrated, but we learn little about know exchanges might take place between teacher and learner. We can consider it from the point of view of institutional and organizational histories and see the ways in which the discipline has been located in the political and economic flows of formal education and produced related lore. But even associations of domain and encoded knowledge do not reach a sense of what we do, what we think, and what we believe. It is only in observing the clear, global commonalities of practices, ideals, and beliefs that we recognize the strength and significance of our human kinship in and through creative writing. That is our real lore, our true, defining lore – all else pales in importance compared to this.

References

Campbell, C. (1987), *The Romantic Ethic and the Spirit of Modern Consumerism*, Oxford: Basil Blackwell.

McGurl, M. (2009), *The Program Era: Postwar Fiction and the Rise of Creative Writing*, Boston: Harvard University Press.

Myers, D. G. (1996), *The Elephants Teach: Creative Writing Since 1880,* Englewood Cliffs, N.J.: Prentice Hall.

Wandor, M. (2008), *The Author Is Not Dead, Merely Somewhere Else: Creative Writing after Theory*, London: Macmillan.

Toward a Unified Field: The Complications of Lore and Global Context

Stephanie Vanderslice
University of Central Arkansas

In both the first and second editions of *Can Creative Writing Really Be Taught? Resisting Lore in Creative Writing Pedagogy*, the editors and I located the definition of lore in Stephen North's landmark book *The Making of Knowledge in Composition*, which classifies lore as one of the eight kinds of knowledge in composition, that is: "the accumulated body of traditions, practices, and beliefs in terms of which Practitioners understand how writing is done, learned, and taught" (1987: 22). Lore also includes the myths about the teaching, learning, and practicing of creative writing today. But should it? Certainly lore *can* sometimes perpetuate myths about the activity of creative writing. It doesn't always, however.

I may be as, or more, guilty of conflating lore and myth in the last decade, but I want to advocate, from here forward, that we separate the two terms. To do that we need to be clear on their definitions. Let's start with myth. The *Oxford English Dictionary* definition of myth that is most salient to this discussion is no. 2a.:

> A widespread but untrue or erroneous story or belief; a widely held misconception; a misrepresentation of the truth. Also: something existing only in myth; a fictitious or imaginary person or thing.

It's fairly straightforward to enlarge this definition to make it salient to creative writing pedagogy. A creative writing myth, then, can be characterized as an untrue or erroneous story or belief about the process of creative writing, a misconception or misrepresentation of the way creative writing is practiced or accomplished, often in a way that inhibits the teaching or learning of the subject. Some of these myths emerge from writers themselves—as Wendy Bishop notes in *Released into Language: Options for Teaching Creative Writing*, writers can be notoriously inaccurate in self-reports about their practice (1998).

One can see why, according to this definition, the perpetuation of creative writing myths in the teaching and study of creative writing is problematic. Sometimes unreflective or unconsidered teaching lore, aided by the damaging cultural myths that surround creative writers and creative writing, *does* perpetuate erroneous beliefs about the subject. Other forms of teaching lore, however, have utility, especially since they are often based on practitioner-led inquiry and experience.

Let's compare North's definition, again, the: "accumulated body of traditions, practices, and beliefs in terms of which Practitioners understand how writing is done, learned, and taught" with the traditional definition below yields some interesting results. From the *Oxford English Dictionary*:

> 5a. That which is learned; learning, scholarship, erudition. Also, in recent use, applied to the body of traditional fact, anecdotes, or beliefs relating to some particular subject, (e.g. as animal lore or plant lore).

So the traditional definition posits lore as something that is learned, but, like North, references it as a "body of tradition[al]" knowledge about a subject, knowledge that *can* be factual but can also be misleading or untested, depending on what it is and how it is used.

In our enthusiasm at locating a problematic characteristic of creative writing teaching in composition scholarship twenty years ago, its dependence on lore, I now think Kelly Ritter and I may have been a bit hasty and dualistic in our approach, relying solely on North's definition without considering its context, especially in light of the fact that by the time we were making connections between North's lore and lore in creative writing, in the early 2000s, the book in which it appeared had been published for twelve years, and such context was already available. In this chapter, I want to unpack some of that context and complicate the subject, reconsidering lore and creative writing pedagogy almost twenty years from the time when Dr. Ritter and I first began examining it and broadening its implications.

In part, this reconsideration stems from the transparency North himself shows in several essays in *The Changing of Knowledge in Composition: Contemporary Perspectives* edited by Lance Massey and Richard E. Gebhardt and published in 2011. In fact, his introduction, "Notes on the Origins of *The Making of Knowledge in Composition*" (MKC), North candidly describes the emergence of the book as partly due to tenure pressure and department politics—he knew he needed a book for tenure and had been told by his chair that a book about writing centers, where he had been working for much of his early career, would not be accepted by the powers that be. He'd have to pursue another line of research.[1] So it was out of necessity that he began thinking about the nascent field of composition knowledge as a whole, eventually producing a book that would *shape* knowledge in the discipline as much as evaluate it, although in an essay describing its significance in the same volume, Ed White acknowledges that with its publication, North "paid a price for his originality and critical perspective on the field" (21).

Indeed, practitioner lore emerged early on as perhaps the most problematic concept in MKC, something that would be debated on and off for the next ten years, before the idea of lore in creative pedagogy was even a twinkle in our eyes[2], and as Richard Fulkerson writes in "The Epistemic Paradoxes of Lore," defining the term and its boundaries remains a sticking point:

> One of the most basic problems about lore is that it is often impossible to distinguish among potential meanings of the term:
>
> 1. Lore as knowledge
> 2. Lore as a hypothesis to be considered as inclusion in the field's body of knowledge
> 3. Lore as a way of making knowledge.
>
> Fulkerson (2011: 48)

Or, putting it another way, Fulkerson cites North's portrayal of lore as "conclusion, possibility, or method" all at once (48). Lore as conclusion might include what he denotes as public "lorisms" like "not using red ink" or the idea that "teaching formal grammar improves prose" (48)—conclusions that have sometimes been misinterpreted in the field. It is "public lorisms" like these that can lead scholars to conflate lore with myth: sometimes they are frustratingly overapplied or inaccurate. Indeed, along these lines, some scholars, including David Bartholomae, saw North's portrayal of lore as "imperialist and condescending" (Fulkerson: 49). Bruce Horner also pointed out that in MKC, "the knowledge constituting lore doesn't stand up to the usual criteria for achieving status . . . in the end, lore doesn't cut it" (qtd. in Fulkerson: 49). Others, at the same time, praised North's recognition of "the contributions of practitioners to the making of knowledge" (49).

---

[1] The ways in which lines of research are and are not supported in the academy and the work that results—both renegade and mainstream—seems ripe for investigation itself. Joseph Moxley published *Creative Writing in America* despite the fact that his department chair informed him it would not count for tenure. In my own experience, it was a supportive chair, David Harvey, and a location in an independent writing department that allowed me to pursue creative writing pedagogy in the early days, when it was not an established field.

[2] Joe Amato and Kass Fleischer.

According to Fulkerson, such diametrically opposed readings "happen because North's treatment of lore in MKC is itself ambivalent" (50). It fails to recognize that lore is itself, "like scholarship or experimentation, a *method* [emphasis mine] of proceeding," not the outcome, and that "any method can be 'ill used'." Moreover, it is worth noting, that this perspective on lore emerged at a time when "rigorous empirical research" was privileged in order to counter what was perceived as "the field's reliance on guesswork and speculation" (59–60), a time when the pendulum was swinging away from practitioner-led research and taking an experimental turn. Fulkerson points out that "non-quantitative [e.g., qualitative] research now dominates," with even journals like *Research in the Teaching of English* publishing significant amounts of ethnography and case study (60). "If lore does not equal bad ethnography/case study," he posits, "then does it make sense to say that ethnography and case study is lore done well?"(61).

What, you may be wondering at this point, does all this talk about lore in composition have to do with lore in creative writing studies? On the one hand we can view it as a means to interrogate the dualistic ways scholars, myself included, have depicted it in creative writing scholarship in the past several years, presenting lore almost universally in the negative. Lore isn't always an effective form of knowledge, but it can be effective if it's based on reflection and practitioner-led research. Likewise, it isn't always an ineffective form of knowledge, but it can be ineffective if it's not grounded in adequate research or if it perpetuates or overapplies the inaccuracies or myths that continue to dog the teaching and learning of creative writing or writing in general.

Another complication: lore and its influence can vary according to cultural context and perception. According to Jen Webb, writing about Australia in *Can Creative Writing Really Be Taught?* (second edition), dependence on lore is less problematic in "Australian or UK creative writing courses, largely because government initiatives and related institutional demands have propelled writing teachers into the logic of the academy" (97). "Writing teachers in Australia," she adds, are "at home with the work of researching pedagogy, interrogating traditions and truisms, producing analysis of process and developing arguments about research in practice … it has been a long time since anyone wondered whether it is possible to teach creative writing" (97).

At the same time, Webb also describes a terroir in Australia that can be ambivalent when it comes to lore, such as the split system in AU universities whereby working writers teach as "casual teachers, transmit[ting] enthusiasm and technical knowledge, in which the tenured writing academics take on the responsibility, or perhaps the burden, of satisfying their institution's requirement for engagement, entrepreneurship, research, and service, as well as teaching and pedagogy" (98). Although this situation is certainly not unrecognized in the US and other countries, it is problematic at best, as it allows the "casual" teacher to continue to reify lore even if it is inaccurate.

In his review of *Can Creative Writing Really Be Taught* in the Australian journal *TEXT*, Ross Gibson also implies that lore is a uniquely American problem—in spite of Webb's examples otherwise—and laments the book's lack of attendance to other national contexts on subject. The latter is an excellent point—creative writing scholars internationally do have a tendency to speak over one another instead of engaging together directly on the subject—a situation I am hopeful this book will begin the process of dismantling. Moreover, editors of scholarly collections like myself, and others, need to be more intentional in seeking contributors.[3] Graeme Harper—through his international conference Great Writing, and in his own work as well as personal conversations—also reminds us over and over that creative writing theory and pedagogy varies in focus according to the national contexts from which it emerged. Understanding these contexts is critical in creative writing scholarship. In doing so, I encourage readers to try to understand these contexts by reading the work of scholars describing them histories in *TEXT*, *New Writing*, and other important sites (the works of Paul Dawson and Harper himself are good places to start, and so is Janelle Adsit's bibliography [https://www.criticalcreativewriting.org/creative-writing-studies.html]). However, instead of dismissing lore as an American problem (Webb has admitted it's not; countless headlines decrying even the existence of creative writing in the UK university in British newspapers indicate the same), it's more important to come together in these explorations, seeking to uncover the challenges we have in common and address them.

Certainly, when I made a study of the teaching of creative writing in the UK for ten years, described extensively in *Rethinking Creative Writing*, I explained the conditions under which creative writing gained a foothold and grew there, as well as how this trajectory meant that creative writing in the UK was in some respects further along than the US.[4] My research into the system in Australia

---

[3] Here I will admit that I invited Jen Webb's contribution because I knew her work and worked with her in the Creative Writing Studies Organization. I should have sought other international scholars, especially from Australia, to weigh in.

[4] Largely based on the Dearing Report and analyses of its effect on higher education in the UK, as well as several study tours of institutions in the UK.

tells me a similar story.[5] And yet in both cases, I also see ways that the systems are not perfect, especially when it comes to the perpetuation of lore.

So back to North and our original posing of the problem of lore, which was grounded in a very specific definition set out by a landmark book in composition studies in the United States. Composition studies[6], writing studies, and their complicated relationships to creative writing studies actually form the landscape that creative writing studies emerged from in the United States. In fact, lacking the centralized governmental structures that influence higher education in other Anglosphere countries, composition studies in the US *is* our Dearing Report, our Dawkins Reforms. Some scholars, such as Dawson, Andrew Cowan, and Claire Woods[7] recognize this and even suggest other scholars keep it in mind when interpreting American scholarship in the field. Others do not, continually infantilizing problems surfaced in the US as "American" and invoking a lack of growth in the field at all that is deeply inaccurate. *TEXT*, an Australian creative writing journal I have long admired, as I enumerate below, is even guilty of this practice by highlighting a quote from, of all things, a medieval-studies scholar in the US denigrating the state of creative writing studies there, instead of looking to the people actually working in the field, people whose work *TEXT* had actually referenced, reviewed, and published, like myself, Tim Mayers, Dianne Donnelly, and many others. To wit, this erroneous comment published on their web page in 2012:

> Kurt compared *TEXT* with Creative Writing discipline publications in North America:
>
>> there is never any research published . . . that I know of in the U.S., on creative writing pedagogy. In fact, there is virtually no scholarly discussion of how creative writing might be taught better; there is little critical thinking along

---

5   Based on my study of Dawson and others and my limited knowledge of the effects of the Dawkins Reforms. I have long believed a study tour of Australia is in order to balance my knowledge of the UK system. Unfortunately, research funding in the US has dried up almost completely since my 2006 study tour. Let this footnote be a notice that I would welcome any opportunities to serve in a visiting or speaking capacity at an Australian university, in order to study, in person, their vibrant creative writing landscape.

6   In the US higher education system, which is four years instead of three, students must take a year of "general education" courses to prepare for their majors. This includes a universal "composition" course to prepare students for academic writing. Over several decades, an entire discipline has grown from theorizing the best ways to teach this subject: composition studies.

7   From Woods, "Literacies in transition: Students and the journey in the discipline of writing" in "While Australian academics have positioned writing in higher education primarily by asserting the value and place of creative writing and, to a lesser extent, business and professional writing, the US context has been driven, on the one hand, through composition, rhetoric and research in written communication (with ongoing debate about how these fit alongside English, literature, or cultural studies) and, on the other, through creative writing courses taught often within fine arts programs. [3] It behoves us to be aware of such debates . . ."

the lines suggested by [the] fruitful research which often appears in the pages of *TEXT*. North America has no "creative writing studies" . . .[8]

Heinzelmen qtd. in Brophy and Krauth (2012)

One wonders why this quote was selected when the editors must have known otherwise and when the quote so obviously misrepresents the field. In fact, I wish they had asked me to speak to the value of *TEXT* instead, a journal I have been reading and recommending to creative writing scholars for years, as have many of my colleagues, instead of a literature scholar in the US who had somehow, as late as 2012, despite several books and special issues of the flagship US journal *College English* on creative writing (edited by myself, Kelly Ritter and others) by that point.

Why, indeed. The problem, I think, is that *TEXT* itself was guilty of something US scholars have often been accused of: looking at only a slice of the story rather than considering the wider picture, a practice it's easy to fall victim to, as I'll describe later. To offer a capsule history of creative writing in the US that will bring us to 2012 and beyond, creative writing in US higher education started with the first course offerings in 1896 at the University of Iowa and developed slowly over the next forty years into the Iowa Writer's Workshop formed in 1936 and initially led by Wilbur Schramm. It was not until poet and entrepreneurial academic Paul Engle took over the workshop in 1941 however, that the program kicked into high gear. After the Second World War, with the help of the GI Bill, the program grew from twelve to over one hundred students, many of whom became major figures in American programs and some of whom then scattered like seeds to develop programs elsewhere, all following the Iowa Workshop Model. By 1967, when the Association of Writing Programs formed, there were thirteen programs. By the 1990s there were hundreds.

Truthfully, conversations about creative writing theory and practice in higher education, did lie fallow, for far too long, for many decades, in fact, as US writers in academia relished the sense of community they had found there more than anything else[9] and considered that community to be enough. It wasn't until Joseph Moxley published *Creative Writing in America* in 1989 and then Wendy Bishop, Hans Ostrum, and Katherine Haake began to investigate the subject in a

---

[8] The author goes on to say that there were no creative writing studies journals at this point in the US. This is true. Special issues of major journals aside, the first issue of *Journal of Creative Writing Studies* in the US appeared in 2016.

[9] Many scholars with many points of view have described the history of creative writing in America. For a more detailed version of my perspective, see *Rethinking Creative Writing*, Frontinus Publishing, 2011.

deep and scholarly way that creative writing research began to appear and then gain momentum. In much the same way Iowa sowed the soil to grow creative writing programs across the US, these early scholars, many of whom who were writers who had also crossed over from composition studies, piqued the scholarly interests (passions, in my opinion) of a long list of scholars who began to interrogate the theory and pedagogy they had been instructed to take as gospel. These scholars included Patrick Bizzaro, Mary Ann Cain, Dianne Donnelly, Anna Leahy, Timothy Mayers, Kelly Ritter, and myself, all of whom had produced important work, books and articles, by 2012. Just five years later, creative writing studies had expanded to include a third wave, many of whom can be found in the significantly expanded second volume of *Can Creative Writing Really Be Taught*, an expansion that was the only way to do justice to a momentum that had begun in the 1990s, exploded in the 2000s, and had expanded exponentially into dozens of scholars in the 2010s who led the charge to found the Creative Writing Studies Organization and Conference and the *Journal of Creative Writing Studies*.

Like the editors of *TEXT*, I have been guilty of looking at only part of the picture and want to use this chapter, in a book I hope will contribute mightily to establishing a foundation for an international portrait of the field, to make a call for looking at the whole, for training our eyes on global creative writing and its contexts rather than using one piece of the puzzle to cast doubt on the others or make our own landscape look better. Examining the broader picture involves setting aside our own assumptions, especially those that support our own theories. To borrow from a business perspective: "The moment you know something with certainty, you become a liability," as career coach Tarah Keech writes in an online career journal, "certainty, of anything, is built on assumptions— and assumptions are risks" (2019).

To provide a personal example and bring the discussion back around to lore: Kelly Ritter and I were off to the races once we found a kernel of theory, a definition that highlighted issues we were having with our own discipline, without looking at the larger context and consequences of that research. It fit our worldview at the time (2007) that creative writing theory and pedagogy were moving too slowly, a worldview that was entirely valid but supported by a definition that had been somewhat cherry-picked to suit our purposes. I reintroduce North, his definition of lore and fields of knowledge in composition and the work of subsequent scholars examining it, to point out that studying lore and its context just *in the US alone* reveals the subject to be deeply complex, much more complex than Kelly Ritter and I first thought. It is precisely because of this complexity that lore demands further study—in the US and abroad, in

Anglosphere countries and others, as creative writing continues to spread to higher education internationally. It is not simply an American problem, although it can be a problem here, to be sure, but one that challenges all of us. Misused, lore remains one of the most significant threats to the learning and practice of the literary arts in higher education simply because it traffics in what really amounts to the "fake news" of the field. Continued attention to the use and misuse of this form of knowledge can help us ensure that practitioner knowledge is honored when it works and promptly discarded when it doesn't.

Ultimately, to dismiss lore as an American problem contributes to a kind of othering that does a great disservice to our field, mimicking the kind of name-calling and polarization that is happening politically around the world. It does not have to be this way. It is past time for the countries in places in which creative writing is studied and where its study is on the rise—too many countries to list now—to come together and honor the paths each has taken to this place, to present creative writing studies as a unified field.

Describing composition studies in 2011, scholar Gregory Smit wrote, "After 45 years [as an academic field] composition studies is still arguing fundamental principles" (25). He argues, "without a common vision of what it means to do research in composition studies or a common vision of writing is, how writing is learned, and how writing ought to be taught, the term '*professional*' [emphasis mine] in composition studies becomes almost meaningless" (228).

Creative writing studies does not have to reinvent the wheel. We can learn from composition studies' struggles and bring, as North himself hoped would happen in his own field, "practitioners, scholars, and researchers," and I must add, creative writers outside academia, together, "to become familiar with and to value each other's methods and knowledge" in order to achieve a unity that will enhance our position, globally. Moving forward from this unified position behooves us not least of all because, in whatever forms they take in the coming years, reifying lore or finally leaving it behind, the literary arts will proceed with or without us. What this unity will ultimately look like, I cannot prescribe or predict, but it begins by approaching our colleagues across borders not with assumptions but with questions, with curiosity, and with respect.[10] It begins with this book, but it will only continue with many more like it.

---

[10] I have also argued for a more collaborative spirit in creative writing than is evident in other disciplines and what that might look like in moving forward here: Vanderslice, Stephanie (2016) "'There's An Essay In That': Wendy Bishop and the Origins of Our Field," *Journal of Creative Writing Studies*: Vol. 1 : Iss. 1, Article 2. Available at: https://scholarworks.rit.edu/jcws/vol1/iss1/2

References

Adsit, J. (2019), *Critical Creative Writing*. Available online: https://www. criticalcreativewriting.org

Brophy, K. and Krauth, N. (2012), "Without TEXT, the practice, research, and pedagogy of creative writing at the university level would be in dire straits," *TEXT: Journal of Writing and Writing Courses*, 16 (2). Available online: http://www.textjournal.com. au/oct12/editorial.htm

Fulkerson, R. (2011), "The Epistemic Paradoxes of Lore," in R. C. Gebhardt and L. Massey, (eds), *The Changing of Knowledge in Composition: Contemporary Perspectives*, 47–62, Logan: Utah State University Press.

Gibson, R. (2018), "'Unloreful' TEXT: Journal of Writing and Writing Courses," 23 (1). Available online: http://www.textjournal.com.au/april18/gibson_rev.htm

Keech, T. (2019), "The four career lessons most women learn too late, according to a career coach," Fairygodboss. September 17. Available online: https://fairygodboss. com/articles/the-4-career-lessons-most-women-learn-too-late-according-to-an-executive-coach

Moxley, J. (1989), *Creative Writing In America: Theory and Pedagogy*, Urbana, IL: NCTE.

North, S. (1987), *The Making of Knowledge in Composition: Portrait of An Emerging Field*, Portsmouth, NH: Heinemann, Boynton, Cook.

North, S. (2011), "Notes on the Origins of the *Making of Knowledge in Composition*," in R. C. Gebhardt and L. Massey, (eds) *The Changing of Knowledge in Composition: Contemporary Perspectives*, 11–16, Logan: Utah State University Press.

North, S. (2011), "Afterword," in R. C. Gebhardt and L. Massey, (eds) *The Changing of Knowledge in Composition: Contemporary Perspectives*, 323–5, Logan: Utah State University Press.

Oxford English Dictionary. Available online: https://eds.a.ebscohost.com/eds/detail/ detail?vid=1&sid=febc7b8d-073c-48c0-bf50-7e11b81e8511%40sessionmgr4006&bd ata=JnNpdGU9ZWRzLWxpdmUmc2NvcGU9c2l0ZQ%3d%3d#AN=uca.50959346 &db=cat04436a

Ritter, K. and S. Vanderslice. (2007), *Can It Really Be Taught? Resisting Lore in Creative Writing Pedagogy*, Portsmouth, NH: Heinemann, Boynton, Cook.

Smit, D. (2011), "'Stephen North's The Making of Knowledge in Composition and the Future of Composition Studies' Without Paradigm Hope," in R. C. Gebhardt and L. Massey, (eds) *The Changing of Knowledge in Composition: Contemporary Perspectives*, 213–35, Logan: Utah State University Press.

Vanderslice, S. (2010), *Rethinking Creative Writing*, London: Frontinus.

Vanderslice, S. and R. Manery. (2017), *Can Creative Writing Really Be Taught? Resisting Lore in Creative Writing Pedagogy*, 10th Anniversary Edition. London, Bloomsbury.

Webb, J. (2017), "The traces of certain collisions: Contemporary writing and old tropes," in *Can Creative Writing Really Be Taught? Resisting Lore in Creative Writing Pedagogy*, 10th Anniversary Edition. London, Bloomsbury.

White, E. (2011), "The significance of North's *The Making of Knowledge in Composition* for graduate education," in R. C. Gebhardt and L. Massey, (eds) *The Changing of Knowledge in Composition: Contemporary Perspectives,* 17–27, Logan: Utah State University Press.

2

Ukubhukuda:[1] Not Sinking in Language but Swimming

Bronwyn Law-Viljoen and Phillippa Yaa de Villiers
University of the Witwatersrand

The Languages of a South African Creative Writing Seminar

Teaching proficiency in English is not the same as facilitating the discovery of a creative voice, although these processes may overlap. They are richly complicated, however, when students bring more than one language to the writing classroom. South Africa has a long history of resistance to language policies, which were, during the apartheid years, deliberately exclusionary and racist, explicitly geared to denying the equality of all languages before the law. After the first free elections in 1994, the Mandela generation recognized eleven official languages. In practice, however, English has become the main official language. As English mother-tongue speakers, therefore, we deliver the official policy by conducting our teaching in English. But as writers conscious of the need to redress inequality in our society, we choose to be attentive to changes in the linguistic and literary landscape, and to the explore these changes in our practice and our teaching.

Thus, though we teach and conduct discussions in English, informing each oral and written submission by our students are the rich repositories of other languages that university-level students in South Africa possess. We aim to consider how these languages might undo the hegemony of the dominant discourse so that our students can produce writing that is risky and self-aware.

The pedagogy of the postgraduate creative writing courses at the University of the Witwatersrand in Johannesburg is practice-driven and seminar-based.[2] At

---

[1] *Ukubhukuda* is isiZulu for "swim."
[2] Postgraduate creative writing degrees (most of these at Master's level) are offered at the following South African universities: University of the Witwatersrand (Wits), Stellenbosch University, University of the Western Cape, University of Durban-Westville, University of Cape Town, Rhodes

the Honors level, seminars for each of the courses are weekly, three hours long, and combine wide-ranging discussion, reading, and writing. Students produce work at a steady pace and are given rigorous feedback by their tutor and peers.

While the medium of instruction is English, the energizing dissent expressed in the recent #Rhodesmustfall movement,[3] and the university's implementation of a new language policy that recognizes the right to be instructed in African languages, indicate a moment of transition that has yet to find its form. This chapter explores anecdotal evidence captured in classes in this transitional moment in order to suggest a pedagogical response to the dynamic political debates at the university and to discover new ways of teaching within the multilingual creative writing seminar.

Our desire to plot a course through this complex political and linguistic terrain—not by applying theories to the teaching situation but rather by traveling through language with our students—is based on our own practice as writers ourselves. Along with our students, then, we are in dialog with a rich, multilingual context, seeking points of entry in order to engage private and communal reservoirs of knowledge and experience.

Though one of the authors of this chapter is a poet and the other a prose writer, we both find that our pedagogical points of departure resonate with the principles and practices of traditional oral storytelling, to which many of our students have been exposed. These are explicated by A. C. Jordan (1973: xi):

> The ethos of traditional society was enshrined in an oral, legal, religious, and literary tradition through which the community transmitted from generation to generation its customs, values, and norms. The poet and the storyteller stood at the center of this tradition as the community's chroniclers, entertainers, and collective conscience.

University, and University of Pretoria and many colleges offer undergraduate creative writing courses, though not full degrees in the discipline. The postgraduate programs (some coursework-based and others requiring a full dissertation in the form of a creative project and a reflective or theoretical essay) are usually situated within literature departments, and staff split their time between instruction in literature and the teaching of creative writing. The program at the University of the Witwatersrand began about twelve years ago under the umbrella of the English Department. In 2011 the first full-time Creative Writing instructor was appointed and the program subsequently separated from English, becoming a fully fledged academic department with three full-time staff members, and offering Honors, MA, and PhD degrees.

[3] Rhodesmustfall is a student movement at South African universities that was set in motion by a range of issues, from the lack of funding for tuition (hence #feesmustfall) to the slow pace of curricular and systemic transformation at these institutions. The movement polarized around debates about the removal of "colonial" symbols from university campuses, such as the statue of the arch-colonizer Cecil John Rhodes at the University of Cape Town.

This description, although relating to amaXhosa,[4] can be generalized, with some variations, throughout the languages of southern Africa, in regard to which our students far exceed us in linguistic adeptness, since many of them are proficient in at least three languages.[5] With this proficiency in mind we will narrate examples of strategies discovered through engagements with students' work in two different courses in the Honors program: a poetry course and a course in short fiction and non-fiction.

Africa is a multilingual continent, yet our literary output is dominated by the colonial languages of English, French, Portuguese, and Arabic. Many indigenous languages were transcribed by missionaries who were not proficient speakers of these languages, and so the orthography they created undermines precision of meaning and presents problems for native speakers. In addition, idiom, the basic unit of abstraction, was often lost in transliteration. For these and other reasons, many African language speakers now choose to write in English.

South African indigenous languages have been further marginalized by an education system that did away with early literacy-learning in mother tongues during the first years after democracy in 1994. In urban areas in particular, local languages were partially abandoned as English was seen as the language of access and aspiration. The halcyon days are now over, and the sobering education statistics attest to poor reading and writing skills across all languages, with poor training in mother tongues given as a reason by many researchers for this decline.

Our Honors cohort is predominantly from what has come to be known as the "born free" generation, and are heirs to English *and* to their familial language legacies. In the last several years, the linguistic topography of the Honors seminars has included various combinations of the following: English first-language speakers, isiZulu first-language speakers (some private-school educated, some public-school educated—there's a vast difference between these two in the quality of the education and the value that is ascribed to indigenous languages), Sepedi first-language speakers, Gujarati first-language speakers, white Afrikaans first-language speakers, black Afrikaans first-language speakers.

These last racial distinctions are not casual but point to a complicated set of relationships to Afrikaans in South Africa as the language of the apartheid regime from 1948 to 1994. Originally a creole from Dutch, Afrikaans came into being through slaves, many of whom were from Indonesia and Malaysia.

---

[4] AmaXhosa: refers to a tribal, ethnic, and linguistic group concentrated in the Eastern and Western Cape provinces of South Africa. Their language, isiXhosa, is the second largest home language in South Africa after isiZulu.

[5] The two writers of this chapter are proficient in English and Afrikaans, and both are learning isiZulu.

Mixed-race citizens of the early Cape Colony were called Afrikaners, yet over centuries white descendants of the French Huguenot and Dutch settlers appropriated the name and the language.[6]

There are a variety of regional "versions" of Afrikaans spoken in the country, and the majority of speakers are, ironically, black, although the means of literary production in mainstream Afrikaans is firmly in white hands. The black Afrikaans poet Ronelda Kamfer (2019: 187) observes, "I knew that there was a glass ceiling, a definite limit in terms of how the Afrikaners would allow my writing, the writing of a Black person writing in Afrikaans, to be assimilated into their culture."

There are now eleven official languages in South Africa. The most widely spoken *first language* is isiZulu, followed by Afrikaans, isiXhosa, and then English, though the latter dominates as the language of classrooms, government, and boardrooms. Our South African students were almost all taught in English, even though their life experiences have enabled varying levels of expertise in multiple languages. Our non-South African students (and the number of international applicants to the program is increasing) bring additional languages (Igbo, isiNdebele, Shona, Somali, Arabic) and complexity to the classroom.

Poetry: Sampling Culture Through the Craft of Memory (Phillippa Yaa de Villiers)

A language is a flash of the human spirit. It's a vehicle through which the soul of each particular culture comes into the world. Every language is an old growth forest of the mind, a watershed of thought, an ecosystem of spiritual and social possibilities.

Wade Davis (2014)

I am fortunate to be teaching a poetry course against the backdrop of a lively poetry community in Johannesburg and across the country. Evidence of this can be seen in the many poetry slams, publications, contests, and fora for presentation and debate about poetry, as well as in the number of spaces that welcome creative

---

[6] Afrikaans became entrenched not only through a cultural movement that produced an Afrikaans literature, but more insidiously through the oppressive policies of the apartheid regime, which imposed Afrikaans as the medium of instruction at high school. A direct response to this was the Soweto uprising of 1976, in which protesting school children were met with the full and violent force of the state.

expressions of traditional African culture, which includes poetry. The pedagogical strategy of my poetry seminar is informed on the one hand by the values of this enthusiastic and diverse poetry community, and on the other by a practice of deep, critical reading that is intended to refine and add substance to creative work.

In addition to this, my teaching has been influenced by what I have learned in regard to style and technique, and equally by values gathered through exposure to indigenous African language communities. I have come to understand, for instance, that for amaXhosa, sensitivity to language and love of poetry is one half of the "gift" of the poet; ability to respond in kind is the other. As much as people can recite the names of all the poets and authors they admire, if they are unable to respond, they are not poets. They might be interpreters, teachers, or archivists, but "poet" is an honorific, bestowed by a collective.

The students in my poetry course have been selected because they are able to demonstrate that they have immersed themselves in a variety of texts and canons, and also because they bring to their writing and to the classroom the critical tools to be able to work, creatively and technically, with the rules and conventions of their own languages as well as English.

Poetry—which is not always written down, as the rich oral traditions of our region demonstrate—is primarily an expression of personal, communal, and even national identity, and situates the speaker or writer within the context of their language and culture. The better the writer knows this context, the more able they are to locate aspects of their own identity and to discover lexicons and idioms that enrich their creative work.

My pedagogical interventions include exploring their memories of poetry and storytelling, mottos, nursery rhymes and word games that, although not intelligible to other class members, provide a sound landscape that is associated with playfulness. These interventions are aimed at bringing to the surface the hidden languages in my students, many of whom have experienced the denigration of their mother tongues, and all of whom are caught up in the complexities of race, class, and gender. The surfacing of hidden languages is accomplished by the reciting of the remembered poems, mottos and nursery rhymes.

The creative work of the course is always accompanied by critical reflection, usually produced after the creative work has been completed. This may take the form of journal entries or a personal essay written in response to other poets. Responding, for example, to Pablo Neruda's poem "Poetry," Abdirizak Muhumed (2017), a Somali student whose literary background is enriched by the thousands of oral poems that accompany every aspect of a nomadic, camel-centered life, writes:

> On arriving on the planet earth from my mother's warm womb, it was the first sound that I heard. The Muslims' melodious call to prayer was recited into my ears, still on the midwife's hands, apparently to scare away any devil to touch my innocent body, and to welcome me into the world of poetry. Its religious significance aside, the adhan is in itself poetic revelation ... Since then, I have been watching people chanting and reciting oral verses on every occasion, whether it was a wedding ceremony, a political rally or a gathering of guerrilla fighters. If Neruda wasn't sure whether he received poetic inspiration 'from winter or river', I'm also skeptical about whether it came to me from the kraals of camels or the hearth outside my mother's hut.

Muhumed's description of the bosom of poetry that nurtures his language reveals his awareness that his writing creates a fragile bridge between his various worlds. He knows that his language is more than a set of signs, it is a way of thinking, mapped by material conditions which persist alongside a notion that the world is homogenous, Anglocentric, and industrialized. A reminiscence on his childhood bedroom expands the category of "childhood bedrooms," because it is not a room at all, but a tent made of grass and leaves that he, as a child, learned to make every night. Through the description, he offers his reader access to his culture through personal experience:

> And the rain poured elsewhere
> I dismantled my room in the morning
> I loaded my belongings on my he-camel
> I reassembled the sheaf of grass
> I erected my leafy room in the evening
> Like the nest of birds

Barely discernible to the reader is the fact that Muhumed effectively had to perform here (and elsewhere in his work) a translation from Somali—his mother tongue lies behind the description of a practice that not only appears in English but is written down for the first time.

Jordan (1973) asserts that the poet is the guardian of traditional values. The language in which these values are inscribed is handed down from generation to generation, and arrives in our classrooms both serendipitously and through complex historical, political, and social phenomena. We see this inscription and transmission happening time and again in Muhumed's work, and in the poetry classroom it soon becomes clear that he is not alone in this act of guardianship.

In contrast to Muhumed, however, whose poem explores an individual's experience, in a poem called "Mokete (A Gathering)" Mo'Afrika Mokgathi (2019) combines Sepedi with English to render her impression of the poetic tradition expressed by her family:

> Ululations
> [...]
> Soundtrack of diphala [horn section band]
> There, my guard of honor to meet her
> parallel—poetry and my bloodline
> pitching ululations
> the crowd's excitement at each mention
> of a name I have heard mentioned before
> [...]
> I wanted to be kgadi kgolo [great aunt]
> Have a share of her wisdom
> Sit at her feet
> Ke rete Direto. [I recite Poetry]

The poem describes how poetry takes place in Mokgathi's family and broadly in Sepedi culture. Besides the words, the poetic event includes musical instruments and the voices of people. This is the lineage that the poet wishes to join.

Besides exposing poets to new canons and poetic forms, we suggest English as a language that can serve a cohesive function and create access. But by encouraging creativity in whatever language the students feel is most effective, we hope to emphasize that proficiency in English should not mean marginalizing mother tongues. We want our students to be free to make their creative and critical contributions in whatever language is most appropriate.

Tereska Muishond (2019: 139), who completed the poetry course in 2018, notes in an essay on Afrikaans and colored[7] identity:

> Poetry in high school ... was a subject I found foreign, written by poets from England and the United States and even those from South Africa: Shakespeare, Robert Frost, Alfred Lord Tennyson, Wordsworth, C.J. Langenhoven, Breyten Breytenbach, and N.P. van Wyk Louw ... and the lone, small, gentle voice of Antjie Krog ... it certainly didn't help matters that the oppressor's language was my mother tongue.

---

[7] While "colored" is a term frowned upon by some as belonging to an old apartheid racial classification system, many colored people retain the word as a descriptor of their mixed cultural and racial heritage.

When she engaged with black women writing in Afrikaans, she experienced a flowering of her own talent. The course offered her a chance to experiment in her mother tongue, and so she created a short poem (Muishond 2013) called "Hulle Roep" (They Call), exploring her Khoisan ancestry in an Afrikaans that mimics the rhythm of drums:

Hulle roep
Hulle roep
Hulle roep na my
Stemme van gister
Stemme uit die donker

Hulle soek
Hulle soek
Hulle soek na my
Geel gevrimmelde hande,
voete,
gesigte
Klap-klap
Stamp-stamp
Skree hul gedigte
. . .
[They call
They call
They call to me
Voices of yesterday
Voices from the dark

They search
They search
They search for me
Yellow, wrinkled hands
Feet,
Faces
Clap-Clap
Stomp-stomp
Their poems scream]

Johannes Davids (2019), also a black Afrikaans writer, inscribes identity and history into his poem "Wie Spreek" (who speaks), which combines Setswana with Afrikaans and identifies with both black and white political martyrs:

Spreek stem die nagtegaal
weergalm uit versmoorde
gegeselde blink bebloede gange
Biko's, Tiro's, Aggetts
ompone o tswa kae?
van apartheidsdrome
swartbewustheidskreet . . .
[Speak voices the nightingale
reverberating out of smothered
flagellated shiny bloodied corridors
Bikos, Tiros, Aggetts
people where were you
in apartheid dreams
black consciousness cry . . .]

What I am learning about the poetic traditions of other languages besides English is that the centrality of the community storyteller and the way in which the craft is trained and deployed are as crucial to the notion of values as the technicalities of grammar and orthography. This discovery has been facilitated by my involvement in the South African Poetry Project (ZAPP), which is engaged in Indigenous Knowledge Systems research, focused on language. At one of our sites, a high school in Tshepisong, Johannesburg, Zukiswa Futha (2018), the isiXhosa language teacher, describes how storytellers/poets are identified: "If I am starting to teach poetry, that child will just start, the child will stand up [and start reciting] let me say this and this and this and this. In that case, we just sit down and allow the child to speak."

The quality of the speaking that the teacher describes here is often emotional and verbally skillful. It uses rhyme and rhythm, and may contain references to existing texts—sung, written, or spoken—to create a heightened expression that is deeply felt by the collective. Thus aesthetic, social, and spiritual values are revealed through the spontaneous creation of oral poetry, an ancient tradition that is still vibrant in many contexts. And at a strategic moment, the creative writing teacher sits down and listens to the student, becoming a learner herself.

Our students grapple with this tradition, orienting themselves in relation to it, finding points of departure, and exploring the possibilities presented to them by their mother tongues. To this end, they are asked to complete writing and reading activities that obliquely confront the politics of their linguistic inheritance. The danger in all of this is that we might fall into a narrow "identity politics" that gives rise to ideology rather than poetry, reproducing stale, "anthropological" reports in a provincialist, mediocre pastiche. In order to dissolve essentialism, and to engage productively with the challenges of writing oral literary forms into a version of English, we draw on poetic traditions from elsewhere: Asia, South America, and Canada, for example.

Part of the aim of the poetry course, then, is to encourage students to contribute to literature in their mother tongues, and to explore the influence of their mother tongues on English. The dictum of Keorapetse Kgositsile, South Africa's late Poet Laureate, was "to tame English to speak Setswana." We hope in some small way to contribute to that decolonizing agenda and to give students the space to become the scribes of their ancestors while faithfully engaging the challenges and narratives of contemporary existence.

Striking Out in the Prose Seminar (Bronwyn Law-Viljoen)

> Walking home from school everyday, I passed a tavern on the corner run by a Mozambican from Xai Xai. The children played outside and spoke a mix of Xitsonga, isiZulu and Sesotho. This was their language of play.
>
> Mbali Sebaeng (2019)

Mbali Sebaeng, a now-graduated student of the Honors degree in creative writing, paints a complex picture of the language pools, ponds, oceans that she has passed through since her early childhood. I realized early on in my encounters with her in the Honors seminar that assigning a language to her, or identifying what we like to think of, too easily, as her "mother tongue," was misguided, because she moved between several registers, codes, even dialects; from moment to moment choosing or finding herself surfacing in one language, swimming for a while in its eddies, and then striking out towards another.

Though my alluvial metaphor suits me, Mbali grew up partly in Soweto, far from anything that might resemble a pond. Soweto is a township of Johannesburg created by the apartheid regime to enforce racial segregation. Though the advent of democracy in 1994 did away with the draconian and racist Group Areas Act, the spatial legacy of apartheid has not yet been properly dismantled and so Soweto, like other black townships in South Africa, lags behind more affluent, white suburbs in regard to service delivery and social services.

Mbali entered the creative writing program in 2017 and went on to an elective called Writing Immersion in the second semester. She thus spent a year in my seminars grappling with her relationship to the several languages that make up her discursive, creative, and intellectual worlds.

Some way into the first semester, perhaps by the second non-fiction assignment, prompted by my suggestion that the students think through, and try to express, the relationship between space (or place) and meaning in a short essay set in a place that was of some significance to them, Mbali had begun to describe her relationship to English (the language in which she had been schooled), to isiZulu (her mother's first language, and the dominant language in her school social circles, though always inflected with a multiplicity of other languages), and to Setswana (her father's first language and, importantly, her paternal grandmother's). She was responding to my encouragement to all of the students to resist the deeply ingrained imperative (learned at school and at university) to write exclusively in English, and instead to consider what their other languages gave them as writers, what resources were embedded in these languages. Mbali was beginning to see that her languages represented different worlds, both actual (school, home, church) and idiomatic, and that even the use of a single word in Setswana, say, unlocked something for her—showed her who she was in relation to her language communities and the places that they "inhabited." The pedagogical approach here was not prescriptive. It involved a valorization of the various languages of the students, enacted largely through class discussion, but also through written and oral feedback that explicitly pointed to places where the use of a language other than English might be considered—in dialog for example, or in the use of titles and names, or in idioms that had no equivalent in English. For some students who had been constrained, all through school and university, to make use of an elusive and "proper" English, this was a revelation. The creative writing class showed them that languages—all of them—are a resource rather than an impediment.

Perhaps the most interesting of Mbali's language worlds was the church she attended with her family in her teens. The pastor was Malawian and used Setswana, Sepedi, and isiZulu translators for his multilingual congregation. The hymnal, however, had hymns in isiXhosa, isiZulu, English, Sepedi, and Setswana; and she, along with all of the other congregants, sang along in whatever language the hymns for the service happened to be in. She knew many of these in more than one language and therefore was able to ascertain the meaning of whatever she was singing by recalling the words in the languages she did know. Thus her entry into the written iterations of her languages was through the rich liturgical language of a church hymnal.

She recalls now, in our interview, wanting to write stories that her grandmother could read but feeling hampered by her limited access to Setswana. Indeed, she finally confronted that uncomfortable reality in the second semester when she wrote an extended fragment about a visit to family members in Botswana (a country adjacent to South Africa where Setswana is the official language), where she felt marooned by her inability to communicate with cousins and aunts, except in the most rudimentary way.

She also understood that because of her schooling, her access to literature was through English, and that therefore her first literary impulse was to write her way into the language that she had encountered in English stories and novels. She was, it should be said, not uncomfortable writing or speaking in this language, but she described wanting to write in a way that more closely resembled and conveyed the textures, scenes, voices, and relationships of her own experiences. As the seminar progressed, and as oral and written feedback to her writing encouraged experimentation, she began, gradually, to allow Setswana (and sometimes isiZulu) into her stories through the dialog of her characters, through names and idiomatic expressions.

Allowing herself to code-switch in her writing opened up a new set of questions about storytelling, technique, and point of view. In the seminars, we looked carefully at her handling of sections of text in Setswana or isiZulu, debating the need for translations (literal or contextual), subtle explanations, or even glossaries. I encouraged her—and other students—to try all of these devices and to gage the success of them through listening to her peers' responses. When did the story or essay need a translation? Was the glossary overly didactic? Could the glossary be used in some new and interesting way, as part of the story rather than as an add-on at the end?

In a story written early in the first-semester course, however, Mbali demonstrates that she is more or less at home in English, and she does not yet venture into Setswana for the dialog between her two characters (who, like her, would have access to languages other than English, and might, in a real-life situation, especially a difficult one such as this, code-switch):

> 'We're dead, Sesi! Dead!' Zinhle's clasped hands are shaking. The sweat beads forming on them are crystal-like in the moonlight.
>
> 'Shut up, Zinhle! Just shut up!' Though her voice is strong in the open field, it isn't steady. Gugu stands motionless with her hands on her head unable to hide her distress.
>
> 'We should switch off the car. We don't know who . . . or what is around. Gugu . . . we're in trouble . . .,' her voice trails off as she makes her way to the driver's side.
>
> 'I know . . .' Gugu mutters under her breath.

The tire burst. Thrice. In the middle of nowhere. That is an exaggeration. The Dlamini girls know where they are. More or less. They are on their way back home from a rendezvous to Midrand because Zinhle wanted to see a boy she liked. Prince. But they had taken a wrong turn and found themselves on a deserted road at 6pm in June.

Mbali Sebaeng (2018)

In my interview with Mbali (Sebaeng, 2019) a year later, she describes to me a more likely language scenario than the one she represents in her story between the two sisters. High school, she tells me, was characterized by easy code-switching. In a group of peers, speakers would choose their own languages and converse comfortably with others who might be speaking another language or a mix of languages. "No offense was ever taken," she points out, "but there was an unspoken expectation that amongst us—we were mostly middle class because of the kind of school we were at—the anchor language would be English."

This experience continues into her work environment but now, she notes, there is what she describes as an "intentional" code-switching, which is slightly different to the easy back and forth between the multiple languages of the school context. Perhaps there is a subtle pressure at play in a professional context, a need to demonstrate one's proficiency to colleagues. But whatever the reason, she describes this intentionality as "a decision to use the language you've chosen consistently." What this more conscious turn brings with it, she says, is an awareness of "correctness" that is usually absent from more relaxed social situations. What it also means is that the speaker who has made this decision must consciously stick with it, must not code-switch or borrow words and phrases from another language. It suggests commitment to a complex process of decision-making in the time-frame of the conversation, a series of language choices that will be determined by the speaker's proficiency and breadth of vocabulary in the language that is now burdened with an overt intentionality rather than the usually more covert or unconscious conversational speech acts. These explanations make much clearer to me, and perhaps to Mbali herself, how complex the multiple acts of speaking and writing are in a multilingual writing class. They help me to improve upon the pedagogy of my seminar, to make more explicit to all of us that these processes are taking place all at once and that we should find productive ways to harness them.

I imagine that for Mbali and others in the Honors class, it is precisely the perceived need to be "correct" that influences their language decisions, both when they are speaking and when they are writing. Indeed, a student in the previous year—whose first language was isiZulu but who studiously avoided using it in his stories, even when he was encouraged to do so—had explicitly conveyed his discomfort with switching out of English, even for a short story in which his characters, as he had presented them, would decidedly not have spoken the kind of English that he ascribed to them, as he himself conceded in discussion.

The assumption with which students seem to enter the program is that what is required in the creative writing seminar is "correctness" in English. The seminar room might at first resemble other classroom situations they have been in, other "formal" environments in which someone is "in charge" and might have certain expectations of them. This may be more charged for the black students in the seminar who are entering the traditionally "white space" of a South African university (various attempts, successful or otherwise, to transform this space notwithstanding) and the classroom of a white, English-speaking writing instructor.

But whatever the reasons, whatever the constraints, whatever the various positions occupied by all of us in the seminar, our work is to deploy a variety of strategies—free writing in any language; using words and phrases in assignments without always feeling the need to translate; searching for the connection between the *way* a thing is said and the language used to say it—to loosen the assumption. At the same time, however, as the ostensible inventor of such strategies, I have to examine my own assumptions about the choices that my students are making. I cannot, for example, decide on their behalf that they should use languages other than English in their assignments. I must navigate this terrain with some care in order to give my students a linguistic autonomy that is not governed by my (potentially misplaced) desire to see them work comfortably across a variety of languages and registers. In other words, I have to help create a writing seminar in which students are encouraged but not constrained to experiment, to take risks with all the languages to which they have access. I do this through open-ended discussion, through writing exercises in which students are asked to code-switch whenever it 'feels' right, by including essays in their course readers that specifically discuss questions of language and translation, by offering students the option to write one full assignment in a language other than English (though this is constrained by the resources we have at the university to provide feedback in any of the languages that students might choose), and by asking them to try things first in one language and then in another. Importantly, the students are each other's readers. They usually share languages from which I am excluded and I make it clear that they are each other's best critics. They must give and receive robust feedback. The aim is to allow them to see their personal repositories of language as resources, as rich worlds of possibility, not unlike the other resources they have available to them: their life experiences, their work environments, their various skills.

In the case of Mbali, the shift becomes visible in an assignment submitted in the Writing Immersion seminar, some eight months after that early piece. Oddly enough (though this "repetition" might be a subtle, half-conscious, poetic resolution of her earlier story) her characters here are also in a car, but now heading to Botswana for a family visit. This is still fiction, but the story mirrors a real event in Mbali's life:

> The drive to Dinokana is a long and dusty one. Baratamang does not seem to notice the winding skyrise horizon that steadily morphs into a mountainous terrain. It is only when the rocky road jostles her aunt's Polo Classic from side to side, therefore disturbing her absorption of the words on the page, does she lift her head. Mildly irritated, she eventually gives in and closes the book on her lap. It is nearing dusk. Her Rre Mogolo, her father's older brother, turns around and sees the preteen looking out and grabs the opportunity to engage her in conversation.
>
> 'Se re le gauswi le go fitlha.' ['We are almost there.']
>
> 'Oh? How far?'
>
> 'Mohlomong 20 minutes.'
>
> 'Ga o ka nka tsela e,' [If you take this road,] her father adds, lifting one hand from the steering wheel to gesture further North West of the N4, 'It will take you to Botswana.' The car veers and the hand promptly returns to secure its place in the ten past ten position.
>
> Although she is forced back to this reality, Baratamang is intrigued. She props herself up on the seat and gazes at the road he had pointed out. 'So, how far to Botswana then?'

The exchange here shows the writer working out what is needed to make meaning clear to a non-Setswana reader, but also, obliquely, to the character Baratamang, who is the one least able to converse in Setswana. Baratamang's journey with her family to visit her grandmother and her extended family becomes a journey into a language in which she feels adrift. Setswana is the "mother tongue" that Baratamang's father speaks but her access to it, like Mbali's, is limited. Her sense of linguistic dislocation is compounded by her guilt that her lack of mastery of her grandmother's language means she is unable to negotiate the nuanced relationships in the family, the forms of address, the gentle protocols.

Some way into the visit, Baratamang gets up in the middle of the night and is dismayed that she can't remember the word for "bathroom":

She walks over and gently opens the door. She is not met with the quiet that she expects. There are still women in the kitchen washing pots and preparing breakfast for the nation. She had hoped that through trial and error, she would find the bathroom. But now, she won't go unnoticed. She prepares herself; trying to remember the word for bathroom in Tswana. It has something to do with house. Something=ntlo? Ntlu-something? Ntloeng? No! Small house. Ntlu enyane. She mouths the words over and over until she reaches the kitchen.

Baratamang asks for directions in her broken Setswana, and when she returns from the bathroom she overhears her aunts conversing in the kitchen, commenting on her inability to speak the language and her use of the phrase "Ntlu enyane" (small house) for "bathroom":

> 'Ea, ke oa Olefile. Bana ba rona ga ba itsi SeTswana. Re nyetse metebele!' ['Yes, she is Olefile's. Our children do not know Setswana. We married Matabele!'] laughs the familiar voice.[8]
>
> 'Ntlu enyane!' ['Small house!'] the second voice cannot contain her laughter.
>
> . . . The laughter is not malicious. Baratamang knows this. But it still hurts. It reminds her of the same toned laughter her parents used to playfully offer to buffer her language fumbles.
>
> 'Mama, uPapa are o kopa izipots!' ['Mama, Papa says he is asking for the pots!'] was the favorite mix match of Zulu, Tswana, and English that they brought up to tease her. But all it did was highlight her linguistic inadequacies She wonders what it would be like had her father relented, despite himself, and let her go ahead with her six year old sweeping declaration, 'Papa, I don't speak Zulu. I speak English!' His 'Not in my house!' she believes crippled her. Now she doesn't know what a toilet is because he didn't use the word enough.

My interview with Mbali is a year after this story was written and when I ask her about its references to her childhood experience of "failing" to speak Setswana she is philosophical. English, she now concedes, is her "most fluent language," her "first language." But what remains is a longing for the "word-world" that might help her to describe a feeling, or a joke, or an onomatopoeic phrase (which are plentiful in isiZulu). "My writing would be at its best," she says, "if it could include all those references." Perhaps the feeling she still has is described in the last sentence of this assignment:

---

[8]   The speaker's use of "Matabele" is a slighting reference to a different ethnic group, who speak an Nguni language (such as isiZulu) rather than a Sotho-Tswana language (such as Setswana).

Baratamang wishes her cousin were here. Kedu is the one she could always rely on when she visited her grandmother to act as a mediator, translating the Tswana words her grandmother would say to her in a combination of Zulu and English, leaving out the obvious disappointment in her eyes that needed no translation.

Mbali's discussion of her relationship to English, isiZulu, and Setswana is both ambivalent and pragmatic. To some extent she has embraced English, or at least she has swum too far out into this big pond to go back to the shore. But nonetheless she has decided to apply to an MA in literary translation in the United States. Here is a further complication: a course in translation suggests a commitment to finding her creative voice in more than one language, but the decision to pursue it in North America, far from the familiar speakers of her home languages, will no doubt present her with a fresh set of challenges.

With the experiences of Mbali and others in mind, I have drawn other colleagues in to the course to assist with the reading of assignments in languages other than English. Each year, I explore with my students the sometimes untapped potential of the language resources open to them for the writing of their stories and essays. We debate the options, they tinker, they risk, they rebel. This year, two students have responded to the invitation to present one of their assignments in isiZulu (which a colleague in the African Languages department will read). I am surprised that there are not more choosing this option, but what this suggests to me is a determination on the part of my students to master a literary language of their choosing (as complicated as this choice clearly is, given the history of the country and the ongoing suppression of African languages). For now, the Honors seminar, presented in English, can only offer them choices, can help them to decode their expectations of themselves, and perhaps, if it is to achieve anything, encourage them to write in an English that is inflected, flexible, colorful, contaminated, in creative discourse with the other jostling language cousins. Perhaps what Mbali and others are reaching for is an English that is a Setswana-English or an isiZulu-English, not quite itself but something more interesting, more fluid, and more true to their experiences.

References

Davids, J. (2019), From an unpublished portfolio produced as part of the poetry course, translations by the authors and Johannes Davids.

Davis, W. (2014), "The Ethnosphere and the Academy", Keynote Speech: Where There Be Dragons. Available online: https://www.wheretherebedragons.com/wpcontent/uploads/2014/09/DavisEthnosphereAcademy.pdf (accessed September 16, 2019).

Futha, Z. (2018), interview with Phillippa Yaa de Villiers.

Jordan, A. C. (1973), *Tales from Southern Africa*, San Francisco: University of California Press.

Kamfer, R. (2019), "There is Another World and it is in This One," in M. Xaba (ed.), *Our Words, Our Worlds: Writing on Black South African Women Poets 2000–2018*, Durban: UKZN Press.

Mokgathi, M. (2019), from an unpublished portfolio produced as part of the poetry course.

Muhumed, A. (2017), from an unpublished portfolio produced as part of the poetry course.

Muishond, T. (2013), from an unpublished portfolio produced as part of the poetry course, translations by the authors.

Muishond, T. (2019), "Searching for Women Like Me," in M. Xaba (ed.), *Our Words, Our Worlds: Writing on Black South African Women Poets 2000–2018*, Durban: UKZN Press.

Sebaeng, M. (2018), from an unpublished portfolio produced as part of the prose writing course, translation by Mbali Sebaeng.

Sebaeng, M. (2019), interview with Bronwyn Law-Viljoen.

3

Workshopping to Better Writing and Understanding

Fan Dai and Ling Li
Sun Yat-sen University

Introduction

Creative writing in English in China was introduced to tertiary education only in recent years against the backdrop of English-teaching reforms (Dai 2012, Kroll and Dai 2013). Dai has been offering one of the few-and-far-between creative writing courses since 2009 at Sun Yat-sen University. In China, other universities that offer creative writing courses are Renmin University of China (since 2006), China University of Petroleum (since 2014), and a few others such as Sichuan University and Xiamen University (Dai 2015, Dai and Li 2017).

Having been run for almost ten years, the creative writing course for English majors at Sun Yat-sen University is conducted in a holistic manner. By this, we mean to say that it introduces various crafts through reading as a writer and lectures on examples of good crafting from previous students' work. Then we, Dai and colleagues, run workshops for students' assignments that account for more than three-quarters of the course. This chapter examines the special elements of the workshop in the Chinese context, in order to see its role in the creative writing classroom and beyond.

Previous Studies on Workshops and on Chinese Culture

The creative writing workshop, which originated in the US in Iowa in the 1930s to 1950s (Myers 1996, Vanderslice 2010), is considered to be the "natural academic mode for creative writing" (Leahy 2010: 63). As the signature pedagogy of creative writing (Meacham 2009, Leahy 2010, Stukenberg 2017), the workshop has been "an epicenter for both critique and defenses" in the academy (Mayers 2017: 8).

Donnelly (2010) and Clark et al. (2017) collected a myriad of voices on the strengths and weaknesses of the workshop model. These include benefits such as "fostering empowerment, improvement of writing skills etc." versus drawbacks such as "hegemonic structure of race and gender" and "limiting students to develop unique writers' voices" (Howe 2016: 491). While the two editions and other related literature explore new ways to run effective workshops and even non-traditional ones like that of the "unworkshop" by Harper (2017: 20), they are mainly inspected through a monolingual and monocultural lens, mostly in English-speaking countries. As pointed out by Whitehead (2016: 376), there might be a risk of cultural imperialism if the local context is not taken into consideration when applying the pedagogy of the Western workshop in Asia.

Taking into account the realities of working in English as a foreign language, the creative writing workshop at Sun Yat-sen University is designed to combine the workshop model with aspects of proficiency training in the Chinese context (Dai 2011).

The Workshop and Critical Thinking

According to Myers (1996: 118), the workshop method is one of "communal making" and "communal criticism". Bizzaro (2010: 38) pointed out that the two tasks central to workshop are "interpretation" and "evaluation," in which analytical tools borrowed from New Criticism, Literary Critical Theory, and related knowledge are relevant for honing student writers' crafts and understanding of the discipline. Cain (2010) proposed that the workshop is an ideal "third space" where students develop their critical capacity and thus expand their creative understanding of how texts work as texts.

Considering that the workshop is a place for students to learn how to read critically, the teacher should be able to provide "a rich and interesting array of reading methods" that "help students demonstrate to themselves that their poems, stories, essays, or plays might be read from a variety of perspectives" (Bizzaro 2010). For example, "In Bed," an essay by Joan Didion, is about migraine. The writer starts with her younger days when she tried to deny the presence of migraine in her life and ignored the symptoms:

That in fact I spent one or two days a week almost unconscious with pain seemed a shameful secret, evidence not merely of some chemical inferiority, but of all my bad attitudes, unpleasant tempers, wrongthink.

Didion (1994: 689–91)

Most students could see that "my bad attitudes, unpleasant tempers, wrongthink" is the writer's thought, which explains why she felt migraine was "a shameful secret." As beginners in creative writing, they might fail to see that the reason for migraine, which is the result of "some chemical inferiority," is inserted in her thought, rendering "my bad attitudes" an incorrect way of understanding migraine, as she herself knew the pain was a physical phenomenon, not the result of her attitudes. Therefore, this thought was her past thought, which is in line with that of those who don't understand migraine. Therefore, "my bad attitudes" evokes the thoughts or voices of other people, and carries both Didion's voice when she could not accept migraine and the voice(s) of those who have little knowledge of it. Such overlap of thought and voices of different people is not something that students tend to be aware of. Close examination raises their awareness on how an effective essay works, thus preparing them for critiquing each other's work.

Close reading like the above would serve as the introduction to critical thinking in that Dai tends to invite students to supply answers with general questions to a given passage followed by more specific questions to encourage them to think in a specific direction. She would start with questions such as "What kinds of voice/thought do you see in the paragraph?" This would likely be followed by "What other voices do you see?" "Do you see any overlapping of voices?" She would give her perspectives, to fill in what is missing in the students' answers, of all the voices and analyse the overlapping voices.

The above process would serve as a mind-opening example for students to think beyond a straightforward answer, a reminder to think critically. The absence of critical thinking of Chinese students has been the concern of many scholars in recent years at home and abroad (Atkinson 1997, O'Sullivan and Guo 2010, Ku and Ho 2010). For those who have taught in China, a common impression is that students tend to be quiet in the classroom, avoiding eye contact with the teacher when asked a question (Wu 2009).

Although the increasing exposure to knowledge has turned some students into active participants over the years, the lack of response is still more present than interaction. This phenomenon is often linked with lack of critical thinking, in addition to other reasons such as L2 learner's "silence of embarrassment, fear, and anxiety" (Smith and King 2018: 325); and the influence of Confucian heritage culture (Zhou, Knoke, and Sakamoto 2005, Wu 2009) which advocates harmony and respect for authority, and which discourages students from questioning or challenging teachers. This also leads Chinese students to exhibit face-saving tendencies in their public behavior (Wen and Clement 2003: 20).

On the other hand, some research argues that the fact that students are silent in class doesn't mean they lack the ability to think critically (Tian and Low 2011, Zhang 2017, Chen 2017, Lu and Singh 2017). The workshop at Sun Yat-sen University resonates with this argument. The workshop, comparatively new to Chinese students, is a model that encourages interaction within the classroom. Students sit in a circle, which makes it hard for anyone not to be noticed. Moreover, the course allocates 20 percent of the grade to participation in workshop. This setting encourages students to speak, especially after the active ones have taken the lead.

One example is when students read "In Honor of . . ." (Dai 2016), a published piece from Dai, the teacher. One student raised a question about the three paragraphs in which the writer sidetracked to talk about her own experiences of going to the toilet, lining up for the swing, and getting hot water in between classes when resources were limited, while that part of the story was supposed to be about QiuQiang, an intellectually disabled classmate who had the privilege of not being restricted by rules. The student pointed out that those three paragraphs seemed to have little to do with QiuQiang's story. Dai praised the student and admitted that she herself was fully aware of that when writing, but she had found it hard to resist the details that revealed an experience that would be difficult for the current generation to believe. She also suggested that those paragraphs were instances of the frustrating aspects of life that QiuQiang's privileges prevented him from suffering. Therefore, they are loosely connected to Qiu's story.

Dai was pleased that students challenged her for a published story. That would have been taboo in a conventional Chinese classroom, since the Chinese educational culture places the teacher in the position of authority: someone students should respect, not question (Wang 2006, Ku and Ho 2010, Li, Rao and Tse 2012). Furthermore, this was also a challenge to the face culture, as this could have caused Dai to lose face. The students' question demonstrates that they understood the coherence of the story, and felt comfortable enough to challenge the authority of the teacher and writer. Dai had frequently encouraged students to express their opinions, and that she would value the fact that they shared their opinion rather than stay silent. This established a practice in which students were ready to critique and were open to criticism. Since every student's work is to be critiqued, every student has the same opportunity to experience both.

The workshop creates an environment in which everyone is free to speak their mind in a critical manner. Students are told that the ability to critique demonstrates their understanding of craft, which in turn would help their own writing. Therefore, the workshops throughout the semester turned critical thinking into a common practice.

Having been in the MFA creative writing program at City University of Hong Kong, Dai knew how active and interactive students in a workshop could be. Having taught the creative writing course in China and knowing the culture, she did not expect the same active participation in the Chinese classroom. Even so, she knew it was important to encourage discussion whether they made a good point or not. Although it is true that her students were not as active as their counterparts outside China, most of them could be motivated to speak if a few students took the lead, especially after the act of speaking in the workshop had been appreciated, usually through Dai praising the students' questions as valid and to the point. Dai also made sure that she praised the student for critiquing her work.

It is clear that the workshop has changed the culture in the classroom, in that students would have to speak more than usual, that they would need to demonstrate what they articulate makes good sense, and that they may even have to challenge a traditional power figure. Therefore, the role of the teacher assumes more importance because he/she is there to give the student encouragement for being "offensive," especially when the student disagrees with the teacher. This is something the teacher has to learn to accept, instead of trying to save their own "face" even when the student's critique is justified. Therefore, this process of critical thinking on the students' part is beneficial both ways. It follows that the workshop becomes an education for both students and teacher. The teacher's being receptive to criticism sets a good example for the students.

The Workshop: Healing and Peer Support

The creative writing course at Sun Yat-sen University has been offered to second-year English majors, most of whom are around nineteen years of age. When Dai first taught the course in 2009, she was concerned that students might not want to open up and write about things they really cared about, but the workshop proved otherwise. Almost every semester, more than one student would cry during a workshop. The first workshop that witnessed a student, Yan, crying was about a story in which the writer expressed her guilt for having kept silent for breaking her grandmother's sewing machine. Like everyone else in the family, she assumed that the writer's cousin had done it. Every Spring Festival, the grandmother would blame the cousin for not admitting to the "crime" during the reunion dinner. The cousin would deny it to no avail. Years later, the writer got into Sun Yat-sen University and learned that her cousin had considered her his role model. That rendered the writer doubly guilty.

When she started crying, her fellow students started sharing their own stories of guilt. That had the apparent effect of easing the student. Such peer support came again in another workshop, in which student Lu talked about herself being deaf in one ear while the other ear was suffering from an infection that could lead to deafness. She received a lot of warmth from her peers during the workshop. She reported that after the workshop, a classmate whom she did not know well shared with her her own story of losing health. Lu was very much touched, and the workshop experience gave her a great deal of strength.

Dai was aware of the difference of these workshop experiences compared to those in English-speaking countries (Dai 2011). In fact, her colleagues had advised her confronting issues such as these ought to be the job of a counselor. However, counseling services are new in China, and students do not seem to understand or trust them enough. Besides, there is so much demand for the service that, more often than not, students cannot get the timely help they need.

Student Ni submitted a short fiction for her workshop. It was about a couple, the husband having been injured in war and then killed on the plane back home. Dai commented that the war part was not particularly authentic but the emotional aspect felt very real, at which point Ni started crying. She was crying so hard that she asked to leave the classroom. Given the unusual situation, Dai asked Ni whether she would like company. Ni said she would. So her roommate left the classroom with her.

Dai checked with the other students to find out what they knew about the situation. A few of them, who had talked with Ni after reading the story, said Ni's story must have come from the fact that her boyfriend was in a military institution, and their meetings were frustrating more often than not: their plans were often restricted by regulations and interrupted by unexpected trainings and happenings beyond their control. The students all said that Ni would be okay. She just needed to get things out of her system. A few classmates knew her well enough to say that the workshop must have triggered Ni's most tender feelings though she had already reconciled with the situation before writing the story.

A few months later, Ni and Dai were in a summer program together in Cologne. They had a walk, and Dai brought up the subject. Ni gave some accounts of how her boyfriend was called to official actions with almost no notice and how heartbreaking for her it was to abandon their plans, especially when she had to travel quite some distance to meet him. Ni hastened to make it clear that her crying at the workshop did not mean that she was very sad. What made her cry was the attention she got in the workshop. The tears were her way of handling the warmth. She said another classmate who also cried in her own workshop shared the same feeling. It was a story about a father and daughter, and it was not particularly sad, and she certainly did not expect herself to cry during the workshop. But the warm responses from the class induced the tears.

It is apparent that the workshop has unexpectedly served as an effective way for peers to give support to each other. In addition to discussing the craft of a student's creative work, it provides a platform for students to find emotional outlet and support. This is a niche that creative writing finds itself to have in the Chinese educational setting, as there is scarcely another course that gives students the opportunity to express their opinions toward life. As a result, students take the initiative to share works outside the classroom, so that on more than one occasion, one student would try answering a question on behalf of the writer because the student had read the story and discussed it with the writer.

What has happened in the workshop, in fact, reveals a gap in the current educational scene. Students do need the emotional space they find through creative works, and they find the workshop helpful for that. Although the question remains whether it is appropriate for the creative writing teacher to offer something close to a counseling service (Linder 2004), Dai's experience is that the workshop in the Chinese context has functioned partially as a platform for students to give each other emotional support, which they otherwise would not find among themselves. The stories workshopped are the media and base for emotional exchanges. They bind the students and the teacher together in a way that is not known in a regular or traditional classroom. Such peer support resolves some actual issues that have troubled students for a long time. In Yan's case, she sent her story to her cousin under Dai's encouragement, and the cousin, now a mature young man, had forgiven Yan and was pleased to clear his name in the family.

The Workshop and Cultural Awareness

One difference between creative writing in one's mother tongue and that in a foreign language is the attention the writer needs to pay to cultural elements. Obviously, each country has something special about its culture, which renders translation difficult. At the same time, creative writing in a foreign language can be understood as a kind of translation, or more specifically, self-translation without the original text (Dai and Zheng 2019). As hard as it is to believe, quite a number of students write without considering whether a native speaker of English can understand expressions such as *Gongfu, Qi, QQ,* and *WeChat,* as they are so widely used in China.

Having been writing and publishing in English for the last ten years or so, Dai herself has been incorporating explanations of cultural elements into the narrative and turning it into part of the story. She has also been doing research in this aspect as cited above, in the hope of raising awareness of writers who write in a foreign language. Throughout the workshops run in the last nine years, Dai has worked on developing students' cultural awareness, which has now taken shape. Initially, expressions such as "her parents *worked outside* since she was a child," "they spent a lot of time *pressing the road*," and "Maybe I should buy it on Taobao" were used frequently without awareness that most English-speaking people were strangers to them. From the context, one may be able to work out that Taobao is likely to be the name of a shop, and sure enough, it is one of the biggest and widely used online-shopping websites in the country. However, *worked outside* and *pressing the road* could be a little mystifying.

In the given workshop, Dai pointed out that *worked outside* is a recent Chinese-specific term. The expression refers to the particular phenomenon of people leaving villages to work in cities where they receive better pay. That served as a reminder for students that when they write in English, they must not assume their readers to have such cultural knowledge about China. Similarly, in another workshop, Dai alerted students that the expression *pressing the road* would be puzzling to non-Chinese readers. It is colloquial, meaning dating: in China, it is common for those falling in love to take long walks as if they are there to press the road.

Another example of a general lack of cultural awareness is as follows:

> But I'm a little concerned about my hands' safety recently, for the double eleven festival is coming and people around are all planning to do something.

"Double Eleven" is an online-shopping promotion occasion first started on November 11, 2009 in China. It has since become the largest scale of online shopping with heavy discounts and has resulted in new records of revenue for just one day. Many netizens ended up spending a lot of money just by clicking the mouse. Consequently, people talked about "chopping their hands off" in order to stop the shopping frenzy; hence, the writer of these lines is worried in anticipation of the coming Double Eleven Day. For someone who is not familiar with the current shopping scene in China, "Double Eleven Festival" can still be understood as a shopping occasion, but the logic between the writer being concerned with her hands and the "Double Eleven Festival" would definitely need explaining.

The above examples indicate the extent of the lack of awareness on the students' part when they write in English, as these expressions are so culturally specific that not all non-Chinese people would understand them. The workshops provide the opportunity for students to develop cultural sensitivity, and their writing reflects such progress. The workshops enable students to see, through cases such as the ones discussed above, how much they have taken for granted some of the facts of life in China. Therefore, they began to incorporate cultural explanations into their writing. For example, student Qing wrote:

> People believed it was the best to have a son and a daughter, which means "good" in Chinese characters

The explanation can enable readers to understand that the word "good" comes from Chinese characters that represent son and daughter. However, it doesn't let readers visualize the word. So suggestions were made to revise the lines into the following:

> People believed it was the best to have a son （子） and a daughter （女） , which means "good" （好） in Chinese characters

Another example of student's progress in explaining a cultural phenomenon is as follows:

> The doctor said she can only live for three days, so Da Bo (Ba Bo's son, my father's elder male cousin, I am supposed to call him uncle) sent her home. (Local people think it is ominous to die in the hospital.)

The explanations in the brackets are very helpful for the non-Chinese reader. However, brackets are an interruption of the narrative. They interfere with the flow of the story. In fact, these lines can easily be turned into the following without brackets:

> The doctor said she can only live for three days, so Da Bo, my father's elder male cousin, sent her home, as the local people believe it is ominous to die in the hospital.

Clearly, students saw the need in the above examples and made efforts to address the cultural issues concerned. Given more time and practice, they would make further progress.

Student Xinlu used a Japanese expression not familiar to the non-Japanese reader in the following:

> *"Yoloshiku."* I shook hands with him, heart pounding vehemently. Nice to meet you. I repeated the meaning in my heart.

Xinlu succeeded in blending the explanation of *Yoloshiku* with her own thought in the narrative, making the narration natural rather than contrived, and the narrative voice remains the same. Dai would draw the students' attention to similar skilled blending of a cultural phenomenon in workshops, showing them the difference that crafting makes in a narrative.

The following student, Yihang, demonstrated similar consideration in her work:

> . . . waiting for *Hongbao*, the money given to children as a lunar new year gift on Chinese Spring Festival, which carries the traditional good wishes from affectionate elders.

Her explanation, which fits naturally into the narrative, gives the necessary details for the international reader.

Student Yichun brings in a Chinese legendary figure in her writing:

> MenShen, the god of doorways in China, was famous for its horrible appearance because it could get rid of evil and ghosts. However, the MenShen in our class did not refer to those big men with heavy features, but meant Dang, the girl whose face was dark and full of acne, with small eyes and a flat nose.

The nickname *MenShen* here is used to refer to Dang, a classmate who was not very pretty. The writer explains the cultural aspect of the term before describing Dang's appearance without using words such as "horrible" or "ugly," which shows her understanding of the principle of "show and not tell," which also reveals her concern and sympathy toward Dang while making an association with *MenShen*.

Another example of evidence for students' progress is cited below:

> We called the circumstance *"Jia Tu Si Bi,"* which means someone has nothing but the bare walls in his house.

The writer uses a Chinese idiom to describe a situation of poverty. The Pinyin *Jia Tu Si Bi* here gives a Chinese touch while the explanation that follows eases the reader's frustration. The use of Chinese idioms and proverbs, which are very rich in daily Chinese, is something Dai, as a teacher and as a writer, often stresses in workshops, so that students come to appreciate the culture-specific wisdom and ideology they convey, which contribute to the Chinese aspect of the story.

Conclusion

The workshop has played a very important role in the teaching of creative writing at Sun Yat-sen University. It allows close reading of the narratives concerned and encourages students to express their opinions about writing techniques, including critiquing the work of authority figures. Consequently, the workshop has become the breeding ground for independent and critical thinking. The workshop also fills the gap where counseling service is not so available in Chinese universities. It functions as a platform for students to give support to each other and benefit from each other's experiences and strengths, a scenario otherwise unlikely to materialize in an academic setting. The workshop witnesses, in addition to the progress in writing techniques such as point of view and characterization, the increasing cultural awareness the students develop in writing in a foreign language as the course advances.

The above characteristics make the workshop special in the given creative writing classroom in China. Its role is facilitated through the supervision of the teacher, who needs to be open-minded, willing, and ready to be challenged by students, who must be sensitive to students' emotional needs, and who keeps alerting the students about the cultural points that demand explanation and elaboration, and pushing students to think of better ways for such explanations and elaborations.

References

Atkinson, D. (1997), "A Critical Approach to Critical Thinking in TESOL," *TESOL Quarterly*, 31(1): 71–94.

Bizzaro, P. (2010), "Workshop: An Ontological Study," in Donnelly, D. (ed.), *Does the Writing Workshop Still Work?*, 36–51, New York: Multilingual Matters.

Cain, M. A. (2010), "A Space of Radical Openness: Re-visioning the Creative Writing Workshop," in Donnelly, D. (ed.), *Does the Writing Workshop Still Work?*, 216–29, New York: Multilingual Matters.

Chen, L. (2017), "Understanding Critical Thinking in Chinese Social-cultural Context: A Case Study in a Chinese College," *Thinking Skills and Creativity*, 24: 140–51.

Clark M. D., Hergenrader, T. and J, Rein (eds), (2017), *Creative Writing Innovations: Breaking Boundaries in the Classroom*, New York: Bloomsbury.

Dai, F. (2011), "Writing, Sharing and Growing Together – Creative Writing in Sun Yat-sen University," *TEXT*, April. Available online: http://www.textjournal.com. au/speciss/issue10/Fan Dai.pdf

Dai, F. (2012), "English-language Creative Writing by Chinese University Students," *English Today*, 28 (3): 21–6.

Dai, F. (2015), "Teaching Creative Writing in English in the Chinese Context," *World Englishes*, 34(2): 247–59.

Dai, F. (2016), "In Honor of . . .," *Ninth Letter*. Special Edition. Available online: http://old.creativewriting.english.illinois.edu/ninthletter//international_feature/dai.html

Dai, F. and L. Li. (2017), "Teaching Creative Writing in a Foreign Language in China," *TEXT*, Special Issue 47, October. Available online: http://www.textjournal.com. au/speciss/issue47/DaiandLi.pdf

Dai F. and W. Zheng (2019), "Self-translation and English-language Creative Writing in China," *World Englishes*, 38(4): 1–12.

Didion, J. (1994), "In bed," in P. Lopate (ed), *The Art of the Personal Essay: An Anthology from the Classical Era to the Present*, 689–91, New York: Anchor Books.

Donnelly, D. (2010), *Does the Writing Workshop Still Work?*, New York: Multilingual Matters.

Harper, G. (2017), "The Unworkshop," in Clark, M. D., Hergenrader, T. and Rein, J. (eds), *Creative Writing Innovations: Breaking Boundaries in the Classroom,* 21–32, New York: Bloomsbury.

Howe, L. (2016), "A Review of Creative Writing Workshop Pedagogy in Educational Research: Methodological Challenges and Affordances," *Journal of Poetry Therapy*, 29 (4): 195–206.

Kroll, J. and F. Dai, (2013), "Reading as a Writer in Australia and China: Adapting the Workshop," *New Writing: The International Journal for the Practice and Theory of Creative Writing* 1–15.

Ku K. Y. L and I. T. Ho (2010), "Dispositional Factors Predicting Chinese Students' Critical Thinking Performance," *Personality and Individual Differences*, 48:54–8.

Leahy, A. (2010), "Teaching as a Creative Act: Why the Workshop Works in Creative Writing," in Donnelly D. (ed), *Does the Writing Workshop Still Work?*, 63–77, New York: Multilingual Matters.

Li, H., Rao, N., and Tse, S. K. (2012), "Adapting Western Pedagogies for Chinese Literacy Instruction: Case studies of Hong Kong, Shenzhen, and Singapore Preschools," *Early Education and Development*, 23(4): 603–21.

Linder, V. (2004), "The Tale of Two Bethanies: Trauma in the Creative Writing Class," *International Journal for the Practice and Theory of Creative Writing*, 1 (1):6–14.

Lu, S. and M. Singh (2017), "Debating the Capabilities of 'Chinese Students' for Thinking Critically in Anglophone Universities," *Education Sciences*, 7, 22.

Mayers, T. (2017), "Notes Toward an Inventive, Processed-Oriented Pedagogy for Introductory Multigenre Creative Writing Courses," in Clark, M. D., Hergenrader, T. and Rein, J. (eds), *Creative Writing Innovations: Breaking Boundaries in the Classroom,* 7–20, New York: Bloomsbury.

Meacham, R. (2009), "Vision and Re-vision in Creative Writing Pedagogy," in Regan A. R., Chick N. L. and A. Haynie (eds), *Exploring Signature Pedagogies: Approaches to Teaching Disciplinary Habits of Mind*, 59–79, Sterling, VA: Stylus.

Myers, D. G. (1996), *The Elephants Teach: Creative Writing Since 1880*, Chicago: University of Chicago Press.

O'Sullivan, M. and L. Guo (2010), "Critical Thinking and Chinese International Students: An East-West Dialogue," *Journal of Contemporary Issues in Education*, 5(2):53–73.

Smith, L. and J. King (2018), "Silence in the Foreign Language Classroom: the Emotional Challenges for L2 Teachers," *Emotions in Second Language Teaching*, 323–39.

Stukenberg, J. (2017), "Deep Habits: Workshop as Critique in Creative Writing," *Arts and Humanities in Higher Education*, 16(3):277–92.

Tian, J. and G. D. Low (2011), "Critical Thinking and Chinese University Students: A Review of the Evidence," *Language, Culture and Curriculum*, 24:1, 61–76.

Vanderslice, S. (2010), "Once More to the Workshop: A Myth Caught in Time," in Donnelly D. (ed.), *Does the Writing Workshop Still Work?*, 31–5, New York: Multilingual Matters.

Wang, L. (2006), "The Differences between the Chinese and English Modes of Thinking and Paragraph Structure in English Argumentative Writing," *J. Shang Luo Teach,* 20: 25–30.

Wen, W. P. and R. Clement (2003), "A Chinese Conceptualization of Willingness to Communicate in ESL," *Language, Culture and Curriculum*, 16 (1): 18–38.

Whitehead, H. (2016), "The Programmatic Era: Creative Writing as Cultural Imperialism," *Ariel: A Review of International English Literature*, 47(1-2): 359–90.

Wu, X. (2009), "The Dynamics of Chinese Face Mechanisms and Classroom Behavior: A Case Study," *Evaluation and Research in Education*, 22 (2-4): 87–105.

Zhang, T. (2017), "Why do Chinese Postgraduates Struggle with Critical Thinking? Some Clues from the Higher Education Curriculum in China," *Journal of Further and Higher Education*, 41(6): 857–71.

Zhou, Y. R., Knoke, D. and I. Sakamoto (2005), "Rethinking Silence in the Classroom: Chinese Students' Experiences of Sharing Indigenous Knowledge," *International Journal of Inclusive Education*, 9 (3): 287–311.

4

Protagonizing the L2: The Case for "Life Writing" in Creative Writing (SL) Contexts

Dan Disney
Sogang University

Life Writing as Self-narrativizing

This chapter seeks to extend from a number of previous studies, each of which has explored responses to specific questions, such as, how to speak with (or into) "a voice in a new language?" (Hanauer 2010: 8) and, alternatively, "how to feel like ourselves in a language we do not quite feel at home in" (Disney 2011: 4)? Indeed, when working toward establishing this interdisciplinary subfield as a legitimate academic discipline in Korea (only partly responding to discourses—or the so-called "lore"—of Creative Writing pedagogies in native language contexts in other parts of the world), Creative Writing (SL) educators may well focus instead toward locating guiding principles sharing ethical kinship with Paolo Freire's notion of *conscientization* (1983: 95). This chapter understands Freire's pedagogical foundations can enable self-advocatory, empowered modes of consciousness, and contends that Creative Writing (SL) classes catalyze new phenomenological possibilities through expanding the potential to engage and express human complexities in a non-native language. In his paper "Toward a New Poetics in Creative Writing Pedagogy," Paul Dawson asks whether pedagogical processes in Creative Writing classes are to be "guided by the idiosyncrasies of each teacher, the practicing writer able to pass on knowledge by virtue of [their] innate talent" (Dawson 2003: web), and then goes on to instead showcase a suite of teachable skills. While the subfield of Creative Writing (SL) is gathering impetus, this chapter agrees with Dawson, and asserts that creative writing classes can cause students to "see themselves as inescapable participants in a social dialog through the practice of writing" (Dawson 2003: web). The emergent discourse of Creative Writing (SL) foregrounds creative processes generating epiphanic, emancipatory protagonisms in both mother and other tongues, and Freire's communitarian theories keep any Creative Writing (SL) syllabus focused toward an inherently liberatory, democratic methodology in which students cultivate skill-sets around reading, thinking, feeling, and articulating engaged, intra-, inter- and extra-personal connection.

Surveying the Korean peninsula, it seems many of the world-class English literature programs in this country foreground canonical studies under the sole aegis of imparting critical literacies. Taking up an alternative pedagogical position with wholly different curricula (but quite possibly similar claims to humanistic objectives and outcomes), and based on the evidence from a range of creative writing classes my forbearing colleagues working in Sogang University's English Department (Literary Studies; Cultural Studies; Linguistics) have allowed me to teach over the last decade, I assert the benefits of creative exploration as no less than a cathartic mode of expansive self-humanization. Incorporating close and critical reading practices, I devise a blended pedagogical slant that privileges both criticality and creativity which expends less energy worrying about whether or not we are engaged in a viable or legitimate academic discipline and more time focusing on acquiring and then mobilizing skill-sets in which students locate and/or invent new modes and means of creatively expressing culturally-bound narratives using a novel non-native material. *Can* creative writing be taught? *Can* creative writing be evaluated objectively (Ritter and Vanderslice 2005: 110–11 *passim*)? It seems that the lores that have sprung up around these questions from other places and other pedagogical contexts answer resoundingly in the affirmative. In my classrooms at Sogang University, we insert the word "how" in front of both questions, and spend semester devising our responses.

As Dawson points out, there is a minor canon of writing handbooks promulgating models in which "Creative Writing offers students more personal freedom and practical skills than an essay-based literary studies class" (Dawson, 2003: web), but reading as a writer in L2 contexts takes on specific inflections: implementing notions of genre (typically understood by our students) alongside a heuristic pedagogical slant (hitherto largely unheard of in literary and cultural studies contexts here), in this chapter I survey the radical innovations delivered by undergraduate students participating in an experimental syllabus and read the writing students produce as a data set displaying the results of a generative methodology that synthesizes previously learned academic behaviors and knowledge. Specifically, these classes mobilize students' criticality (the much-practiced ability to analyse, explicate, and critique) and knowledge of canonicity (where texts are read as exemplary models) to augment genuinely novel, creatively literate original writing. At Sogang University, the interdisciplinary and often trans-genred life writing delivered by each critical co-investigator placed in charge of their own narratives (Freire 1983: 68) indicates these groups authentically engage real questions for lives within which each student writer is demonstrably protagonizing. Of course, Creative Writing (SL) educators shift away from the hermeneutic tradition's critique and analysis of literary texts and textuality, toward instead an explicit foregrounding of the materiality of a learned language in all its potential (Disney 2014: 2). In this chapter I seek to contribute to the emerging discourses of Creative Writing (SL) in Korean contexts, by exploring processes at play in classrooms while also proposing responses to a specific question: namely, which pedagogical benefits (if any) are conferred in learning to write creatively in a second language?

Just as L2 proto-poets in poetry writing classes at Sogang University have "view[ed] literature as a cluster of plausible models" (Disney 2014: 3), students enrolling in the university's life writing classes are equally encouraged to read a supplementary range of both L1 and translated literary texts. Encountering writers including (but not limited to) Theodor Adorno, Walter Benjamin, Ryszard Kapuściński, Hermoine Lee, Primo Levi, David Sedaris, and Rebecca Solnit, students read neither as analysts nor critics but instead as opportunistic language-instrumentalizers with an eye and ear toward how others have manipulated language into stimulating shapes and sequences. Quite simply, students are encouraged to read for fun and for function, and under the gaze of these attentive readers, a more direct question may drive toward creative inquiry: "how might I do something *materially akin*" to what has been done in this canonical text before me (Disney 2014: 3)? Herein, "[t]raditional boundaries between reading and writing, the creative and the critical, [are] challenged" Dawson, 2003: web), and when considering life writing deploys plausible, belletristic, re-readable language on a sentence-by-sentence basis, it seems we may well be limited only by our imaginations and, importantly, our knowledge of the learned language (to say nothing, yet, of those literary structures playing out within that language). Working toward a definition, we may say that while life writing is never purely imaginative literature, the remit of this literary mode remains expansive, and will certainly include photo essays, montage, confessions, historical studies, psychogeographical meditations on place, manifestos, hagiographical studies of people, travelogues, auto/biography, interviews, dream diaries, perhaps even philosophical tracts, and so forth. And so the trick therein lies with each reader: what have others done structurally, indeed generically, that I might seek to emulate?

In her seminal *Body Parts: Essays on Life Writing*, biographer Hermoine Lee works toward the following definition of Life Writing:

> what we want from it is a vivid sense of the person. The reader's first question of the biographer is always going to be, what was she, or he, like? Other questions (like why, or how do you know, or do we approve, or does it matter) may follow. But "likeness" must be there. And when we are reading other forms of life-writing—autobiography, memoir, journal, letter, autobiographical fiction or poem—or when we are trying ourselves to tell the story of a life, whether in an obituary, or in a conversation, or in a confession, or in a book—we are always drawn to moments of intimacy, revelation, or particular inwardness.
>
> Lee (2008: 3)

Lee's definition can be turned slightly, and to great effect: instead of asking, "what was she, or he, like?" so as to tell the story of a life, in contexts where L2 writers deploy language as a radical technology delivering newly-expressive L2 identities, we may instead seek for explicatory means by which to inform our readers what *we* are like, and do so in full awareness that ours are stories that only we can tell, and that these stories remain legitimately no less than fascinating. This is part of the so-called *conscientization* that remains so central to these classes: when students learn how to read without the specter of a term paper looming, but in service to fulfilling their own intellectual curiosity, something important may be gained: critically attuned readers may also become well-versed readers of self and others. Those able to see the depth structures of how stories are composed seem able not only to empathize with but also predict human behaviors; therein, those who can imagine how and why things happen are only a short distance from replicating those patterns in dynamic, creative narratives.

What comes next, of course, in capturing our readers' attention is largely a matter of style. Novelist George Saunders catalyzes proto-writers toward plumbing language for its stimulations when exploring the ethos of textual exploration and invention:

> I think a good story is one that says on many different levels, "we're both human beings, we're both in this crazy situation called life that we don't really understand; can we put our heads together and confer about it a little bit at a very high, non-bullshitty level?" Then all kinds of magic can happen.
>
> Saunders (YouTube 2017)

Perhaps this is where a heuristic life writing syllabus demanding wholesale creative exploration will work on fundamentally different levels to those classes gearing toward knowledge produced by critique and analysis: indeed, it is no exaggeration to assert that within the procedural realms of sentence-making where a learned language is treated as an experimental, malleable, material, in arriving at Saunders's so-called non-bullshitty authenticities, these moments of intimacy may well be a matter of self-revelatory expansion. When L2 student writers act as investigative *litterateurs*, each is engaging an imaginative and then linguistic process by which to self-protagonize and, for some, this signals no less than a radical methodology toward new sensibilities, new expressivities, indeed a renewed lexicon by which to narrativize our pronouns. Far from an imperialistic Englishization of these students' imaginarium, then, this pedagogical slant insistently dwells in possibility, and in seeking for what Freire asserts as a liberatory education by prioritizing "acts of cognition" over "transferals of information" (1983: 67), so often what conjures is no less than unexpected moments of arresting L2 textuality.

"Useful Precepts"?

One fear inevitably paralyzing almost every student at some stage in their life writing classes is conveyed in the question, "what makes our writing 'good'?" (and, perhaps equally inevitably, that question is compelled by economies which push attention necessarily toward final grades). Of course, similar anxieties have long been part of the discourse of Creative Writing as an academic discipline in native language contexts, and there endures an "ever-present myth of the unteachability of creative writing" (Ritter and Vanderslice 2005: 110). Some of those fears seem assuaged when students are told "ambition" will factor greatly in final marks (regardless of the writer's textual outcomes). In the first weeks of semester, a new group circles the omnipresent question of value and make a series of claims: good writing can demarcate truths and beauty; good writing can humanize us, and expand those vistas (psychic, affective, intellectual) that unfold us as individuals going across social and cultural worlds. Rather than just enabling the output of more detailed descriptive sentences, in these classes our best writing may cause us to feel at once uncomfortable and at home. Throwing open the question of "value" can energize and motivate, while also initiating the important groundwork of democratizing the classroom. These conversations also steer us back toward reading in the hope that our future encounters with texts written by others might well reveal tricks we too can learn how to play: to somewhat turn Whitman's famous credo, then, to be excellent self-narrativizers we might attempt first to become excellent readers.

Three points serve (I hope) to aid L2 proto-writers as they begin to excavate, invent, discover, confabulate, and arrange their narratives. First, good writing seems to observe and precisely notice details. Consider this from Ryszard Kapuściński's "Central Asia—the Destruction of the Sea," contained in his masterful *Imperium*:

> The airplane delimits a wide circle, and when its wing dips one can see sand dunes stretching down below, wrinkled by the wind. It is the new desert of Aral Kum—or, more precisely, the bottom of the sea that is disappearing from the face of the earth.
>
> Kapuściński (1995: 254)

This opening paragraph seems "nonchalant, so confident" says one student, and the text also seems effortlessly populated with a richness of kinetic details as we sit tight, at a circling plane's window, gazing onto vistas below. Action, drama, tension: all are foreshadowed in this verb-filled setting, and I suspect most of Kapuściński's readers will glide toward the second paragraph, eager to see what happens next. Good writing can immediately draw us in, and so it is with Tiziano Terzani's "The Peddlars of the Trans-Siberian Railway," from his book of long-form travelogues, *A Fortune-Teller Told Me*:

> In Ulan Bator the summer sunsets are slow and glorious. The mountains glow with beautiful pastel colours that change from green to blue to violet, like the colours of the silk sashes that Mongolian men and women wear around their waists like belts. I watch it for the last time, absorbing the lofty purity of the sky and yearning sweetness of the hills. The sun never seemed to disappear, casting longer and longer shadows over the crowd that stood with raised arms to wave at the train, and over the pickpocket who, at the last moment, tried to steal my little Minox.
>
> Terzani (1997: 304)

These two exemplary paragraphs use language in such painterly fashion (one recalls ancient theoretician Horace's *ut pictura poeisis)* and chime with surprise and delight: a disappearing sea? A frenzy of color on a faraway train station? These imagistic settings crystallize that which Horace claims for poets, those language-users who (allegedly) "aim at giving either profit or delight, or at combining the giving of pleasure with some useful precepts for life" (1965: 90). This then may well serve as our second characteristic of so-called "good writing," which seems always to avoid cliché and well-worn turns of phrase when hooking readers, working instead toward image and figuration where the skies you invite readers to imagine are always the color of silk sashes, etc. Writing like this seems to know we must amaze and stir those we seek to stimulate; finally, then, the third hallmark of "good writing" works toward what Aristotle refers to in his "Ars Poetica" as "organic unity," which might most simply be understood as the interrelation and interconnectedness of well-observed, re-readably stimulating language: famously, the philosopher asserts "whatever is beautiful, whether it be a living creature or an object made up of various parts, must necessarily not only have its parts properly ordered, but also be of an appropriate size, for beauty is bound up with size and order" (1965: 42), and herewith possibilities of structuring narrative seem endlessly fit for exploration.

In these ways, then, part of the lore of life writing in a learned language may involve delimiting language as a material. If "the limits of my language mean the limits of my world" (Wittgenstein 1922: 68), then part of the auto-humanization of these L2 life writers entails semantic, syntactical, lexical, grammatical expansion of who, what, and how they can be. Reading opportunistically toward a range of so-called tricks of the trade, the attention of these reading writers is directed unrelentingly toward seeking for examples by which to know answers to the following questions:

(i) CONTENT
     Is the text "showing" or "telling" its readers, and what is shown or told?
     From which point of view? How do these impact on tone and theme?
(ii) STYLE
     Is the narrative unified as a coherent whole? Which language is used, and
     to what ends? In which ways do sentences probe for impact and effect?
(iii) STRUCTURE
     Which genre devices are at work in the text, and how do these develop
     unity and coherence?

An example: when reading Neil MacGregor's careful *flânerie* across long-absent cultural spaces via his reading of historical objects, we may come to better understand the many ways in which language can be fabulously manipulated to ardent and evocative effect. This writer's meditations on a Chinese Han lacquer cup (AD 4, discovered near Pyongyang), and a Korean roof tile (AD 700–800, from Kyongju) demonstrate the novel ways by which to intensively read objects into stimulating textual events, and both the cup and the tile are archeologized by MacGregor writing in the manner of an elaborate survey. When he claims that the "cup is a powerful document" (2012: 185), intellectually curious readers seeking advances on their own creative tricks to play will want to know *why?*, and may well ask next, *and how have we been made to care?* When the roof tile is said to "have been some sort of status symbol" (268), we may look at rooftops around us and wonder *how so?*, immediately engaging with MacGregor's quietly outrageous claims. In short, we are being manipulated, and this writer's tone remains both scientifically detached and gently awed, as if these objects are portals to shift us impossibly backward into once living, forgotten places. It seems that part of the wondering mind must also wander, generatively, and if these classes expand linguistic parameters, then the ability to creatively express and narrativize will also expand.

MacGregor is always careful to include readers in his meditations, and this is "our cup" (182) and "our roof tile" (268); in terms of Horace's so-called useful precepts, through MacGregor's transportational explorations we not only understand the lost contexts from which these objects derive but also come to understand our present contexts, and he asserts as much: the "lacquer cup of 2000 years ago takes us into territory that is disconcertingly familiar" (186). MacGregor moderates his approach to these subjects so as to write from a position whereby history is a setting, objects are treated as if characters, and his elaborations lead finally toward a unifying dénouement; MacGregor's punchily philosophical last sentence, "how you read history depends on where you're reading it from" (270), shows proto-writers a structure wherein exploration and enumeration can finally arrive at aphoristic explanation, and this can work spectacularly as a unifying device causing readers to linguistically perform no less than their own "acts of cognition" (Freire 1983: 67).

Of course, this may all be a quantum leap from where most beginner-writer students will be situated, and so (to begin at the beginning) in order to initiate processes by which to protagonize our language, George Saunders calls for careful interest to be paid to sentences where actions, dictions, and settings indicate underlying emotion. Thus it is, with all the care of an attendant imagination given full permission to wander, that Saunders' rudimentarily declarative "Frank was an asshole" shifts toward a much more interesting, "Frank snapped at the barista who reminded him of his dead wife" (Saunders 2017) to which, in the early weeks of semester, our class then adds further clauses, experimentally amplifying this swarm of complex textual affectivity: Frank snaps at the barista who reminded him of his dead wife, (a) whom he'd divorced last week; or (b) who was his childhood sweetheart, and whom he'd only married a month ago; or (c) whom he hadn't thought of for years, since getting out of jail. In telling the stories only we can tell, the same expositionary approach can apply: "Dan ~~was nervous on the first day of class~~ raised his voice too loudly, squeakily anxious to be heard by the people he'd guide over the semester that stretched ahead," or "~~I was feeling~~

~~protective and anxious~~ glanced around the sun-filled field amid the dead grass where cows dared not venture, and whispered to her, 'get behind me; please don't talk!'" From the outset, our early investigations can be suffused with language in which actions imply emotion, and so often proto-writers in L2 domains must be carefully encouraged and shown how to change focus from the explications they rehearse endlessly in literary and cultural studies contexts. Early in the semester sentences are so often merely descriptive, rendered with characters tentatively populating atonal or anodyne settings, whose motivations may be gradually coaxed toward antagonistic problematization, before a climactic moment then dénouement, as if one guideline is immediately useful: as to prose fiction, so to life writing (at least, to an extent). Other considerations loom, by which to create writing that shimmers with intent: which kinds of language does a protagonist use? How do they act? Which other physical traits do we see? Consider the human form as a palette: what of facial features? Body shape? Clothing? Hair (and indeed levels of hairiness, etc.), and what do these details each imply? Is your protagonist a sympathetic character, or not, and do you know why? Who narrates the text—is the voice reliable?—and which effects are produced? Another way of organizing our creative approaches toward language is to understand we are literarily concocting answers to a series of pseudo-questions (to wit: characters = who? Setting = where + when? Plot = what? Theme = why?) and the very nature of the enterprise entails that, from the outset, we probably know only the barest of details. The writing itself supplies answers to *who, where, when, what* and often these emerge unexpected and epiphanic as the *why,* that final arrival of *conscientization* through newly aware self-knowing. This is the "value" of Creative Writing (SL) classes: through reading, then reflecting, wondering, exploring, and experimenting, we finally come to expand our abilities to engage, cathartically, with self and our others.

Something Tangible in Our Minds?

So far, this short chapter has somewhat explored the possibilities and parameters of an experimental life writing syllabus by which top-ranked literary and cultural studies students working in L2 contexts at Sogang University have been encouraged to seek for ways to creatively protagonize their own narratives. But beyond merely heightening orthographic sensitivity, it remains to be seen whether any pedagogical benefit is conferred when learning to write creatively in a second language. In his study of L2 creativity, *Poetry as Research: Exploring*

Second Language Poetry Writing, David Hanauer asks "[c]an poetry writing be considered a form of knowledge" (11), and his evidence implies that, indeed, "linguistic, creative, intra- and interpersonal knowledge transfers when students undertake the practice-based research of making poems in a foreign language" (Disney 2011: 6). In this life writing class, where high caliber students explore wholly different generic modes of creative engagement to those taught in Hanauer's classes, two folios are required, accompanied by an exegetical statement that will be both critically framed by the theories we consider (Freud, Lacan, Benjamin) and suffused with examples from closely read canonical texts which have somehow been instructional. The content of these documents makes clear just how varied the advances are between these language-instrumentalizers spending a semester together and taking boldly experimental excursions into, through, and across the English language. By semester's end I field thirty-six folios, totaling 119,213 words (or, between the eighteen students in this particular group, 6,623 words each over eighteen weeks); their words traverse themes as varied as loneliness and K-pop, blind dating and bullying, insomnia and falling in love, blocked toilets, racism, weird religiosity, etc. The evocations start from first sentences, and I am struck by the attention to detail some of this writing displays:

"It is late afternoon, or to be more precise, nearly evening; through the dusty air, I see the red sun sinking down toward the earth." (Eun Ji)

"A shaft of eyeballs is pinned to a single mouth reigning over the table." (JuHee)

"His eyes were as if someone had carved small slits on his cream-colored face and two blue drops of blood had collected in the middle." (Jiyang)

"I used to think that the language in my brain worked too slowly to process all the logic, ideas, and visuals popping up in my web of neurons." (Sangjin)

"We all have those moments where we have a glimpse of the silhouette of 'something' in our mind that we'd like to make tangible and share with others." (Na Hyun)

Of course, this captivating and syntactically elegant language is the result of painstaking attention to detail, not only in each student's text but, firstly, the exemplary writing they read in this class: and so it is that skill-sets acquired while working within the pedagogical contexts of the hermeneutic tradition seem indeed a generative precursor to our creative engagements. In this literary and cultural studies department, these incredible students are more than able to read toward how other writers manipulate language into genre effects, and the evidence compels my understanding that their criticality enables and augments creative emergence. To which ends, though? Rather than a "separatist site of teaching and learning, whose practice and traditions are rooted in a powerful lore that sustains such separation" (Ritter and Vanderslice 2005: 102–3), if Creative Writing (SL) is to finally find a legitimate position within the institutions we work in (and those of course steered by national research foundations, political policy makers, et al.), an ongoing conversation will require constant attention to the results our students deliver. To wit: the many linguistic advances, developments in expressivity, gains in intra-, inter-, and extra-personal skills (all gearing toward catharsis, competence, confidence, and ultimately humanization) I leave to students from this life writing class to assert:

> One of the most effective tools that helped me during the life writing class in becoming a more engaging writer to readers is "reading as a writer." Reading other writers' works has given me an insight on how they perceive people and their environment. A few literary works we tackled this semester—Levi's "Gold" and "Iron," and Sedaris's "Cyclops"—inspired me to be more detailed in my characterizations. Reading their character descriptions gave me the impression that writers are observant with the people they encounter because not only do they describe the physical attributes of their characters, there are reasons as to why a character might appear in a certain way.
>
> (Yujin)

> When I started to write, it was mostly in the style of reportage but not in an interesting way. I had come to my first roadblock, thus I revisited some of the texts we analysed this semester to seek help; I especially paid attention to re-reading "Farewell, Burma." Terzani says that "history exists only if someone relates it," and that only with "every little description of a thing observed one can leave a seed in the soil of memory" (47). As a creative writer my goal is to leave the reader with an impression, in this folio's case I wanted my memories to become part of their memories; I want readers to experience what I experienced. This re-reading led me to realize that while reportage is an important aspect within the folio, to truly leave an impact on the reader there needs to be a balanced amount of showing (embellishment) to counterbalance telling (reportage).
>
> (Lucy)

> Reading Kapuściński's "Central Asia: the Destruction of the Sea," the first thing that came to my mind was that if it were not for this story, I would never have known the tragic ruination of the Aral Sea. This can happen if we are not

interested enough to learn what has happened to certain archeological sites. Even if we know, history can slowly vanish in people's minds if we do not ruminate, think critically, and discuss what has happened in the past. In terms of Kapuściński's writing, his text effectively provokes many thoughts and feelings that allow readers to not forget terrible incidents; after reading, rather than feeling hopeless, we may feel anger towards self-seeking political leaders neglecting the lives of innocent people and exploiting nature for their own sake. Thus, I thought it would be necessary to deal with another historical event that happened to the royal palace of Korea, Changgyeonggung, so as to bring about the same levels of raised consciousness in my readers.

(Gyuri)

Meditating on friends, foes, families, and beyond, by the end of our semester together these virtuosic English majors present a complex array of intimacies (and sometimes also acrimonies) swarming through a series of settings both familiar and surreal, each story whispering to its readers in well-imagined and strangely recognizable truths. In their own idiosyncratic ways, each writer seems energized toward crafting experience into a rigorously stylized language, and so often the effects are simply thrilling. Of course, and as noted in previous studies, these classes cannot be simply an arena in which the "power/knowledge endgames of colonization" play out; therewith, Creative Writing (SL) educators, and especially "native speaking writer-academics mobilized to English (SL) domains should feel [ourselves] compelled to work against the specters of Englishization [and the] attendant alienations, disempowerments, and deauthorizations" (Disney 2016: 38). Encouraging students to find a linguistic means to tell stories only they can tell, these classes actively adopt a Freirian platform, and assume all participants to be "anything but empty vessels waiting to be invested with information" or knowledge (Disney 2016: 35). Deploying the highest levels of critique and analysis, life writing classes at Sogang University catalyze a hybrid pedagogy which prioritizes critical reading (of exemplary texts, and indeed of our peers' work) in order to arrive at rarefied versions of our own stories. Therein, criticality and canon do not merely co-exist alongside this creatively-focused class: life writing inherently repurposes conceptual tools first picked up in literary and cultural studies classes, and these enable student writers to enlarge their imaginative possibilities. In Korean contexts, it seems that the creative output of these ambitious, dedicated, perhaps post-critical language-instrumentalizers entails nothing less than contact with a self in relation to myriad others; by these means, socialized and syncretic new dimensions of consciousness can emerge.

References

Aristotle (1965), "Ars Poetica," in *Aristotle, Horace, Longinus: Classical Literary Criticism*, trans. T. S. Dorsch, New York, Penguin: 31–75.

Dawson, Paul (2003), "Towards a New Poetics in Creative Writing Pedagogy," in *TEXT*, 7 (1). Available online: www.textjournal.com.au/april03/dawson.htm

Disney, Dan (2011), "'Is this how it's supposed to work?' Poetry as a radical technology in L2 Creative Writing classrooms," *New Writing: The International Journal for the Practice and Theory of Creative Writing*, 9 (1): 4–16.

Disney, Dan (2014), "Introduction: Beyond Babel?" in Dan Disney (ed.), *Exploring Second Language Creative Writing: Beyond Babel*, 1–10, Amsterdam: John Benjamins Publishing.

Disney, Dan (2016), "Creative Writing (SL): Notes toward an Inter-discipline?", in Graeme Harper (ed.), *Exploring Creative Writing: Voices from the Great Writing International Creative Writing Conference*, 33–48, Newcastle: Cambridge Scholars Publishing.

Freire, Paolo (1983), *Pedagogy of the Oppressed*, trans. Myra Bergman Ramos, New York: Continuum.

Hanauer, David (2010), *Poetry as Research: Exploring Second Language Poetry Writing*, Amsterdam: John Benjamins Publishing.

Horace (1965), "On the Art of Poetry," in *Aristotle, Horace, Longinus: Classical Literary Criticism*, trans. T. S. Dorsch, 77–95, New York: Penguin.

Kapuściński, Ryszard (1995), *Imperium*, New York: Vintage International.

Lee, Hermoine (2008), *Body Parts: Essays on Life-Writing*, London: Pimlico Books.

MacGregor, Neil (2012), *A History of the World in 100 Objects*, New York: Penguin Books.

Ritter, Kelly and Stephanie Vanderslice (2005), "'Teaching Lore' Creative Writers and the University," *Profession*, 2005: 102–12.

Saunders, George (2017), "On Story." YouTube, uploaded by Redglasspix, October 26. Available online: www.youtube.com/watch?v=1-1xNNrABw8

Terzani, Tiziano (1997), *A Fortune-Teller Told Me*, New York: Flamingo.

Wittgenstein, Ludwig (1922/2001) trans. D. F. Pears and B. F. McGuiness, *Tractatus Logico-Philosophicus*, New York: Routledge.

5

From the Shadow of a Myth to an Academic Subject: Teaching Writing from a Cognitive Base

Nora Ekström
University of Jyväskylä

Introduction

> As any good story of creativity teaches us, we often need to look back in order to keep moving forward.
>
> Wegener (2016: 187)

As a novice teacher about twenty years ago, I did not enter the classroom alone; I had an invisible army of my former teachers with me. My educational history manifested itself as principles, practical exercises and stories I told. However, at the time I wasn't conscious about this. There is a certain feeling of belonging that arises when remembering one's previous teachers. Their presence protects the young teacher. Yet imitation is not always wise. This is especially true in a field such as creative writing, which has more limited research on which to base its instruction. An army can do harm, too.

In my doctoral thesis, I tried to outline the principles of teaching Writing in the University of Jyväskylä at both Basic and Advanced levels (Ekström 2011). I have experience as both a student and a teacher in these studies, and yet the task was not easy. I found educational principles I agreed with, but which had no analogy in my own classroom practice. I found methods that had proved to be effective, yet I couldn't explain why. Finally, I ended up having to study both my own history—how I became a teacher of writing—and the history of creative writing in Finland.

The main purpose of research is to acquire new knowledge. I pointedly say in my thesis that I will try to get rid of the patterns of the past and find a better alternative wherever possible. My approach to history, however, is appreciative (Ekström 2011: 19–20). As cognitive science has shown, without memory you cannot imagine (Mullally and Maguire 2014). Furthermore, when you know the past, you can also anticipate the future.

Manifold Impact of Fennomania

Today Finland is a bilingual country.[1] However, as Nilsson notes, "In fact Finnish-language literature was very unusual before the Romantic nationalist revival at the beginning of the nineteenth century and the first publication of the Kalevala epics by Elias Lönnrot in 1835-1836" (2010: 135). Finland belonged to Sweden from the Middle Ages until 1809, and during those years the Swedish-speaking minority was the dominant group (Broomans 2015: 18). When the Russian Empire subdued Finland, it became an autonomous Grand Duchy. One could speak about the issues arising from Russification (Hoeven 2015: 91–2), but on the other hand during autonomy Finland was able to grant all adult citizens the right to vote as the first country in Europe.[2] Finland declared its independence in 1917, just after the Russian Revolution. Yet even during the years of Russian rule, Swedish remained an important language for the culture and institutions (Mäkinen 2015: 288). Finnish-language literature was only beginning to develop, and the first known attempt to educate Finnish-language writers was an interesting reflection of the national situation.

Elisabeth Järnefelt held an unofficial literary salon for writers in the later part of the nineteenth century. Järnefelt, a Russian native who married a Finnish governor, chose to support Finnish-language literature, no doubt because she and the members of her group were Fennomans. (Kopponen 1985.) They wanted Finland to be independent and thus needed the support of the majority of the Finnish-speaking population (Kirby 2006: 91–8). At the time, Finland was in fact an area inhabited by several tribes (Pulkkinen 1999: 118). To Fennomans, arts were an important vehicle for depicting the "common folk" as united. Literature was especially important, as language unified the majority of people. Writing in Järnefelt's group was therefore clearly connected to the Fennoman movement. For example, dialects were often used in written texts in order to reflect a naturalistic style (Kopponen 1985: 85).

---

[1] Officially, the languages are Finnish and Swedish. There is also a recognized Sámi minority, who live in Finland, Sweden, and Norway. Their main language is Northern Sami.

[2] More can be found at http://www.helsinki.fi/sukupuolentutkimus/aanioikeus/en/index.htm

The writers of Järnefelt's group were successful, especially Juhani Aho. His novels are still highly valued in the canon of Finnish literature. Aho has been described as a collective author (Niemi 1985: 42). He benefited from Järnefelt's group, for instance, when developing ideas for his novels (Aho and Niemi 1881/1986: 61). In this sense, it is a shame that Järnefelt's salon is not more widely known in Finland. I still encounter many students who feel that somehow it is less worthy to write in a collective way (Ekström 2018: 148–9). This is one of the sad legacies of the Romantic myth, which I will later discuss more specifically.

Nowadays I often mention Aho in my teaching: with his versatile texts he is a good example of a modern writer. An important theme to him was the relationship between nature and culture (Niemi 1985: 24–5, 33, 46). This theme is most timely and a good example of a motive for writing that does not require personal tragedy, as some theories of creativity have claimed.

Romanticist Fennomans believed that only vernacular language could express the soul of the people (Hoeven 2015: 85). At one point, Fennomans considered language as having the same status as a person's homeland (Virtanen 2002: 265). Eventually, Finnish and Swedish cultures began to diverge (Nilsson 2010: 135–8) and today only about 5 percent of the population speaks Swedish as their first language. There are no academic writing programs in Finland that operate in Swedish. All the information I managed to gather about teaching writing in Swedish was about short courses in community colleges. In fact, it is quite revealing that it was only writing this article which made me think about this issue for the first time.

Some of the Finnish Swedes speak Finnish so well that they can study writing in Finnish. Meanwhile, Swedish language writers can also travel to Sweden for education. There appear to be a number of similarities between the curricula of the Swedish University of Lund (2019) and University of Jyväskylä (2019a). Both focus upon the same theme; namely, the ability to give and receive feedback as a knowledge-based target for learning. This is an important difference with, for instance, the University of Iowa (2019a), whose online general catalog only says that the courses will involve "critique of class members' work." In some course descriptions there is a little more detail, such as that "students will be expected to read the submitted story beforehand and respond with a letter as well as respectful and constructive in-class critique" (University of Iowa 2019b). However, there is no information detailing when and where the skill of giving feedback will be learned—and there is no mention at all about learning to receive feedback. So, it seems that at least in these two Scandinavian examples kindred culture leads to similarities in educational principles: learning to learn is emphasized.

Finnish Guidebooks for Creative Writers

It took a long time after Järnefelt's group before organized writing programs were established in Finland. Fennomans put literature on such a pedestal that it seemed almost impossible to teach fiction writing. The ideas of the Romantic era suited the Fennomans well: art, especially literature, was seen as representative of nature, and thus stood in opposition to the industrialized and organized society. During the Romantic era writing gained political dimensions (Eagleton 2008: 17). In Finland, even as late as the 1960s, only published authors were able to really deal with sensitive national topics (Jokinen 1997: 8–9). The Romantic concept concentrated one-sidedly on the unconscious part of creative process. Writing was primarily seen as a spontaneous activity: inspiration and ideas were considered more important than implementation. (Bennett 2005: 60–6; Weiner 2000: 76; Bolter 1991: 21; Ekström 2011: 37.) Authors remained outside of the society—or at least outside of the education provided by the society. As a result, organized teaching of writers started late compared to, say, that of the visual arts.

In the twentieth century writing guides were important ways of advising creative writers.[3] Studying the development of these guides reveals how the teaching of writing in Finland was slowly becoming possible at various level. In my thesis I peruse more than fifty Finnish writing guides for writers. In this article, it is possible to only mention a few. I therefore concentrate on those published before creative writing programs started up at universities in Finland.

Best-selling authors Vihtori Peltonen and Mika Waltari wrote the first two writing guides. Although these books have much in common, they reflect different aspects of Fennomania. In his foreword Peltonen (1900) regrets that he did not manage to write a better guide. Meanwhile, Waltari (1935/2005: 5–7) reports feeling a certain amount of hilarity when he wrote his text, which is an objectively less important book.

Peltonen published *Kynäilijä* (Scribbler/Penman) in 1900. He compares writing to building houses while also making his connection to academic studies clear. For example, he refers to Socrates when describing how true beauty depends on expediency. He describes how the demands of beauty and harmony guide approaches to narrative, letters, and scientific research. In this way, Peltonen portrays all humans as born with a natural sense for beauty—though

---

[3] Some writing guides are connected to foundations, which aim to educate both through short courses and by giving feedback through the mail. Read more at https://kansanvalistusseura.fi/briefly-in-english/ and https://nuorenvoimanliitto.fi/in-english

he notes that aesthetic preferences are cultural and vary across different continents (Peltonen 1900: 5–9).

Peltonen published his novels under the pen-name Johannes Linnankoski. He was a journalist and the founder of a newspaper, as well as being an eager spokesperson for universal education (Laitinen 1998: 130). For a short while Peltonen studied teacher training, and both his book and career in general are examples of rapid national development. According to Söderhjelm neither of his parents could even write their own name. Yet they both were able, and eager, to read and willing to educate their children (Söderhjelm 1919: 18–21). This was probably due to the historical situation. As Mäkinen notes:

> Still, as a legacy from Snellman and the *fennomania*, Finns see themselves even now as a nation of readers, where the circulation statistics of public libraries and the annual sales figures of book market are important pieces of news. This does not mean that everybody reads regularly. It is more a question of ideology and a feature of the national identity.
>
> (2015: 297)

Peltonen did not romanticize writing, even though he mentions that genius is innate. Yet even a genius needs a lot of practice. He makes it clear that the skill of writing, then often considered a gift from birth, can be developed through practice and exercise (Peltonen 1900: 10–11). On the whole, Peltonen believes in the power of education, and he applies this directly to creative writing.

What Qualifications are Required from an Author?

Mika Waltari (1935/2005), author of the next writing guide started a tradition of focusing on the importance of the personality of the author. Indeed, I borrowed the title of this chapter after his guide's first heading. The title of his book is *Aiotko Kirjailijaksi?* (*Are You Going to be an Author?*).

The Romantic myth[4] about the innate genius of the writer makes it difficult to believe that writing can be taught, and Waltari's book is a good example of this. On one hand, he gives a lot of information and advice on how to become a writer, while on the other he belittles his own advice and therefore provides contradictory content. In fact, Waltari actually explicitly states that it is a good result if someone gives up writing after reading his guide and understands

---

[4] As Andrew Bennett (2005, 53–71) has pointed out, the concept of the literary genius was not as one-dimensional as some literature about the period has suggested.

how demanding writing really is (1935/2005: 10). The distrust of education is explicit.

According to Waltari, an author needs to be cultured, but there is no necessity to study in an organized way. Emphasizing the importance of personality, he claims to only give advice based on his experience as a writer, and for instance as an inspector of manuscripts offered to publishers. He even mentions avoiding taking example from guides published in other countries (Waltari 1935/2005: 6–7, 18, 59). He also makes no reference to Peltonen, which seems peculiar.

In addition to the Romantic myth, Waltari was also likely affected by contemporary biographic trends in literary study and research. In Finland, the focus of this research tended to emphasize the author's psychology (Koskela and Rojola 2000: 16–19). Correspondingly, there is a special emphasis on the author's personality and its importance when writing guides discuss fiction in the 1950s and 1960s (Ekström 2011: 47).

Waltari's description of a writer is somewhat contradictory. According to him the true author will experience a passionate youth and a restless adulthood. Furthermore, the new generations will push old authors aside. On the other hand, Waltari frequently uses terms such as "great" and "destiny" in an admiring way (Waltari 1935/2005: 12–15, 82, 147–9, 177). On the whole, Waltari makes many distinctions between different genres and kinds of authors: in particular, between the great ones and the ones who have to *settle*. These generalizations further emphasize the cult of the author's personality.

There is a principle in Waltari's guide that has strongly influenced my experiences both as a student of writing and my early years as an instructor. Waltari argues that authors should never explain their works or publicly oppose their critics (1935/2005: 211). This principle applied to classrooms in Finland even through to the beginning of the 2000s. In a typical feedback situation, the teacher and other students in the class discussed the work-in-progress almost as if the writer was not present at all. At least the writer was quiet—sometimes the rule was to talk only after everyone else had been given the opportunity to speak.

In 2006, I made a small-scale study about feedback with students at the very beginning of their creative writing studies. It was clear that these respondents also assumed the writer's role to be passive in feedback situations. I realized that I had also been instructing to take notes while receiving feedback, rather than to answer queries or discuss their own work. (Ekström 2008). In a humorous way, one could say that a student focusing on his notes was like a passenger in an airplane preparing for an emergency landing, head between the knees. I therefore noticed a big difference between my concept of learning as an active constructivist process and my teaching practice.

Though I did not abandon guides for writers—and their advice—after this, I started to read them in another way: I paid more attention to whether the author leaned more on their pedagogical knowledge or their own experiences.

Different Generations Meet in the Classroom

An author and a scholar have in common the need to research. Peltonen (1900: 15) describes how writers both interview experts and engage in personal research through observation. Waltari (1935/2005: 20, 176) also mentions that authors often experience and explore the world, but he warns not to explore too much. Like a scholar, an author too is in danger of getting carried away in the exciting process of gathering information.

These suggestions by Peltonen and Waltari are central to recent studies of writing. Nevertheless, Erno Paasilinna emphasized the "explorer" metaphor in another way: "one should live a life that makes a writer" (1979a: 8). This quote became famous in Finland.[5] Paasilinna (1979b: 18) argues that education will unify writers and their way of observing. In fact, he claims (albeit vaguely) that there are examples of this from other countries. I believe these ideas reflect his experiences during his school years—he was educated during a time when behavioristic principles held sway, and when experts therefore concentrated on the tangible and observable, and were not as interested in the inner life of people (Bower and Hilgard 1981: 74).

Behaviorism focused on evaluation, and so did writing guides affected by this conception of learning. It was common for them to speak about evaluation instead of feedback. It therefore seems funny that some examples of rude evaluations were not only written but also reprinted. As a famous author, Hannu Salama describes the way he responds to a writer is to give a "rough response" which often includes swear words (Kylätasku and Linnilä 1970: 34). It appears to me that this phenomenon was due to the Romantic myth of the difficult genius, whereby authors did not care about appearing polite or civilized.

---

[5]   Yet the author is questioned even in the editor's preface (Korolainen 1979).

Paasilinna's ideas reveal an important lesson: the learning concepts of students might differ. This is why it is important to start education by discussing how one learns writing: what does feedback really mean? Why are the intentions of the writer important? Who is responsible for learning?

Literature Research in Guides

Paasilinna (1979a: 9) says that language is the author's only tool and it therefore has to be personal. Although Paasilinna opposed writing programs, it is probable that this statement and overall formalistic literary research supported the creation of creative writing studies in Finland. Formalists spoke in the 1960s about literary language that deformed ordinary language (Eagleton 2008: 3). However, where should one learn this kind of language?

The most important literary theory in writing guides seems to be New Criticism, which put aside the personality of the author. It first appeared in Finland in the 1950s, but continued to appear in the guides twenty years later. At the same time, proper writing exercises begin to appear in these books. It seems that both in the United States and Finland, there was a clear connection between New Criticism and educating writers. Both educators and New Criticism emphasize a pragmatic approach to literature and the making of new texts (Myers 2006, 130–1; Ekström 2011, 48–9).

One of my former teachers, Liisa Enwald (1980) wrote a guide which also described New Criticism. As a young teacher I often taught close reading to my students as well. But since then I have grown more skeptical about applying the concepts of literary theory to teaching writing. Analysing the text simply shouldn't take more time—or pages—than writing it. Sometimes the concepts and methods of literary studies are too exact.

Waltari (1935/2005, 24–6) had already noticed the difference between literary theory and writing: he urges writers to respect literary studies, but emphasizes that a writer reads differently to a scholar. I believe that close reading frequently leads to feedback that is too specific, thus overwhelming the writer with information. Väinö Kirstinä (1976, 16) criticizes New Criticism for ignoring the text's relationship with reality. Maybe it should also be criticized for forgetting the writer, their capacity to receive feedback, their intentions, and their emotional connection with the text.

Enwald's (1980) guide is noteworthy because she gives advice on how to teach writers. This is a whole new level of thinking: how to improve the education of writers instead of asking whether they should or should not be taught (Ekström 2011: 53–4).[6] At the same time, cognitive science was providing increased vocabulary and metaphors for the human mind (Anderson 1995, 11), and thus the practice of imagining and the process of creating was not seen as such a mystery anymore.

Writers were also gradually released from the expectation—as previously articulated by Fennomans—that they had a political duty. Waltari (2005/1935: 74–7) makes an important distinction between describing a social phenomenon and agitating for change. Väinö Kirstinä (1968) argues in his preface that the 1960s demand too much politics from writers. At the same time, the Arts Council's contemporary report stated that it is the government's responsibility to promote and develop the arts (Rautiainen 2008: 25). Instead of focusing on the author's responsibility to support national pursuits, the coin was flipped; an artist scholarship scheme was planned in the 1960s and put into action in the 1970s and 1980s (Rautiainen 2007: 50). On the other hand, portraying Finnish common folk seems to be a consistent part of the Finnish literary canon. As Lyytikäinen points out, even parodies tend to replicate this theme and extend this emphasis on regular people. She also notices that even as late as 1999, "The popular media, however, seems to favor national subjects, and traditional literature is a constant source in this regard. Indeed, cinema appears to have become a central vehicle of 'national' art." (Lyytikäinen 1999: 139 and 164).

One of the more recent guides refers back to Waltari in its title: Taija Tuominen wrote *Minusta Tulee Kirjailija (I am Going to be an Author)* in 2013. In a way, it closes the circle. At the end of the book there are references to both domestic and international writing guides, as well as novels and even creative research. Alongside writing guides, research is becoming increasingly important for writers. In the curriculum of Basic Studies, for example, students are asked to read an article about how to evoke vivid imagery in a reader's mind (Suvanto 2016). Meanwhile, theses are often helpful, as they offer practical advice—or catalog a range of advice from a collection of writing guides.

University of Jyväskylä: Studies in Writing

A comprehensive set of basic studies in writing courses were developed at Jyväskylä in 1992. A few years later specific subject studies were launched. Advanced studies begun in 2002. Behind the development of academic studies

---

[6] Short courses in Creative Writing had also been growing more common in community colleges since the middle of the 1960s.

in writing were the wishes of amateur writers and authors in Central Finland. Officially, the initiative came from the Regional Artist for literature, Markku Laitinen. Meanwhile, the advisory board consisted of members from several departments of the University of Jyväskylä: Communication, Literature, Art Education and Teacher Education. The board also had members from the Writers' Association of Central Finland (Vuori 1998: 10–11).

At least one member of the board, Pirkko Heikkinen (1999: 2) from the Youth Institute of Mikkeli, was familiar with the models of UCLA and Iowa. On the other hand, the first coordinator and teacher of the studies, Miisa Jääskeläinen (2002: 6–9), does not mention foreign writing programs at all when she summarizes her influences as a teacher. This corresponds with my experience as her student from the autumn of 1994 onwards.

Instead of seeking direct models, studies in writing in the University of Jyväskylä were developed by conducting a survey and asking about the wishes of the students (Vuori 1998). In 1997, teachers Miisa Jääskeläinen and Petri Pietiläinen mention that creative writing is taught in the United States and United Kingdom. Instead of describing these models in detail, however, they emphasize the value of research—in a book dedicated to introducing proseminar works written by the students. Furthermore, they criticize Anglo-Saxon education for concentrating on texts and genres, and claim that this focus should change. As a highly revealing example of successful change, they refer to the process writing method, which was created in an international research project which was itself joined by some educationalists from the University of Jyväskylä. They were thus seeking something similar for the development of teaching creative writing: an interdisciplinary component which involved active new research. (Jääskeläinen and Pietiläinen 1997: 1–3.)

Over the course of time, the title of the writing program at Jyväskylä University has been influenced by administrative policies as well as the natural development of the academic subject. The Writing Program changed first into Studies in Creative Writing, and finally into Studies in Writing. The omission of the word creative is meant to reflect the idea that all writing is creative in nature. This view of literature is related to pre-Romantic beliefs (Eagleton 2008: 15). It also reflects a key tenet of creativity research in recent decades: that creativity is natural to all humans, and it should therefore be encouraged in all teaching. Like Peltonen (1900), the curriculum in the writing program at Jyväskylä seeks to highlight the similarities between different genres and styles of writing.

At the moment, both basic studies and subject studies are organized by the Open University of Jyväskylä, and "creative writing is a line of specialization in the advanced level of studies in Literature" (University of Jyväskylä 2019b). In advanced studies, students are able to write both scientific and creative texts as a part of their coursework and master's thesis. Some doctoral theses have also been reviewed.

I choose to present here the curriculum overview of Basic Studies in Writing, since quantitatively such courses reach more students. Basic studies also plants a seed for all that comes later. Each course is worth five ECTS credits.

Basic Studies in Writing
Compulsory courses:

- Artistic and Scientific Approaches to Writing
- The Writer as a Reader

Optional: choose one

- Fact and Fiction in Writing
- Creative Autobiographical Writing

Optional: choose two

- Prose
- Drama
- Poetry
- Non-fiction

Optional: choose one

- Text Collection
- Writing as a Creative Process

From the very beginning, the aim has been to form an investigative relationship with writing. In Basic Studies in Writing, students rehearse this, for example, by searching for new perspectives on family members during the course "Creative Autobiographical Writing." Students interview relatives and gather information from sources such as diaries, old letters, or archives.

Permanent employees tend to be professional educators and researchers. Although one's own writing experience is valuable, teaching expertise is also needed in the design of the study structure. This permanent staff ensures that the pedagogical ideas remain consistent through the study modules and that the teaching is based on research. During the introductory course, they will ensure that all students have certain basic skills both as students and writers. Creativity is viewed holistically, influenced by motivation, discipline, and the surrounding community. It is as important to be aware of the cognitive processes behind creativity, as it is to be conscious of its communal nature (Sawyer 2012).

One of the next big questions at Jyväskylä—and other writing programs in Finland—is again a question of the language. We already have some (Finnish) students who would prefer to write in English, especially science fiction. Immigration is also expanding. Sweden is ahead of us with an international program in creative writing and thus a possible model for our future (University of Stockholm 2019). Since the University of Jyväskylä is also an active member of the European Association of Creative Writing Programs (EACWP), the basis for international co-operation is solid.

In Education, Diversity is a Benefit

There is a difference in educating authors and writers. In a language area of about five million people, it makes sense to educate writers who are able to make their living by producing many kinds of texts. Yet, the evaluative distinction that Waltari earlier made between different kinds of writers is unnecessary.

In Finish Open University students come from different backgrounds. Some have a doctoral degree and some haven't studied at all since primary school. Students have different professions and usually they are of various ages. Studies in writing often plays a role in the examinations of teachers and journalists. Some of the students are already published authors. Even though they share an interest in writing in common, as readers they differ. It is possible to lean on the knowledge of the participants. The classroom is filled with students who have an expertise in their mother tongue, and knowledge of various fields of literature as well as a wide range of genres.

My taste in literature is narrow; I have my likes and dislikes. But together with the group of students, we can overcome personal taste. Another way to overcome this is through research. This is why all education should be based on it. This principle does not exclude the writing guides. However, guides should be tested to prove their usefulness and validity.

Researching writing guides shows how attitudes towards writing and creativity have changed over time. It helps to understand and question the methods of one's teachers—and hopefully to question one's own methods too. For me, personally, it was extremely important to identify the relationship between my concept of learning and my teaching practice. Teaching creative writing should not start with the text but instead with the ability to learn. How one learns writing? Who is responsible for learning? When we give up talking about natural-born gifts or "living a life that makes a writer," the teacher's responsibility grows a little bigger. At the very least, each instructor is responsible for thinking about teaching instead of repeating old models or sharing personal experience as generic. The academic tradition of systematic questioning is actually very beneficial in this sense. A writer, a teacher, and a scholar have lot in common, indeed.

Learning diaries are also a good example of the power of research. It seems to me that I knew their creative potential for a long time, but it was only after my colleague, Anne Mari Rautiainen started to research them for her doctoral dissertation that the opportunity of writing a learning diary in a creative way found its way into the actual written instructions of the courses. Naturally, more and more students have become interested in this new kind of learning diary since then.

In education, it is not the success of the teacher that counts, but the success and satisfaction of the students. I believe learning to write is a craft, but it cannot be learned only from the master or by reading a writing guide. Connecting with other apprentices is even more important. Rather than lecturing, it is the master's task to create a framework for peer learning. With peer support it is also easier to question the instructor's advice.

Maintaining a critical attitude towards writing studies means questioning whether the information gained is personally applicable. An important way to do this is through writing learning diaries. Writing these diaries is an opportunity to study different genres too; students are encouraged to write them in a creative way, for instance, in the form of a dialog in a drama course. I believe this also provides an important way to rehearse a new kind of writing, through playing with genre expectations while remaining objective. This form of expression can therefore also help bridge the gap between writing and the research of writing.

References

Aho, J. and J. Niemi (1986), *Juhani Ahon Kirjeitä*, Suomalaisen Kirjallisuuden Seuran Toimituksia, Hki: Suomalaisen kirjallisuuden seura.

Anderson, J. R. (1995), *Cognitive Psychology and its Implications*, 4th edn, New York: Freeman.

Bennett, A. (2005), *The Author*, The New Critical Idiom, London: Routledge

Bolter, J. D. (1991), *Writing Space: The Computer, Hypertext, and the History of Writing*, Hillsdale, N J.: Lawrence Erlbaum Associates.

Bower, G. H. and E. R. Hilgard (1981), *Theories of Learning*, The Century Psychology Series, 5th edn, Englewood Cliffs, N.J.: Prentice-Hall.

Broomans, P. (2015), "The Importance of Literature and Cultural Transfer – Redefining Minority and Migrant Cultures," in P. Broomans (ed.), *Battles and Borders: Perspectives on Cultural Transmission and Literature in Minor Language Areas*, 9–38, Groningen, Netherlands: Barkhuis.

Eagleton, T. (2008), *Literary Theory: An Introduction*, Anniversary edition, 2nd edn, Malden, MA: Blackwell Publications.

Ekström, N. (2008), "Tarvitaanko Muutakin Kuin Hyvät Lukulasit? Kirjoittamisen Oppimista Edistävä Palaute," in J. Joensuu, N. Ekström, T. Lahdelma and R. Niemi-Pynttäri (eds), *Luova laji. Näkökulmia kirjoittamisen tutkimukseen*, 35–55, Jyväskylä: Atena.

Ekström, N. (2011), *Kirjoittamisen Opettajan Kertomus: Kirjoittamisen Opettamisesta Kognitiiviselta Pohjalta*, Jyväskylä Studies in Humanities, Jyväskylä: Jyväskylän yliopisto.

Ekström, N. (2018). "Kukaan Ei Kirjoita Yksin," in A. Riikonen, J. Kauppinen, M. Auvinen, E. Tapionkoski, S. Hannula, M. and E. Törmä, (eds), *Kirjoittamisen käänteitä*, 145–61. Helsinki: Äidinkielen opettajain liitto.

Enwald, L. (1980), *Luova Kirjoittaja: Nuoren Voiman Liiton Kirjoittajakurssi*, Jyväskylä: Gummerus.

Heikkinen, P. (1999), *"Tekemällä tehty: Syntymässä olevan henkilön poetiikkaa,"* Licentiate thesis, Jyväskylän yliopisto.

Hoeven, A. v. d. (2015), "The Discovery of Finland. Patterns in Cultural Transfer," in P. Broomans, G. Jensma, E. Jiresch, J. Klok and R. v. Elswijk (eds), *Battles and Borders: Perspectives on Cultural Transmission and Literature in Minor Language Areas*, 83–95, Groningen, Netherlands: Barkhuis.

Jokinen, K. (1997), *Suomalaisen Lukemisen Maisemaihanteet*, SoPhi, Jyväskylä: Jyväskylän yliopisto.

Jääskeläinen, M. (2002), *Sana kerrallaan: Johdatus luovaan kirjoittamiseen*, Helsinki. WSOY.

Jääskeläinen, M. and Pietiläinen, P. (1997), "Kirjoittaen etsitään kirjoittamistiedettä," in M. Jääskeläinen and P. Pietiläinen, *Kirjoittaja opissa: Kirjoittamisen taitoa ja tiedettä etsimässä*, 1–13, Jyväskylä: Jyväskylän yliopiston kirjaston julkaisuyksikkö.

Kirby, D. (2006), *A Concise History of Finland*, Cambridge Concise Histories, Cambridge: Cambridge University Press.

Kirstinä, V., ed. (1968), *Kirjoittajan Työt*, Hämeenlinna: Karisto.

Kirstinä, V. 1976. "Työ ja harrastus," in J. Lehtonen and I. Tiihonen (eds) *Kirjoittajan eväät: Näkökulmia Luovaan Kirjoittamiseen*, 154–61. Jyväskylä: Gummerus.

Kopponen, T. (1985), "Järnefeltien Koulu," in E. Melville and T. Melville (eds), *Kuopiosta Suomeen: Kirjallisuutemme Aatesisältöä 1880-Luvulla*, 79–89, Kuopio: Kustannuskiila.

Koskela, L. and L. Rojola (1997), *Lukijan ABC-Kirja: Johdatus Kirjallisuuden Nykyteorioihin ja Kirjallisuudentutkimuksen Suuntauksiin*, Tietolipas, Helsinki: Suomalaisen Kirjallisuuden Seura.

Kylätasku, J. and K. Linnilä, eds, (1970), *Kirjoittajan Aapinen 1*, Hki: Nuoren voiman liitto.

Laitinen, K. (1998) "The Rise of Finnish-Language Literature, 1860 – 1916," in G. C. Schoolfield (ed.), *A History of Finland's Literature*, 64–147, Histories of Scandinavian Literature, Lincoln: University of Nebraska Press: American-Scandinavian Foundation.

Lyytikäinen, P. (1999), "Birth of a Nation," in Lehtonen, T. M. S. (ed.), P. Landon (trans), *Europe's Northern frontier: Perspectives on Finland's Western identity*, 138–65, Jyväskylä: PS-kustannus.

Mullally, S. L. and E. A. Maguire (2014), "Memory, Imagination, and Predicting the Future: A Common Brain Mechanism?" *Neuroscientist*, 20 (3): 220–34.

Myers, D. G. (2006). *The Elephants Teach: Creative Writing since 1880*, Chicago: The University of Chicago Press.

Mäkinen, I. (2015), "From Literacy to Love of Reading: The Fennomanian Ideology of Reading in the 19th-century Finland," *Journal of Social History, 49* (2): 287–99.

Niemi, J. (1985), *Juhani Aho*, Suomalaisen Kirjallisuuden Seuran Toimituksia, Hki: Suomalaisen kirjallisuuden seura.

Nilsson, A. (2010), "One Nation – Two Literatures? From Finnish to Swedish: Some Themes in the Translation of Finnish Literature into Swedish, 1900–1950 ," in P. Broomans and M. Ronne (eds), *In the Vanguard of Cultural Transfer: Cultural Transmitters and Authors in Peripheral Literary Fields*, Groningen: Barkhuis.

Paasilinna, E. (1979a), "Lyhyt Oppikirja," 8–9, in T. Korolainen, H. Mörsäri and S. Nopola (eds) *Kynäniekka: Harrastajakirjoittajan Tukikurssi*, Hki: Yleisradio.

Paasilinna, E. (1979b), "Kokemusta ja kirjatietoa," 15–19, in T. Korolainen, H. Mörsäri and S. Nopola (eds) *Kynäniekka: Harrastajakirjoittajan Tukikurssi*, Hki: Yleisradio.

Peltonen, V. (1900), *Kynäilijä: Helppotajuinen Opas Kirjoitusten Sepittämisessä: Nuorisoseuroja, Kansakoulun Jatkokursseja Ja Itsekseen Opiskelevia Varten*, Porvoo: WSOY.

Pulkkinen, T. (1999), "One Language, One Mind," in Lehtonen, T. M. S. (ed), P. Landon (trans), *Europe's Northern frontier: Perspectives on Finland's Western identity*, 118–37, Jyväskylä: PS-kustannus.

Rautiainen, P. (2007), *Taiteen Vapaus Perusoikeutena*, Tutkimusyksikön Julkaisuja / Taiteen Keskustoimikunta, Helsinki: Taiteen keskustoimikunta.

Rautiainen, P. (2008), *Suomalainen Taiteilijatuki: Valtion Suora Ja Välillinen Taiteilijatuki Taidetoimikuntien Perustamisesta Tähän Päivään*, Tutkimusyksikön Julkaisuja / Taiteen Keskustoimikunta, Helsinki: Taiteen keskustoimikunta.

Sawyer, R. K. (2012), *Explaining Creativity: The Science of Human Innovation*, 2nd edn, New York: Oxford University Press.

Suvanto, K.-L. (2016). "Inspiring Imagery: An Introduction to Evoking Vivid Mental Imagery in Creative Writing," *Scriptum: Creative Writing Research Journal*, 3 (1), 17–31.

Söderhjelm, W. (1919), *Johannes Linnankoski*, Helsinki: Otava.

University of Iowa (2019a): https://myui.uiowa.edu/my-ui/courses/details. page?id=777480&ci=155915

University of Iowa (2019b): https://myui.uiowa.edu/my-ui/courses/details. page?id=777478&ci=155915

University of Jyväskylä (2019a): https://korppi.jyu.fi/kotka/course/student/ generalCourseInfo.jsp?course=237732

University of Jyväskylä (2019b): https://www.jyu.fi/hytk/fi/laitokset/mutku/en/ disciplines#autotoc-item-autotoc-3

University of Lund (2019): http://kursplaner.lu.se/pdf/kurs/en/LUFA05

University of Stockholm (2019): https://www.hum.su.se/english/education/master-s-level/programmes/master-s-programme-in-english

Tuominen, T. (2013), *Minusta tulee kirjailija*, Helsinki: Kansanvalistusseura.

Virtanen, M. (2002), *Fennomanian perilliset: Poliittiset traditiot ja sukupolvien dynamiikka*, 2nd edn, Helsinki: SKS.

Vuori, S. (1998), *Mitä mieltä kirjoittajakoulutuksesta?*, Jyväskylä: Jyväskylän yliopisto.

Waltari, M. ([1935] 2005), *Aiotko Kirjailijaksi?: Tuttavallista Keskustelua Kaikesta Siitä, Mitä Nuoren Kirjailijan Tulee Tietää*, 2nd edn, Helsinki: WSOY.

Wegener, C. (2016), "Upcycling," in V. P. Glăveanu, L. Tanggaard, L. and C. Wegener (eds) *Creativity, a new vocabulary*, 181–8, New York: Palgrave Macmillan.

Weiner, R. (2000), *Creativity & Beyond: Cultures, Values, and Change*, Albany, NY: State University of New York Press.

6

Scenes of Judgment: Genre and Narrative Form in Literary Memoir

Jonathan Taylor
University of Leicester

Divided Narratives

Many critics have suggested that, of all modern memoirs, Blake Morrison's *And When Did You Last See Your Father?* (1993) had a formative influence on the genre, how it is understood, and how it developed in Britain over the last twenty-five years or so. As Sam Miller puts it, Morrison's memoir "is often said to have inspired a generation of confessional writing" (Miller 2017). Morrison, I would argue, established a pattern for subsequent British memoirists, including myself, to follow—one which makes "confessional writing" seem possible in a British context.

It is a commonplace that confessionalism and its concomitant emotional expression are traditionally problematic in British autobiographical writing. Eve Claxton, for example, talks of the "stiff ... upper lip" and "dignified reticence" (Claxton 2005: xviii–xix) of traditional Victorian autobiography. But alongside this reticence, there developed a reaction, a counter-tradition, which can be traced back at least as far as William Wordsworth's poetry and Thomas De Quincey's *Confessions of an English Opium-Eater* (1822), and then forward to Edmund Gosse's *Father and Son* (1907), J. R. Ackerley's memoirs—for example, *My Father and Myself* (1968)—and ultimately to Morrison's memoir. In their very different ways, these works try to accommodate the confessional impulse within a British framework, finding their own balance between the reticent aesthetics of British autobiography (stiff upper lips, as it were) and the desire to express intense emotions. Morrison's memoir in particular provided a model for subsequent works in the genre, because it demonstrated how it might be possible to find a place for an explicit confessionalism, emotionalism, even judgment (what might, in creative writing terms, be called "telling") within a form which, at least in Britain, is traditionally dominated by the aesthetics of reticence (and hence what might, in creative writing terms, be loosely associated with mere "showing").

The latter form of expression dominates the opening of Morrison's memoir—as if he is easing the reader into the narrative, initially abiding by the (British) reader's expectations of traditional autobiography. The memoir famously begins with a detailed description of "a hot September Saturday in 1959." Morrison's family is "stationary in Cheshire" in a "queue of cars ... [for] the Gold Cup." His father is desperate to see the motor-racing and "does not like waiting in queues," so, through various ruses, contrives to jump the queue, and gain privileged access to the paddock, despite not having paid for it (Morrison 1998: 9–13).

This scene would not be out of place in a novel or film (and, of course, the memoir was made into a movie in 2007): it is, by and large, a straightforward, chronological, first-person narrative focused on an exemplary and formative moment in childhood. The scene is vividly realized, using real names ("Graham Hill, Jack Brabham, Roy Salvadori, Stirling Moss and Joakim Bonnier"), tactile details ("sweet-smelling upholstery," "pall of high-rev exhaust"), vivid imagery ("a stethoscope ... hangs ... like a skeleton"), and dialog ("Well, I'm not going to bloody well wait here any longer") (Morrison 1998: 9–11). As Judith Barrington notes, many American and British memoirs "employ fictional techniques and read much like novels or short stories" (Barrington 2002: 49). In teaching memoir in UK universities over many years, this has always been my starting point: emphasizing the fundamental importance of *storytelling*, which the memoir form shares with fiction. "In order to create a [memoir] ... that anyone would possibly care to read," writes Ben Yagoda, "a writer must express ... [past] impressions in the form of narrative" (Yagoda 2009: 265)—a narrative which, as with fiction, is communicated (primarily) through specific, telling scenes.

This emphasis on specific scenes helps students understand one of the characteristics of the memoir form, which has been used to distinguish it from other types of autobiography: namely, that it focuses on specific moments, on particular relationships, on fragments, on themes, rather than encompassing a whole life. Most modern memoirists seem, at least ostensibly, to follow De Quincey's dictum, that "to tell nothing *but* the truth – [is] ... an unconditional moral law: to tell the *whole* truth is not equally so" (De Quincey 1986: 199). A memoir is, on most definitions, not the "*whole* truth": "an autobiography is the story *of a life*," writes Barrington, "[and] the name implies that the writer will somehow attempt to capture all the essential elements of that life ... Memoir, on the other hand, is a story *from a life*. It makes no pretense of replicating a whole life," and its form is determined by "the selection of . . . [a] theme or themes" (Barrington 2002: 22–3). As Sara Haslam and Derek Neale put it, "a memoir . . . can . . . be structured in a fragmentary, snapshot fashion . . . . The silence between episodes is intriguing . . . – who could, or would want to, write everything down?" A memoir usually "in no way has, or attempts, the feel of a 'complete' record" (Haslam and Neale 2009: 65–6). Such definitions, however fallible, are useful as starting points for students—as well as liberating, in that they free up writers to work in fragments, snapshots, instead of trying to sustain a complete, linear narrative of a life.

Still, "snapshots" (or, for that matter, "impressions") alone do not make a memoir; and, although the focus on telling scenes is crucial as a starting point, general reflections on *aspects* of the past—if not the "whole truth"—do play a part in the form. Such reflections often emerge from the individual scenes. This is certainly the case with Morrison's memoir: after a few pages, he interrupts the initial scene with a section break, which is followed by a more reflective passage about his father's behavior in general:

> This is the way it was with my father. Minor duplicities. Little fiddles. Money-saving, timesaving, privilege-attaining fragments of opportunism. The queue-jump, the backhander, the deal under the table . . . 'They' were killjoys, after all – 'they' meaning the establishment to which, despite being a middle-class professional, a GP, he didn't belong . . . He envied and often praised to us those who had pulled off ingenious crimes, like the Great Train Robbers . . . He was not himself up to being a criminal in a big way, but he was lost if he couldn't cheat in a small way . . . I grew up thinking it absolutely normal, that most Englishmen were like this. I still suspect that's the case. My childhood was a web of little scams and triumphs . . . He failed only once . . . [and] I was indignant. I discovered he was fallible. I felt conned.
>
> Morrison (1998: 13–14)

The narrative voice here is markedly different, in its scope and tone, to that of most post-Victorian, British fiction; it exceeds the usual confines of fictional discourse—to the extent that it does not merely suggest a pattern to the father's behavior, but even extrapolates something from the scene about Englishmen's behavior in general. This is the aspect of contemporary, Anglo-American memoir that Patrick Madden terms its "meditative quality," whereby

> events and experiences narrated are not simply recounted or recreated in language; they are considered – weighed – in thought. The memoirist may utilize all the devices and techniques of fiction to establish vivid scenes, . . . but she will

not simply lead readers to the edge of a hinted meaning and expect them to do the work. Instead, she will take them inside her own mind's engagement with the stories, to process them and to make meaning.

Madden (2014: 224–5)

There are various synonyms used for this "meditative quality" in memoir: summary, exposition, explanation, "telling," confession. Barrington calls it "musing," and also refers to Georg Lukacs's term, "the process of judging":

> The kind of judgment necessary to . . . the memoir, is . . . the willingness to form and express complex opinions, both positive and negative. If the charm of memoir is that we, the readers, see the author struggling to understand her past, then we must also see the author trying out opinions she may later shoot down, only to try out others as she takes a position about the meaning of her story. The memoirist . . . must be willing to share her intellectual and emotional quest for answers . . . Self-revelation without analysis or understanding becomes merely an embarrassment to both reader and writer.

Barrington (2002: 29–30)

According to Barrington, such analysis, understanding, judgment forms a vitally "important ingredient of literary memoir" (Barrington 2007: 110).

As many students have pointed out to me, this ingredient of memoir-writing rather conflicts with what Philip Lopate calls the "nefarious taboo of Creative Writing programs everywhere: 'Show, don't tell'" (Lopate 2005: 144). In the Anglo-American tradition, successful memoirs often *do* include moments of "telling"—moments where immersive storytelling techniques are superseded by judgments, explanations, summary. As Lopate points out,

> literary nonfiction is . . . one arena in which it *is* permissible to 'tell.' In . . . memoirs, we must rely on the subjective voice of the first-person narrator to guide us, . . . [to] explain, summarize, interpret, or provide a larger sociological or historical context for the material.

Lopate (2005: 145)

In this way, the memoir form implies and even enacts what Shirley Geok-Lin Lim calls "a reverse practice" to "Show, don't tell"—one which "begins with show, then tell":

> My opening position is to ignore the 'show, don't tell' doctrine. Instead, I offer a reverse practice; . . . students are encouraged to 'show *and* tell,' to begin their writing projects with concrete, clear, definable things/objects/memories, and to tell about these material and remembered objects, particular scenes and events

in whatever way they choose. That is, my creative writing pedagogy begins in opposition to generally standard practice; it begins with show, *then* tell.

Lim (2015: 341: my italics)

Maybe the memoir form, as it has developed in recent years, is one of the genres in which this "reverse practice" is most evident, at least in an Anglo-American context, where other genres—and particularly fiction—can seem so dominated by the stringent aesthetics of "show, don't tell." If, as Namrata Poddar suggests, the aesthetics of "show, don't tell" is a case of "cultural particularity masquerading itself as universal taste" (Poddar 2016), perhaps it is also a case of *generic* particularity masquerading as universal taste—that is, one which applies more to some genres than others. At a profound level, the two cases are linked: perhaps Anglo-American fiction is more dominated by the "show, don't tell" dictum than memoir because the latter form is popularly perceived as less "central" to the culture, less "universal" in scope. As has been seen, autobiographical forms arguably have a problematic relationship with British codes of reticence, and have sometimes provided a space for individual, even culturally marginalized voices denied access to mainstream fiction—as in, to give one well-known example, the genre of slave narratives in the late eighteenth and nineteenth centuries. Given their didactic and rhetorical properties, slave narratives obviously do not adhere to any aesthetic criteria dominated by reticence and "show, don't tell" (see, for example, Taylor 2003: 84–100).

As Lopate suggests and Morrison demonstrates, the nature of "telling" in relation to memoir is immensely variable: it might consist of character or psychological exposition ("he was not himself up to being a criminal in a big way"), sociological observation ("most Englishmen were like this"), political analysis ("'they' meaning the establishment to which, despite being a middle-class professional, a GP, he didn't belong"), emotional openness or confessionalism ("I was indignant ... I felt conned"), a personal connection between then and now ("I still suspect that's the case"), or a link with wider histories ("he envied and often praised to us those who had pulled off ingenious crimes, like the Great Train Robbers"). What all of these possible judgments have in common is that they arise from the preceding scene: they are all, as Madden suggests, meditations on the images and ideas thrown up by the experiences described.

They also gesture towards the ensuing scene: in Morrison's memoir, the judgment is immediately followed by a sequel to the scene in Cheshire, 1959, as his father's "web of little scams and triumphs" is further exemplified in practice. In this sense, it might be said that many British memoirs are structured in a wave-like formation, moving from scene to judgment to scene, and so on. They "get away"—it might be said—with judgment, confession, telling, by alternating these elements with more conventional storytelling. I have written elsewhere about the ways memoirs oscillate between a sense of sameness and otherness, "difference and ... similarity," "sympathy and empathy," writerly "uniqueness" and readerly "identification" (Taylor 2009: 22–3); and this oscillation is sometimes ingrained in their very structure, as they move between narrative scenes—which, for the reader, enact difference, otherness, and potentially elicit sympathy—to moments of judgment, which attempt to establish some kind of connection with the intended reader, to elicit feelings of identification or empathy. In Sam Meekings' words, the latter sections move beyond the independent self to establish the narrator's "situatedness within the world," a world he or she shares, in some way or other, with the intended reader. Memoirs hence depend upon "a fine balance between the specific and the general," the "smallest of details" and "the universal" (Meekings 2019: 414, 421).

Personally, I think memoir-writing classes should always problematize the notion of so-called "universal" values that a narrator might share with *all* readers. In terms of their ostensible content and form, memoirs are necessarily context-bound, linguistically, temporally, socially, geographically specific. As Matthew Salesses argues, it is vital, in workshop situations, to keep "acknowledging the culture behind the craft, ... all the time, including in the bias of the workshop" (Salesses, 2015). Nonetheless, it is still worth emphasizing the central importance of students considering what common ground they might share with their *intended* readers—intended readers who might well be different for different students. No doubt Morrison's actual readership (for example) is very wide—but there are aspects of his narrative which imply certain kinds of cultural knowledge, certain shared contexts, which both include some readers and (partially) exclude others. His opening chapter would presumably be experienced differently by someone who did not know what the Great Train Robbery was, or someone from an adoptive family, or a female reader, or a reader from a non-British family, or a reader from beyond the UK, or a reader who has not experienced parental bereavement—and so on.

These differences in readerly experience would affect *both* the narrative scenes *and* the moments of judgment. In that sense, it is not the case that these sections respectively elicit feelings of difference and sameness, in any kind of monolithic way. Rather, feelings of difference and sameness, sympathy and empathy, alienation and identification are also experienced on a moment-to-moment, sentence-by-sentence basis within a text: if there is a wave-like contour to many memoirs, this is only in a very general sense, and there are also waves within waves (within waves). After all, in Morrison's memoir, there are moments in the main scene which move away from single-minded focus on the here-and-now of "A hot September Saturday in 1959," and take on a wider perspective: even at the end of the first paragraph, the narrator comments that "My father has always loved fast cars, and motor-racing has a strong British following just now." Conversely, the judgment section is not all summary, but includes some dialog, and a specific memory of a skiing holiday in Aviemore (Morrison, 1998: 9, 14).

There remains a slight difference, though: this memory, embedded as it is in the judgment section, is told in the past tense, unlike the scene in September 1959. The memory is framed as retrospect, as the one time his father's little scams "failed" (Morrison 1998: 14). On Barrington's definition, this element of retrospection—of reflecting back on the memory—is precisely what makes it part of the judgment, differentiating it from the earlier storytelling: the memoirist, claims Barrington, tries to "tell a good story . . . using . . . fictional techniques . . . but unlike the fiction writer, . . . can also reflect out loud on [the] . . . story, bringing *retrospection* to bear on the events" (Barrington 2007: 110: my italics). For Barrington, this is what makes memoir "similar to personal essay . . . When you write memoir, like the essayist, you invite the reader into your thinking process, going beyond the telling of a good story to reveal how, *looking back on it*, you now understand that story" (Barrington 2007: 110: my italics).

Divided Narrators

As Barrington might expect, the opening of Morrison's memoir moves from "telling . . . a good story" towards an understanding of that story in retrospect. The opening scene is immersive, in present tense and stays (by and large) within the child's perspective; the subsequent commentary changes to summary, is in the past tense, and looks back from a mature perspective on childhood years. This is no doubt the kind of "double perspective," which Lopate associates with memoir. "In writing memoir," he suggests,

> the trick, it seems to me, is to establish a double perspective, which will allow the reader to participate vicariously in the experience as it was lived (the confusions and misapprehensions of the child one was, say), while conveying the sophisticated wisdom of one's current self.
>
> Lopate (2005: 143)

In James Olney's words, there is often an "emotional and intellectual divide" in autobiographical writing that "distances the past narrated self from the present narrating self," such that the "'I' narrating understands every event in the narrative differently from the understanding possessed in the past by the 'I' narrated" (Olney 1984: 197). As Micaela Maftei puts it, "something like a splitting of selves is required in order to feature within the text while constructing it" (Maftei 2013: 59).

The split selves of autobiographical narrators have a long literary history—back through Gosse's self-mockery in *Father and Son*, where he "look[s] back upon [a] ... tragic time" through "mirthful recollection" (Gosse 2004: 43), via William Wordsworth's idea of (semi-autobiographical) poetry as "emotion recollected in tranquility" (Wordsworth 2008: 611), to Jean-Jacques Rousseau, to Michel de Montaigne, and ultimately to St. Augustine's *Confessions* (AD 397–400), the structure of which depends upon a radical divide between sinful youth and Christian maturity.

For Olney, this divide often encodes an ironic, and sometimes even humorous distance between mature narrator and narrated self. As Gosse suggests, there is a "mirthful recollection" at work in memoir, whereby the older narrator looks back wryly upon his or her youth. The narrative distance of memoir is, in this sense, analogous to the kind of "comic distance" (see Carroll 2014: 31) which many critics find in humor. As Olney suggests, in relation to W. B. Yeats,

> the ... variety of irony that distances the past narrated self from the present narrating self is surely what Yeats intends in a letter written to his father *à propos* of *Reveries over Childhood and Youth*: 'While I was immature I was a different person and I can [now] stand apart and judge.' What Yeats describes is present-tense judgment ('I can stand apart') of a past-tense condition of being ('While I was immature I was a different person') ... This kind of indulgent and semi-comic irony, exercised at the expense of a younger self, is not uncommon in autobiography.

Such "semi-comic irony" or "gentle self-mockery" (Olney 1984: 197–9) is certainly apparent in Morrison's memoir, *And When Did You Last See Your Father?* While its complex mode of narration often wobbles between voices and selves—between a simulated child's voice, and even free indirect discourse—the dominant voice remains that of sophisticated adult narrator standing apart from, and judging a "younger self." The narrative stance depends on an ironic distance between past and present selves—as the adult narrator himself acknowledges towards the end of the memoir, when he goes to see a therapist:

I sit in a white canvas chair, the sort film directors have, and I play her back bits of my life. She catches me smiling at critical points of my psycho-story, and this, she says, or gets me to say, is because I'm trying to distance myself ironically from my emotions.

Morrison (1998: 214)

I have written extensively elsewhere about the "ironic distance" which characterizes narratives like Morrison's, as well as, more widely, the crucial role of humor in the memoir form, with its mixture of laughter and tears—something which may be particularly evident in British memoirs, where emotional confessionalism is permitted and contained within an ironic framework (see Taylor 2019: 89–160). Here, it suffices to emphasize the structural role that "semi-comic irony" plays in Anglo-American memoir—something which is often overlooked by students. Despite the popular association of confessional memoir with trauma—as evinced by the so-called misery memoir, or survivor memoir, which was hugely popular in the wake of Dave Pelzer's *A Child Called It* (1995)— and despite the idea that, as Elizabeth Grubgeld suggests, "readers bring expectations of seriousness to . . . autobiography" (Grubgeld 1994: 106), memoirs can also be *funny*; and this aspect of the form can come as a revelation to students.

Indeed, as an antidote to "expectations of seriousness," and the association of memoir with trauma, I often approach the subject in exactly the opposite direction: that is, I start teaching autobiographical writing with an exercise intended to elicit work which is playful, entertaining—work which concerns pleasurable experiences and memories, rather than painful ones. For this, I introduce students to J. B. Priestley's semi-autobiographical (and semi-comic) book of personal essays, *Delight* (1949). I then ask them to write a short personal essay on something apparently minor in their lives which has provided them with a sense of delight. I suggest the essay should include three sections: a detailed description of the form of delight, memories of it (for example, the first time it was experienced), and a final paragraph which discusses what it means to them, its significance, and how the experience has changed over time. The exercise has various aims: hopefully, it helps to emphasize the close formal connections between essay and memoir, as highlighted by Madden, Barrington and others; it demonstrates that both essay and memoir incorporate elements of storytelling, memory and judgment; it sets that most difficult of challenges—to write about pleasurable and happy memories, rather than merely painful ones; it stresses the importance of entertaining the reader, providing pleasure, whatever the subject matter. And, potentially, the exercise also implies the central role of

time, change, and narrative distance in autobiographical forms: the last paragraph
of the essay, in particular, is intended to imbue it with the sense of time passing,
of change, of a divide between now and then.

The divide is so fundamental to our experience and expectations of
autobiographical writings that it is almost a marker of the genre or genres; and
texts which attempt to provide a wholly immersive, present-tense perspective on
events are necessarily attempting something different, working against the
generic grain. Of course, there *are* memoirs which do just that: Frank McCourt's
Angela's Ashes (1996) is one of the most famous examples; and, more recently,
Tom Preston's *The Boy in the Mirror* (2015) describes the author's experience of
cancer and its treatment using present tense, a purely immersive, scene-by-scene
immediacy, and, oddly enough, a second-person mode of narration ("You're
lying on your back, arms raised above your head, your whole body perfectly still,
air held uncomfortably in your lungs"). Only at the end of the memoir, in the
Afterword, does the narrative voice slip into first person; yet even here Preston
explicitly disavows narratorial distance or judgment:

> I know I'm supposed to infer some deeper meaning or profound sense of self,
> but all that happens is I remember the pain and the terror, . . . and the way I saw
> in my own reflection the slow but tangible erosion of everything that I was; and
> here and now I can do nothing but exhale deeply and walk lazily to the bathroom,
> where I stand in front of the mirror and I stare right into the depths of my own
> eyes, and I see myself not as healthy and older and secure like I am, but young
> and frail and bald and dying and crying out for help from someone, from anyone.
>
> Preston (2015: 7, 86)

Nevertheless, despite the overt disavowal of "deeper meaning," this passage
still constitutes a kind of reflection—literally so, given the mirror. This is still—
however ambivalent—a retrospective summary, a kind of judgment on a past
self. Even in this most immersive of narratives, the apparent disavowal of
judgment itself becomes a kind of judgment; and the narrative self, which has
been so unified up till now, inevitably divides between past (mirror) self and the
self in remission, who is writing the memoir. They may overlap—the narrator
may see his old self in the mirror—but that very overlap still implies a division,
a bifurcation of selves.

If such bifurcation is more central to Morrison's mode of narration, there are
sections of his memoir which do attempt to provide a wholly immersive, visceral
experience for the reader. For instance, the chapter Tonsils, set in a hospital ward,
is narrated in the present tense almost entirely in the child's voice ("I close my

eyes, and pretend I'm at home, and think of my presents, . . . and I do not cry, Daddy, I do not, I do not"). Still, the chapter is only one small part of an overarching narrative dominated by an adult's voice; so, unless read in isolation, there remains at least an implied ironic distance, and even a gentle humor at the child's expense. At one point, for instance, the child narrator wishes "there were bubbles coming out of [the nurse's] . . . head with words" because "thought bubbles would be a useful invention in real life" (Morrison 1998: 33). Presumably, the intended adult reader would find this idea funny, even though the child narrator is being deadly serious; so there is, in the passage, an implied division between child narrator, on the one hand, and overarching adult narrator and reader, on the other. It would seem that, in Preston's experimental mode and Morrison's more conventional narrative, the split perspective of memoir, along with a concomitant ironic distance and judgment are *almost* inevitable, unavoidable aspects of the genre—at least as it is understood in an Anglo-American context. Barrington goes so far as to suggest that "without [the] . . . attempt to make a judgment, . . . stories [become] becalmed in the doldrums of neutrality, . . . neither fiction nor memoir, . . . an embarrassment to both reader and writer" (Barrington 2002: 29–30). Without judgment, that is, a memoir is not a memoir—it hardly belongs to the genre, as she understands it.

Divided Endings

Even if I do not *entirely* agree with Barrington in this respect, given the cultural specificity of her aesthetic criteria and claims, there is still no doubt that an entirely immersive memoir, where the narrator is portrayed as still in the midst of the emotions and experiences described, is a difficult thing to pull off. This is partly because an immersive, present-tense memoir necessarily brings attention to its own artificiality or fictionality: it is clearly impossible for a narrator to be experiencing and narrating (let alone writing) simultaneously. To put this another way: in a form which invites the reader to identify writer and narrator as one and the same, an immersive memoir must demand a special kind of suspension of disbelief, in its attempt to maintain the illusion that writer, narrator, and narrated self are all experiencing what is described in the here-and-now.

There are other problems, too, with immersion on the part of narrator and, indeed, writer. In my experience, students understand that there is a qualitative difference between writing about ongoing personal experiences versus those in the past. It is almost impossible to gain a (narrative) distance or perspective on ongoing experiences, or to give them narrative shape. "In the lived chaos," writes Arthur Frank, "there is no mediation, only immediacy ... The person living the chaos story has no distance from her life and no reflective grasp on it. Lived chaos makes reflection, and consequently storytelling, impossible" (Frank 2013: 98). As Maftei points out, the memoirist can "see ... the patterns and themes only in retrospect," and hence "the construction of the story involve[s] a profound temporal division in terms of the distance between events and writing" (Maftei 2013: 60, 94).

Temporal division is a kind of ending: the events described belong, to a lesser or greater extent, to the past, and have finished. No doubt all stories, whether true or fictional, imply some form of temporal division, some kind of ending, or closure; as Andrew Bennett and Nicholas Royle put it, "every literary work must have an ending—however open, suspended or apparently non-conclusive" (Bennett and Royle 2014: 312). A few years back, one of my literature students flippantly suggested that to write about ongoing events or experiences is journalism, while to recollect something which has ended is memoir (or, in Bennett and Royle's terms, a "literary work"). While the distinction has all sorts of problems, there remains a sense in which, as the critic J. Hillis Miller puts it, "storytelling is always after the fact, and it is always constructed over a loss" (Miller 1982: 61).

The close relationship between storytelling and loss is particularly acute for the memoirist, and is presumably why so many memoirs are written about parents, siblings, partners who have died: their deaths provide the endings necessary for the stories to arise. In this way, it might be said that memoirs are often narrated from a point *after* the ending: storytelling, memoir-writing are what come *after* death—the narrator-detective investigating a murder scene, as it were; as Roger Porter suggests, memoirs are often "crime stories, variants of detective fiction" (Porter 2011: 3). Morrison's memoir, for instance, is narrated from a point after the death of his father—a death which is both gradually unveiled by the narrative, and also continually foreshadowed, even immanent, within it.

Likewise, the first chapter of Meghan O'Rourke's memoir, *The Long Goodbye* (2012), opens with the death of her mother—the ending, in a sense, starts the book—and, significantly enough, causes her to feel "split ... in two, like a tree struck by lightning." She feels "divided into two parts" - a part submerged in the past, versus a part who maintains a "'rational' experience of the present" (O'Rourke 2011: 119). Here, as is often the case, the division of past, remembered self from present, narrating self, which is so integral to the memoir form, is caused by traumatic loss. As Maftei suggests, "memoirs … that focus on a period of crisis … of intense stress and heightened emotion" might cause "a disassociation between the author … and the central figure within it" (Maftei 2013: 68). Similarly, Meekings writes that "loss complicates the self; a narrative depicting … loss and its effects thus performs this complication"; such grief narratives, he argues, serve to "dramatize the splitting of the self-concept and its aspects" (Meekings 2019: 414, 426).

As well as depicting and performing loss, grief narratives also represent an attempt to construct something over that loss. They enact, at one and same time, "deconstruction *and* reconstruction", because, as Meekings suggests,

> the narrative impulse – the urge not only to document, but also to structure, to imagine and to create – is vital to the memoirist's self-concept. The act of writing the text establishes a possibility beyond the stasis of grief … One common concern among many grief memoirists is that of trying to make sense of a state of being that seems illogical, irrational, and uncertain.
>
> Meekings (2019: 418–19)

As Miller might expect, the memoirist's "narrative impulse" is to construct something over loss—storytelling represents an attempt to construct a bridge between past and present, between divided selves; it is an attempt to make sense of absence and uncertainty, to impose meaning in retrospect.

This is not just the case for the memoirist him or herself, but also for the reader: storytelling constructs something over loss for the recipient of the text, as well as its creator. That is why we read others' memoirs—because others' stories help us impose meaning on loss, absence, change; and that is also why memoirs themselves are frequently full of others' stories and texts. To illustrate this, I sometimes ask students to bring in a text—a book, a piece of music, a film—with which they personally have long-running associations. They are then asked to describe the text in general—both orally and in written form—and the memories, emotions, relationships, contexts they associate with it. This simple exercise enacts a radical form of "personal criticism" (see Bennett and Royle 2014: 12); it enacts, through creative practice, the ideas of reader-response theorists such as Wolfgang Iser, who argues that interpretation is

> inevitably … colored by our own characteristic selection process. For it is not given by the text itself; it arises from the meeting between the written text and the individual mind of the reader with its own particular history of experience, its own consciousness, its own outlook.
>
> Iser (1972: 289)

If Iser's words here imply a separation of "written text" and "individual mind," the writing exercise, by contrast, suggests an overlap: the text is part of the individual mind's "particular history of experience," part of the reader's consciousness, part of his or her memory. The exercise, that is, emphasizes the textuality of memory—that texts themselves are experiences which serve, in part, to construct consciousness.

Hence why so many memoirs are packed with allusions and citations: the form is often explicitly intertextual; and this is not just because narrators use other texts "in an attempt to make sense of … experience," as Meekings suggests, but also because experience and selfhood are inherently textual, so "memoir[s] cannot help but reaffirm the extent to which we are defined and produced by … language" (Meekings 2019: 417). Memoirs, and autobiographical writings in general, are inevitably also reflections on the textuality of the self; as Linda Anderson suggests, "Autobiography, so this multiplicity of discourses suggests, already has a relation to other texts; there is no singular text of the self or no autobiography which is only one's own" (Anderson 2011: 74). Similarly, Grubgeld remarks that "autobiographical acts are intrinsically forms of reading and present a model of interpretive activity" (Grubgeld 1994: 139). Many recent "autobiographical acts" have understood this: Francis Spufford's *The Child That Books Built* (2002), as its name suggests, attempts to describe the construction of selfhood through childhood reading and interpretation; and Alison Bechdel's well-known graphic memoir, *Fun Home* (2006), captures the fraught relationship between narrator and father partly through the one thing they have in common: reading. Bechdel even uses the term intertextual at one point to describe what she is doing (Bechdel 2006: 207). In my own memoir, *Take Me Home: Parkinson's, My Father, Myself* (2007), I include a whole chapter, called "Bottom of the Bookcase," about texts which both reflect and somehow shaped my relationship with my father: "In remembering my father, I can't help also remembering things which aren't him, which are inadequate substitutes for the real person. I can't help remembering books, records, films which have survived him, and now stand in his place" (Taylor 2007: 113).

Following detailed descriptions of these various books, records, and films, I go on to reflect that "of course, none of these works quite work. None of the texts listed above manage to understand my father entirely. They don't even understand my understanding of him" (Taylor 2007: 125). The reflection at the end of the chapter marks the failure of understanding or judgment—it represents a kind of non-conclusion, rather like Preston's, where he disavows a "deeper meaning" to his narrative. Similarly, in the Afterword (called "Aftercare") to *Take Me Home*, I admit to failing in my quest to understand my father: "I'm not sure who my father was ... My father was all sorts of fathers, husbands, brothers, symptoms, heroes, villains and paradoxes to different people at different times" (Taylor 2007: 261). In the final chapter of *And When Did You Last See Your Father?*, Morrison says something similar: "Now I see that the doors are locked. Now I know I'll never know the truth ... There is no missing piece, only grief" (Morrison 1998: 213).

In this way, the memoir form is always promising to reveal a truth which never quite arrives: memoirs at once promise truth, revelation, judgment, and withhold them, defer them. Each moment of reflection in a memoir is partial revelation, partial judgment, partial truth—and also failed revelation, failed judgment, failed truth. There is what Meekings terms a "perpetual incompleteness" (Meekings 2019: 416) about memoirs, even in their final chapters or Afterwords. As Maftei puts it, drawing on Roland Barthes, encoded in many memoirs is an "'infinitely deferred' meaning" (Maftei 2013: 64). Barthes himself states the case most directly when he declares in *Roland Barthes by Roland Barthes* (1975) that:

> What I write about myself is never *the last word* ... my texts are disjointed, no one of them caps any other; the latter is nothing but a *further* text, the last of the series, not the ultimate in meaning ... What right does my present have to speak of my past? Has my present some advantage over my past?
>
> Barthes (2010: 120–1).

For Barthes, the divide which so often structures memoir and autobiography, between mature narrator and younger narrated self, is at best questionable, implying as it does some dubious moral or intellectual advantage on the part of present self over past self. All there can be, for Barthes, is a series of "further texts" over time, none of them providing the "ultimate in meaning."

In this respect, Barthes seems to disavow the retrospective judgment which Barrington claims is a fundamental part of memoir-writing. As with Preston's memoir, however, even that disavowal of judgment is itself a kind of judgment; and maybe, more importantly, what he brings to consciousness is something which is at least implicit in all sophisticated memoirs: namely, the idea that there is never a "last word," that judgments are always contingent, never absolute, that the present self may prove as wrong and misguided in retrospect as did the past self. Judgments in memoir are always, as Barrington and Lukacs make clear, a *"process,"* not an absolute end-point—in Lopate's words, "a live, candid mind thinking on the page ... slowly and uncertainly" (Lopate 2005: 156). Always in process, always uncertain, the judgments in memoir are hence themselves part of the story, part of the ongoing and unfolding narrative, not separate from it—like the narrator, they change, develop over time. As Barrington writes: "If the charm of memoir is that we, the readers, see the author struggling to understand her past, then we must also see the author trying out opinions she may later shoot down, only to try out others," to the extent that "she may never arrive at a definitive verdict." Barrington advises the memoirist not to "fall prey to what has been called the 'triumphalist imperative', which favors completion over complexity" (Barrington 2002: 29, 58). As I make clear to students, sophisticated memoirs do not provide simple triumphs, straightforward answers, closed endings; and their judgments are usually presented as contingent, provisional, uncertain, ambivalent, ironic.

And that, it seems to me, is a nicely uncertain way to end this essay.

References

Anderson, L. (2011), *Autobiography*, Abingdon: Routledge.

Barrington, J. (2002), *Writing the Memoir*, Portland: Eighth Mountain Press.

Barrington, J. (2007), "Writing the Memoir," in *The Handbook of Creative Writing*, ed. Steven Earnshaw, Edinburgh: Edinburgh University Press, 109–15.

Barthes, R. (2010), *Roland Barthes*, trans. Richard Howard, New York: Farrar, Straus and Giroux.

Bechdel, A. (2006), *Fun Home: A Family Tragicomic*, London: Jonathan Cape.

Bennett, A. and Nicholas Royle (2014), *An Introduction to Literature, Criticism and Theory*, London: Routledge.

Carroll, N. (2014), *Humour: A Very Short Introduction*, Oxford: Oxford University Press.

Claxton, E. (2005), "Introduction," in *The Book of Life: A Compendium of the Best Autobiographical and Memoir Writing*, ed. Eve Claxton, London: Ebury Press, ix–xxvii.

De Quincey, T. (1986), Letter, December 1821, in *Confessions of an English Opium-Eater*, ed. Alethea Hayter, Harmondsworth: Penguin, 117–20.

Frank, A. W. (2013), *The Wounded Storyteller: Body, Illness, and Ethics*, Chicago: Chicago University Press.

Gosse, E. (2004), *Father and Son: A Study of Two Temperaments*, ed. Michael Newton, Oxford: Oxford University Press.

Grubgeld, E. (1994), *George Moore and the Autogenous Self: The Autobiography and Fiction*, New York: Syracuse University Press.

Haslam, S. and Neale, D. (2009), *Life Writing*, Oxon: Routledge.

Iser, W. (1972), "The Reading Process: A Phenomenological Approach," *New Literary History*, 3:2, 279–99.

Lim, S. G. (2015), "Creative Writing Pedagogy for World Englishes Students," *World Englishes*, 34:3, 336–54.

Lopate, P. (2005), "Reflection and Retrospection: A Pedagogic Mystery Story," *Fourth Genre*, 7:1, 143–56.

Madden, P. (2014), "The New Memoir," in *The Cambridge Companion to Autobiography*, ed. Maria DiBattista and Emily O. Wittman, Cambridge: Cambridge University Press, 222–36.

Maftei, M. (2013), *The Fiction of Autobiography: Reading and Writing Identity*, New York: Bloomsbury.

Meekings, S. (2019), "Writing through Loss: The Rise of Grief Narratives through the Lens of Linville's Self-complexity Theory," *Life Writing*, 16:3, 413–27.

Miller, J. H. (1982), *Fiction and Repetition: Seven English Novels*, Cambridge: Harvard University Press.

Miller, S. (2017), "Top 10 Books About Fathers," *The Guardian*. Available online: https://www.theguardian.com/books/2017/mar/29/top-10-books-about-fathers (accessed September 5, 2019).

Morrison, B. (1998), *And When Did You Last See Your Father?*, London: Granta.

Olney, J. (1984), "The Uses of Comedy and Irony in Autobiographies and Autobiography," *Yeats*, 2, 195–208.

O'Rourke, M. (2011), *The Long Goodbye*, London: Virago.

Poddar, N. (2016), "Is 'Show Don't Tell' a Universal Truth or a Colonial Relic?," *Literary Hub*. Available online: https://lithub.com/is-show-dont-tell-a-universal-truth-or-a-colonial-relic/ (accessed March 10, 2020).

Porter, R. J. (2011), *Bureau of Missing Persons: Writing the Secret Lives of Fathers*, Ithaca: Cornell University Press.

Preston, T. (2015), *The Boy in the Mirror*, Scarborough: Valley Press.

Priestley, J. B. (2009), *Delight*, Bradford: Great Northern Books.

Salesses, M. (2015), "Pure Craft Is a Lie (Part 4)," *Pleiades Magazine*. Available online: http://www.pleiadesmag.com/pure-craft-is-a-lie-part-4/ (accessed March 10, 20).

Spufford, F. (2002), *The Child That Books Built: A Life in Reading*, New York: Metropolitan.

Taylor, J. (2003), *Mastery and Slavery in Victorian Writing*, Basingstoke: Palgrave Macmillan.

Taylor, J. (2007), *Take Me Home: Parkinson's, My Father, Myself*, London: Granta.

Taylor, J. (2009), "Share Your Family's Story," *Family History Monthly*, 166, 22–6.

Taylor, J. (2019), *Laughter, Literature, Violence, 1840-1930*, Basingstoke: Palgrave Macmillan.

Wordsworth, W. (2008), "Preface to *Lyrical Ballads*," in *Major Works*, ed. Stephen Gill, London: Penguin, 595–615.

Yagoda, B. (2009), *Memoir: A History*, London: Penguin.

7

Skeptical, Polyglot, Disaggregated: Creativity, Authorship, and Authority in the Australian Context

Ross Gibson

University of Canberra

The first years of Australian colonization, at the end of the eighteenth century, produced more damage than creativity. Dire enough were the privations within the English penal society—ignorant, poorly provisioned, and under-skilled—that had been decanted into an alien realm. But even worse were the horrors suffered by the people who called themselves "Eora," the aboriginal custodians of the harbor reaches and fishing coves and lightly timbered hunting plains that comprised the beguiling environment known nowadays as Metropolitan Sydney. The Eora endured the obliteration of habitats and ecosystems, bewildering pestilence, and a cataclysmic campaign of displacement and murder.

Even so, amidst the dolor, there was some wonder. A prime example was the complex pedagogical collaboration that occurred between a young Eora woman named Patyegarang and a Marine lieutenant named William Dawes (Gibson 2012). We have some nuanced understanding of their relationship because two small notebooks have survived. They are the lieutenant's private record of an intimate process of language exchange that bloomed as seasons circulated and emotions thickened. The notebooks record a highly imaginative deployment of oral and written communication reaching across mutual inscrutability, connected by curiosity that burgeoned genuinely into affection. These hundred pages of handwriting are the first intersectional pedagogy written in Australia. Together Patyegarang and Dawes produced a treatise, in writing, responding to the great creative challenge of their enmeshment. The notebooks constitute a kind of genesis-text for imaginative prospection in Australia. Only now, very slowly, the non-Indigenous population is beginning to understand the brilliance of the creative writing that Patyegarang and Dawes produced and theorized together.

The notebooks commenced in orthodox fashion. Dawes compiled word-lists. Verbs in one column. Nouns in another. He also tried to formulate principles for tenses and voices. Plus some rules of grammar. Then before long Dawes supplemented his method. Bilingually, with Patyegarang's editorial supervision, he took to writing compressed narrative scenes or vignettes. Here is one example:

Dawes. Minyin mnyin bial piabuni whiteman?

Why don't you (learn to) speak like a white man?

Patyegarang. Wianabunina bial

> Not understanding this answer I asked her to explain it which she did very clearly, by giving me to understand it was because I gave her victuals, drink & everything she wanted, without putting her to the trouble of asking for it.

> I then told her that a white man had been wounded some days ago in coming from Kadi to Waran & asked her why the black men did it.

Answer. Gulara.

Because they are angry.

Dawes. Minyin gulara eora?

Why are the black men angry?

Patyegarang. Inyam nalwi whitemen.

Because the white men have settled here.

In the notebooks, such scenes are usually concerned with a slippery authority, a 360-degree attentiveness to one's place in the dynamic system of existence, and they display a creative use of language such that every speaker is always aware of the necessity to be a listener and a servant of forces larger than one's own identity (Jones 2018).[1] As the scenes get written into the notebooks, Dawes dramatizes his apprehension of an ever-emerging understanding, linguistically freighted via a heuristic or discovery-based process. In an immersive fashion, he began to imbibe the relationally contingent worldview that the Eora language served. The

---

[1]   A commonly invoked Indigenous axiom emphasizes that everyone has two ears and two eyes and only one mouth, a distribution of powers that proves the connective, forensic, relational quality of knowledge, multiply more important than one's ability to assert authoritative precepts or proclamations. Highly respected Indigenous artist and scholar Dr. Jonathan Jones, guided by the esteemed Indigenous elder, Uncle Stan Grant, uses a term from Wiradjuri (south-eastern-inland) language to describe this creative method: "Yindyamarra Winhanganha," meaning "respectful thinking" which is fostered by deep listening, respectful actions, and the humble process of "looking after country," all of which informs truthful talking, when the time is right for talking.

notebooks show a pedagogy, shared between Dawes and Patyegarang, that is robust, interrogative, skeptical, but also mutually considerate and cordial even as the exchanges sometimes befuddled Dawes into a crisis of authority.

Perhaps the most telling vignette is when Patyegarang comes to him, somewhat perturbed, and insists that Dawes must adjust the record of a scene that was written down earlier, for she has just realized that when she performed and then described the actions and utterances that Dawes has written in the notebook, she was not aware that a person named Pundul was in the proximity. Because of Pundul's presence in a particular place at that time, laws of kinship and seniority insisted that Patyegarang should have been speaking and performing in a particular manner, a manner organized by the specific configuration of people and forces that made up the scene at that moment. The world and its vivacious agents were arrayed in a way that dictated how Patyegarang should have been engaging with the energetic world, how the grammar should have been activated under those particular contingencies, and she had failed to attend to those dictates. Her implication was that every moment in time and space is *sui generis* and must be grasped, contextually, by attending to all the imbricated particulars. Patyegarang noticed that there was a systemic disphasure to fix, something far more important than her personal complacency.

Reflecting on moments like this, Dawes began to understand how the meanings of the Eora world altered constantly, depending on who and what configured that world at any moment. Shadowing the eventfulness of Indigenous ecologies, Eora words and phrases were much less nominally stable or reified than English words tend to be. Communal awareness prevailed over self-assertion. No one person or viewpoint could claim to be sovereign or solid. Indeed, an individual's identity dispersed, slipped, and re-formed from moment to moment, depending on how the constitutive energies of the world were arrayed, moment to moment, in lively space, in what Australians (Indigenous and non-Indigenous) have come to call "country." (Think of "country" as a super-organism that is animated both by natural procreative urges and by organizing rituals attentive to the significance of animals, vegetables, minerals, and meteorology.) To learn how to express oneself well in such a context is to learn to subsume one's self to the larger cohesions of the living host-environment, all of it comprehended moment-by-moment as an emerging system organized by generational memory or tradition.

I offer the parable of Patyegarang and Dawes to show that Australians are historically predisposed to looking and listening for a contentious range of authorial standpoints. Even as colonial habits continue to impugn Indigenous wisdom, Australians are aware that intersectional negotiations (person-to-person, species-to-species, time-frame to time-frame) are inherent to sense-making in ancient-Australian consciousness and that the privilege of any one person's authority is only provisionally installed in any place at any time.

It follows that in pedagogical circumstances, there are preconditions in Australia that allow, indeed *require*, individualism to yield to a system of distributed authority—the system that most Indigenous people call "country"— whereby instructions-for-living are dispensed by an entire, galvanized ecology in which *people* are not always the determinant agents. Add to this Australia's past fifty-year history of legislatively mandated multiculturalism: a panoply of different ethnic, linguistic, and cultural heritages are recognized and heeded in the national discourse.[2] Moreover, the history of Australian feminism adds substance to the texture, meaning that masculine chauvinism does not prevail unperturbed. To say it simply, there is a majority insistence that authority should not take it itself too seriously. Thus we have a culture that, for all its placidity and political disengagement, is coded to be intersectional. Rather than blending into a patriotic homogeneity of values and attitude, the Australian citizenry tend to be a disaggregated jumble of types, ethnicities, cultures, affiliations, and loyalty-sets, each group with its own laconic skepticism about the likelihood that their differences could ever be unified around anything more than the wish for material security and spiritual privacy. There is no daily patriotism, no Declaration of Independence, no normalizing Bill of Rights. And this tends to feel like something good: dubiety and a disdain for uniform authority make for a democratic temper that is healthily deprecating.

The same skeptical scrappiness applies in the classroom. Each time I return from a biannual stint reviewing tertiary education programs in Hong Kong (a consultancy I have dispensed for almost thirty years), I am struck by the absence of Confucian gravitas or professorial prestige accorded to instructors in Australia. No one gets away easily with "lording it" over anyone else, teachers included. And every university professor has heard the following skepticism pitched at them: "Why are you telling us this?" In Australian polity, therefore, authority tends to get distributed across networks of people, places, and times, rather than being centralized in lionized individuals. This is a fact even at the same time as the electorate outsources the tedium of its own administration to a ruling class

---

[2] I don't want to be too blithe about this national open-mindedness. Presently multiculturalism is being inched backward in regulatory amendments and in mass-media prejudice. Even so, it is a deep code and it is not budging quickly or meekly, particularly in a context where a huge proportion of business titans and billionaires proudly attest to their migrant or refugee backgrounds and biographies.

(ensconced in business, law, and politics) which is still overwhelmingly male, upper-middle class, and ethnically Western European, and which tries to centralize its power and to anesthetize its discontents via tactical tax breaks and populist media squabbles.[3] This is to show the context in which a "charismatic," inspiring, or individualistically authoritative approach to creative writing tuition is not customarily endorsed.

Furthermore, it is important to remember that education in Australia is still generally regarded as a public good that must be governed by regulated civic codes of accountability rather than as a private enterprise that should be market-driven by profit-quests and entrepreneurial carpetbaggers. (Granted, such rogues have proliferated during the past twenty years of neoliberal administration. Proliferated—but not yet dominated.) Which means that teachers and students still tend to cast their minds toward communal benefit and responsibility as much as they look to their own self-aggrandizement.

Jen Webb is probably the pre-eminent analyst of creative writing pedagogy in Australia. Her fact-checking observations harmonize to the tune I've been humming:

> [Individualistic or charismatic teaching authority] is less evident in Australian or UK creative writing courses, largely because government initiatives and related institutional demands have propelled writing teachers into the logic of the academy. The requirement of the Australian government that universities deliver good citizens and good professionals as graduates means that in all subject areas there needs to be a focus on generic skills. That means we must train students not only in the specifics of their chosen discipline area, but also in people skills (collaboration; communication); thinking skills (problem-solving; decision-making); and personal skills (self-direction; integrity). As a consequence, the free-range, idiosyncratic, "seat of the pants" pedagogies depicted by Ritter and Vanderslice [in their article from 2005 entitled "Teaching Lore: Creative Writers and the University"] are less likely to occur, and certainly less likely to be tolerated, in Australian creative writing classes. What we lose in … creative individuality we gain, perhaps, in a more examined, more defensible approach to our students.
>
> Webb (2017: 97)

---

[3] Perhaps the most famous, influential, and persistently true account of this paradox resides in Donald Horne's classic book from 1964, *The Lucky Country*, in which he skewered the national character with these two immortal sentences: "Australia is a lucky country run mainly by second-rate people who share its luck. It lives on other peoples' ideas, and, although its ordinary people are adaptable, most of its leaders (in all fields) so lack curiosity about the events that surround them that they are often taken by surprise."

In fact, resonating to this tone of civic breadth and communal accountability for a paragraph longer, and contra the thrust of neoliberal self-serving, I report that in-classroom peer-assessment regimes, cohort-distributed dialogic disquisition, and chat-room pedagogies in Australia have all tended recently to ingrain attitudes that force each student's mentality out over to *other mentalities* whenever propositions and analyses get bandied about the classroom. I can report also that, demographically assayed, those other mentalities are embodied in a plethora of cultural backgrounds and identity-positions, given that just about every classroom-cohort now has no single ethnic, class, or sexual identity routinely ruling in it with an inevitable majority. And the waning enthusiasm for tuition via the format of the one-way-broadcast lecture has further diminished the allure and stature of the charismatic author-avatar in the multicultural Australian classroom.

So it transpires, messily, that Indigenous plus multicultural plus ecological philosophies all compel Australians to understand—contra the conservative precepts of the nation's political ruling class—that there are aesthetic intensities and semantic specificities distributed throughout the world's numberless animal, vegetable, and mineral entities and that these influences all integrate to produce everyday experience. And so it transpires that many creative writing teachers in Australia have improvised a loosely democratic and demotic new pedagogy that resonates to this "distributed" consciousness. Many creative writing teachers have purposefully developed philosophies and attendant methodologies that encourage writing students to think more about their communal affiliations and obligations than about their lyrical self-assertions. This means the classrooms tend to babble with multiple conversations as paired-off students report to each other, preparatory to representing each other's work in highly interactive plenary review sessions; it means that students are learning, from each other, under guidance from the teacher, much more than they are learning from a centralized, sovereign author standing at the front of the room and trading on a meager stock of celebrity. The methods are myriad. And there are many variations on the foundational philosophy of such creative writing pedagogy. But all the philosophies tend to draw light away from the author as a sovereign visionary, focusing instead on the writer as an interlocutor obliged to engage with fellow readers who are all negotiating to arrive at some provisional comprehension that gets brokered between the stored wisdom of communal understanding (or tradition) and the momentary utterance of some distinctive authorial proposition (or "individual talent").

To bring some specificity to this talk of a local creative writing pedagogy, and to extend my riff on T. S. Eliot's canonical essay "Tradition and the Individual

Talent," I will now explain the gist of a learning-mode that I offer to students. I present it here as something concrete to think with and against, rather than as a decree about how teaching *must* be done. Having said that, I observe that the mode has worked well enough in many classrooms across my hotchpotch society during my past thirty years of heuristic teaching and learning.

In Australia, I start my creative writing courses with some variation on the following question: "where do our utterances come from?" How much is memory, how much is imagination? Then I remind everyone that, in Australia, we get to pursue this question across a vast expanse, from the epic reach of Indigenous knowledge systems through to the intimate scale of lyrics and lullabies and prayers drawn from our multitude of immigrant cultures. But no matter what the context, every writer transmits from a matrix of what-has-gone-before. From a tradition.

Then I offer an example of tradition producing utterance, like this: In *Chronicles: Volume One*, Bob Dylan reminisces about the months when, barely out of his teens in the early 1960s, he began hustling for gigs in New York City. Dossing in strange apartments stuffed with record collections, letting go of the Zimmerman family name that he never felt described him, listening to the nonstop verbiage of obsessive almanackers like Dave Van Ronk, Dylan discovered his creative self in the hubbub of the reprised songs that make the American folk repertoire:

> I could make things up on the spot all based on folk music structure . . .You could write twenty or more songs off one melody by slightly altering it . . . I could slip in verses or lines from old spirituals or blues. There was little headwork involved. What I usually did was start out with something, some kind of line written in stone and then turn it with another line—make it add up to something else than it originally did.
>
> Dylan (2005: 228)

Thus Dylan might start exploring a Blind Willie McTell blues song on a Monday. By Friday, a hundred renditions later, the song had mutated—in riffs and rhymes—into something as new as it was old, as Dylan kinked a line here, changed a verb there, bent a stray melody around a "wrong" run of similes, and lost McTell while being guided by him. This was nothing mystical. It was the output of erudition steeped in tradition and cooked with innovation. His creative writing was founded on attentive transactions between individuality and communality.

This mode of creativity is *rhapsodic*, in the original sense of the expression deriving from the two ancient Greek words *rhaptein* and *oide* denoting "a sewn-together ode." Extant elements get meshed and altered in the reiteration and recombination such that a startling new sonic fabric—stronger and more stimulant than the sum of its old parts—unfurls between the performer and the audience. The process starts with tradition. As T. S. Eliot explained, the creative mind is best understood as a "receptacle for storing up numberless feelings, phrases, images, which remain there until all the particles which can unite to form a new combination are present together" (1921: 49). These particles can come from each individual's lived experience, but they are spawned as well in the culture that steeps every citizen's cognition. And culture is nothing without the archived remembrances that are structured by tradition. When creating original cultural work, Eliot contends, one dissolves into and rises up from tradition in such a way that the "progress of an artist is ... a continual extinction of personality" as one submits oneself to "something which is more valuable" (47). To learn to be a creative writer is to learn how to let go of one's individuality even as one utters it.

This willing self-surrender is the obverse of the "anxiety of influence" that Harold Bloom has controversially asserted to be the impetus of the great men who jostled for authority in the canon of twentieth-century English literature (1973). For thirty years or more, Bloom's lore attracted disproportionate attention, but now in the age of digital culture and social media, Eliot's theory seems to have returned and grown more compelling as an account of creativity amidst all the mashups, the hip-hop bites, and the great, global bursts of poesies that have generally become known as the aesthetics of remediation (Bolter and Grusin 1999).

Borrowing from Eliot, I contend that the creator is best understood as a "medium in which special, or very varied, feelings are at liberty to enter into new combinations" (Eliot 1921: 48). Whereas Bloom portrayed the great poets as *sui generis* entities struggling, Vulcan-like, to stoke atavistic fire out of their nonpareil subjectivities, Eliot's exemplary poets are not so much makers as melders who encourage their own dispersal and momentary disappearance in order for distinctive new creations to get alloyed through themselves.

The new creation comes not from some *urwelt* where ever-originating inspiration burns, but from the everyday world where all that is extant is ready to be re-fashioned, including sentences, poems, artworks, and myriad elements of culture that previous generations have produced and worked to preserve. From all that is extant, the culture makes the new things from the old things, *relationally*, as much as the artist does. Or to endorse Robert Pogue Harrison's startling claim: "[all human cultures] compel the living to serve the interests of the unborn" such that "culture perpetuates itself through the power of the dead" (2003: ix).

So creative writing comes from the transformation of given things, from relics and remembrances. And in that transformation, there is usually a kind of *treason*, a *betrayal* of the given thing. By which I mean that in being tricked into a new form, the given thing becomes other to its original state. Treason, betrayal, traducement: these are usually thought to be sinister actions, coming from the wrong side of virtue, from left field, insufficiently reverent. But benefits can loom in such treasons. Consider the chance to remake a given thing by infusing it with new elements, by putting it in new relationships with other found and mutable things. Think of Dylan betraying but also bowing down to Blind Willie McTell.

Etymologically, the French word for "translation" ("*traduction*") lurks close alongside the English word "traduce"; and "treason" (or "*trahison*" in French, which leads to the English word "betrayal"). Treason's many variants echo through a translation because of the way the original thing can be betrayed, warped, and abducted (as well as "traducted") to a new state as it is moved from one language to another or from one medium or aesthetic form to another.

So I am proposing that wherever creativity roils, good can come from carefully traducing a given thing. Dylan's "Like a Rolling Stone" can come from McTell's "You Was Born To Die." And the greatness of the original song stands firm even as the new song crashes into being.

Thus far I have been extolling "creative treason" by examining translations from an influential first-author to an aspiring next-author. But what of the translation from medium to medium? Which is to say, from cognitive mode to cognitive mode, whereby the ideas and feelings that are couched in one medium (appealing to one system of cerebral-and-affective appreciation) are then translated to a different medium (which galvanizes other systems in one's intellection and sensorium).

One of my personal favorites in this multi-modal drift is Dave Hickey's dexterous essay "A Life in the Arts," in which he analyses the influence of social and natural environments while orchestrating a sinuous, backcutting line of argument that investigates the languorous melodics in the trumpet-playing of Chet Baker. Intuiting that Baker's art is definitively *Californian*, Hickey delves into the bodily pleasures of the music, appreciating the way the listener is taken on a ride with the trumpeter's sparse glissandos and ethereal feints. Hickey notes how the flowing patterns of Baker's sound originate in the same lulling world that impels the "cool economy and intellectual athletics of long-board surfing" (1997: 77)!

When Californian board-riders translate the ocean swell, they express their full incorporation with the spirit of their place; commensurately when Baker "speaks" with his trumpet and his barely breathed crooning, he utters the easeful sociability of bohemian communities strewn across LA and north along the Pacific Coast Highway, communities that take their tempo and mojo from the ocean. The surfers translate the fluid lineaments of the natural elements with their bodies, which are also their means of knowing and their medium of expression. Baker takes all this, adds a wary conviviality brought by his address to an audience, and he translates the full cool flux into sound via the artful movement of air.

Hickey notes how in each case—in the surfing and in the music—"a lost art of living in real time" is fashioned from the loll of experience. From one extant thing or system—ocean, breath, vibrational energy amongst elements and beings—constitutive factors are relationally realigned and translated so another thing arises. A fresh creation. (I am reminded of an observation in one of Stephane Mallarmé's letters, where the poet declares that because there are already enough objects in the world, there is no need to invent new things, and thus poets must create new relationships among the things that already exist [1961: 871].) Translating the surfers' arcs and scything cutbacks, Baker's trumpet glides out a keening gambit of oozed notes. Furthermore, in consideration and translation of these two mellifluous phenomena, Hickey makes his own original prose that is liquid and buoyant whilst also being perspicacious.

Consider this passage where Hickey evokes the moments immediately after a friend has phoned him to say that Baker has died:

> I sat there for a long time in that cool, shadowy room, looking out at the California morning. I stared at the blazing white stucco wall of the bungalow across the street. I gazed at the coco palm rising above the bungalow's dark green roof. Three chrome-green, renegade parrots had taken up residence among its dusty fronds. They squawked and flickered in the sunshine.
>
> Above the bungalow, the parrots and the palm, the slate-gray Pacific rose to the pale line of the horizon, and this vision of ordinary paradise seemed an appropriate, funereal vista for the ruined prince of West Coast cool.
>
> Hickey (1997: 73)

In the classroom, I suggest to my students that we know this writing is art because of the shift it makes in our understanding, and we know it is high quality. Let's waste no breath debating whether or not it is original or inspired. Hickey's prose in "A Life in the Arts" comes from phenomena that already exist.

It is informed and enriched by Hickey's attentiveness to local practices and environmental conditions that can be translated again and again—from anonymous surfers through Baker to Hickey—into new forms and insights. Hickey's prose resonates in that portion of cognition where the reader appreciates form before disquisition, a zone of consciousness other than the zones that Baker and the longboarders simulate so slickly. What we have traced across these three expressive media is a run of translations through different cognitive modes, from the improvising board-riders, to the tonal innovations of Baker, to the melodic analytics of Hickey. There is tradition here. Plus individual talent which finds and utters itself in the creative act of losing the original influence in the wash of the new relationships that each author establishes amongst what already exists.

In some aesthetics primers, this kind of translation would be called "ekphrasis": the practice of glossing one mode of expression with another mode. Words rendering painting, for example, or music formed in response to dance. For me, the most galvanizing version of this "cognitive-mode translation" comes from the German philosopher, lawyer, filmmaker, and avant-garde bureaucrat, Alexander Kluge.

Kluge has long espoused the power of silent cinema: not necessarily its market force; rather its imaginative élan, which I can summarize thus:

> Viewers encounter a pictorial sequence; they generate an interpretation of the sequence; then an inter-title presents some words (appealing to a cognitive mode that is radically different from the pictorial and proprioceptive faculties that the movie sequence has been agitating thus far); this linguistic sense contends with the interpretation that the viewers have just supplied for themselves; *and then* the viewers decide whether to accept the proffered interpretation or to adapt or stay true to the one that they invented.
>
> Then the next sequence runs.

Thus viewers are goaded to know their own minds, to use their minds to make contentious versions of sense, to know that every consciousness observing the silent movie has several different cognitive modes whirring in it at any one time, even as the filmmaker also contends with the meanings by providing the inter-titles as guidelines for interpretation. The audience is an imaginative, disputatious, and discursive assembly, skeptical and *politicized*. And the significance of the film—simultaneously intellectual and emotional—comes from each viewer's speculative psychology contending in skeptical sociability with every other self in the cinema (including the filmmaker's self, of course) as images and words abrade each other, offering different, medium-specific takes on experience (Kluge 1988). On the screen and inside each viewer's sensibility, moving images and words translate the represented experience across each other. In order to know what is being represented, each viewer has to extract an authoring self from this tumult.

When I import this notion to the classroom, I suggest to students that the creative self forms when the author becomes a highly participant viewer or reader translating across media and drawing lines of new understanding out of memory and tradition across the multicultural texture of the society that hosts us.

This ability to cast out past oneself into the communal domain of all our tangled traditions in order to utter something pertinent to the present moment: this is what we can encourage in the creative writing classroom.

References

Bloom, H. (1973), *The Anxiety of Influence: A Theory of Poetry*, London: Oxford University Press.

Bolter, J. and R. Grusin (1999), *Remediation: Understanding New Media*, Cambridge, MA: MIT Press.

Dawes, W. (1790–1), *Notebooks on the Aboriginal Language of Sydney*, London: Hans Rausing Endangered Language Project and SOAS Library Special Collections.

Dylan, B. (2005), *Chronicles: Volume One*, New York: Simon & Schuster.

Eliot, T. S. (1921), "Tradition and the Individual Talent," in *The Sacred Wood: Essays on Poetry and Criticism*, by T. S. Eliot, 49–56. New York: Alfred A. Knopf.

Gibson, R. (2012), *26 Views of the Starburst World: William Dawes at Sydney Cove 1788 – 91*, Perth: UWA Publishing.

Hickey, D. (1997), "A Life in the Arts," in *Air Guitar: Essays on Art & Democracy* by Dave Hickey, 66–78, Los Angeles: Art Issues Press, Los Angeles.

Horne, D. (1964), *The Lucky Country*, Ringwood: Penguin.

Jones, J. (2018). *Murruwaygu: Following in the Footsteps of Our Ancestors*, PhD thesis, University of Technology, Sydney.

Kluge, A. (translated by W. Reinke, E. Reitz and M. Hansen) (1988), "Word and Film," *October: Special Issue on Alexander Kluge: Theoretical Writings, Stories, and an Interview*. Vol. 46 (autumn), 83–95.

Mallarmé, S. (1961), *Oeuvres completes*, Paris: Gallimard.

Pogue Harrison, R. (2003), *The Dominion of the Dead*, Chicago: The University of Chicago Press.

Vanderslice, S. and R. Manery (eds) (2017), *Can Creative Writing Really Be Taught? Resisting Lore in Creative Writing Pedagogy*, 10th Anniversary Edition. London: Bloomsbury.

Webb, J. (2017). "The Traces of Certain Collisions: Contemporary Writing and Old Tropes," in Vanderslice, S. and R. Manery (eds), *Can Creative Writing Really Be Taught? Resisting Lore in Creative Writing Pedagogy*, 10th Anniversary Edition, 95–9. London: Bloomsbury.

8

Creative Portfolios: Adapting AWP Goals for EFL Creative Writing Courses in Japan

Holly Thompson
Yokohama City University

Introduction

Japan has a long literary history arcing back hundreds of years. Celebrated Japanese authors and poets from across the centuries are widely translated and taught, and Japan boasts a healthy publishing industry, receding since its peak in 1996 (" An Introduction to Publishing in Japan" 2017–2018: 8) yet resilient, if ever evolving. Japan remains a literary powerhouse.

This robust publishing industry and rich literary canon exists, in part, because Japan implemented standard Japanese in the nineteenth century and, in part, because Japan was never colonized. After the Meiji Restoration in 1868 when Tokyo-style *hyōjungo* Japanese became standard throughout the country, regional dialects and languages of Japan began losing widespread use. Standard Japanese language was imposed on indigenous Ainu and Ryūkyūan peoples, and though the result was linguistic unity, eight languages in Japan are now endangered, and many dialects threatened (National Institute for Japanese Language and Linguistics). Standard Japanese became a hallmark of colonialism in the twentieth century during Japanese rule in Taiwan, Korea, Malaysia, Singapore, Indonesia, occupied China, Micronesia, and Manchuria as described in "Colonial Language Policies and Their Effects" (Miyawaki 2002). Although occupied by the Allied Powers after defeat in the Pacific War, Japan is one of few Asian countries never to have been colonized. Even during postwar American occupation, the Japanese language was not suppressed, and significant standard Japanese mother-tongue loss has not been widely experienced in Japan—although the rise of globalization with increased use of English as an "international" language is seen by some as threatening the Japanese language, as explored by author Minae Mizumura in *The Fall of Language in the Age of English* (2017).

It may be argued that this language power has helped enable a rich body of Japanese literature to develop. Thus, given Japan's vibrant literary climate, one might expect creative writing opportunities to abound in the Japanese education system. Yet this is not the case. Creative writing has long been absent from most high school and university experiences in Japan.

Creative writing courses and majors have been prevalent in American universities and colleges for decades, and the US-based Association of Writers and Writing Programs (AWP) outlines nine goals in teaching creative writing to undergraduates. AWP also provides a comprehensive list of twelve instruction methods and general advice for grading and developing curricula. Might these goals and methods be adapted for use in undergraduate classrooms in Japan, and particularly in EFL contexts? And what might be the benefits to Japanese university students?

Writing in the Japanese Education System from Elementary School to Higher Education

Students in Japanese elementary, middle and high schools study the national language in *kokugo* classes. In elementary school, children have engaged in expressive writing since the 1920s when the *seikatsu tsuzuri kata* movement began, evolving into a writing philosophy focused on "children's development as observers and writers ..." and "cognitive growth through writing" (Kitagawa 1982: 20); currently, "diary writing and life-experience writing ... provide a vehicle for life guidance by teachers, classmates and parents" (Spence and Kite 2018: 66). In elementary grades 5 and 6, language activities include opinion and persuasive writing, and writing "poems, tanka or haiku" and "stories or essays based on what they have experienced or imagined" (MEXT "Courses of Study: Elementary School" 2011). In middle-school English classes, writing aims set by the Japan Ministry of Education, Culture, Sports, Science and Technology (MEXT) are "to accustom and familiarize students with writing in English and to enable them to write about their own thoughts using English" (MEXT "Courses of Study: Lower Secondary School—Foreign Languages" 2011).

At the middle- and high-school level, in general, students are offered limited academic writing instruction whether in Language 1 (L1) or Language 2 (L2), with students typically taught in class sizes of 30–40 students, making writing instruction challenging. Although "active learning" and interactive classrooms are promoted by MEXT, and university entrance systems have been undergoing modifications in recent years, Kimura and Tatsuno note that "The government has gone through various education reforms (jurisdiction, course of study, and action plans) for decades, but school-level education does not seem to have significantly changed, particularly in high school education. One of the possible reasons is the university entrance exams" (2017:12). The report also noted that "high schools remain focused on traditional classroom teaching (preparation for multiple-choice tests)" (17).

In his close examination of what is being studied at Japanese high schools, Mulvey concluded that "there seems to be no evidence of systemic, cohesive academic writing instruction at the high school level, either in the L1 or L2" (2016: 5–6). He noted that high-school L2 writing in English classes tends to consist of "line-by-line translation exercises," and in Japanese L1 classes, "essay organizational strategies, recognizing and applying critical analysis, and using factual or scholarly support for opinions are not covered in the typical Japanese high school classroom" (5). It remains to be seen whether recent university entrance examination system reform will result in systemic changes in Japanese secondary school writing instruction.

By middle and high school, creative writing of any type has virtually disappeared from the curriculum. Students in my Yokohama City University creative writing classes, when asked to share previous experiences in creative writing, typically reach back to draw on elementary school examples of story writing, or occasionally, to some formal poetry writing—haiku, tanka, senryu—in middle or high school. Other university instructors in Japan who teach creative writing units or creative writing courses report similar responses from students.

In Japan, writing is arguably the least taught of the four language skills (speaking, listening, reading, writing), both in Japanese (most students' L1) and in English (most students' L2). In higher education EFL programs, heavy emphasis has been placed on TOEFL (Test of English as a Foreign Language) scores and "practical English" in recent years. Writing courses, when offered, prioritize academic writing and short essay test writing. Regrettably, writing is often considered by Japanese faculty and administrators as too time intensive and difficult to teach effectively within the system. Perhaps evidencing the dearth of writing specialists hired in Japanese universities is the fact that among the twenty-eight Special Interest Groups (SIGs) operating within the Japan Association of Language Teachers, none is specifically focused on writing (JALT Chapters and SIGs, 2019).

Creative Writing in Japanese Universities

At the undergraduate level, L1 Japanese-language courses in creative writing are rare. If offered, they are likely situated within literature or media departments, or art or film schools. A few creative writing programs do exist though. Tokai University has a Japanese-language Department of Creative Writing course of study, in which undergraduates study the "literary universe" in their first and second years and have the option of undertaking a creative writing project in their third and fourth years (Tokai University Department of Creative Writing, 2019), thus meeting one of AWP's basic tenets that "an expert writer must first become an expert reader" ("AWP Recommendations" 2020). In Waseda University's School of Culture, Media and Society, a Japanese-language program of study in creative writing and criticism is offered with "training in authorship, research, criticism and translation ... covering various literary genres (such as novels, poetry, drama, screenplays) ... in the areas of publishing, editing, broadcasting, the media, and the circulation of cultural artifacts" (Waseda University 2019). Some Japanese universities have *sōsaku* (creative) clubs or a creative writing component for upper-level literature study, but overall, creative writing courses and creative writing programs in Japanese humanities programs are rare.

Within Japanese university EFL (English as a Foreign Language) programs, the main writing focus is inevitably academic writing. While writing centers have in recent years become more common in English-language programs in Japanese universities, their focus, too, centers, sometimes exclusively, on academic writing. At Yokohama City University (YCU), the Practical English Center user guidelines state that the writing center serves students writing "academic papers" (YCU "PEC Writing Center User Guidelines" 2019), in contrast to the more global model of writing centers in the US long employed by programs such as the Writing Center at New York University, which serves students working on "any piece of writing except exams" (NYU Writing Center 2019). Maloney asserts, "CW [creative writing] may be the most under-used tool in the ELT box. A combination of prejudice against non-academic forms of writing, an assumption that play is inherently trivial and has no place in an academic institution and a misunderstanding of the prerequisite language skills are regularly cited as reasons for eschewing CW in favour of academic writing" (Maloney 2019: 17). He also argues that the singular focus on academic modes of writing in Japan "ignores two rich and vital aspects of linguistic development: creativity and self-expression" (1).

Nonetheless, although academic writing remains the main focus of any EFL writing program in Japanese universities, creative writing is increasingly being inserted as a unit component or one-off exercise into EFL courses, and many university English instructors are active proponents of creative writing in EFL contexts. Stiller of Tsukuba University found that "creative writing exercises can be used not only to engage students' imaginations and increase enthusiasm for writing skills development, but also to raise critical consciousness" (2013: 164). Kamata and Guenther instituted an extracurricular course at the University of Tokushima in which the goal was to "write and revise a full-length short story" (2014: 523). Meanwhile, Williams advocates for more creative writing, contending that "While even an advanced L2 writer may occasionally find holes in their knowledge—i.e., specific genres that they have no experience writing in—the goal of L2 writing instructors should be to expose students to as wide a variety of rhetorical styles as their language proficiency level would allow" (2017: 158).

While creative writing is typically relegated to unit components or exercises, some universities such as YCU, Tokyo Women's Christian University, and Meiji Gakuin University have offered full semester EFL courses in creative writing. Meiji Gakuin University produces the literary magazine *Crop* to which current students and recent graduates can submit poetry, essays, short stories and other creative work (CROP). Meiji Gakuin English Department CROP faculty advisor Pronko comments in the current volume:

> The work in this issue of CROP shows how completely students are capable of expressing themselves in metaphors, symbols, themes, characters and the rich, lush, passionate language that has driven the best, wisest and most positive visions of people and the world all through history. This is literature here, another addition to the reserve of human accomplishment.
>
> Pronko (2019)

Yet he goes on to lament "the lack of spaces for students to let out their inner selves in creative forms. Students in Japan are forced into multiple-choice exams, rigid report formats, micro-managed experiences and hyper structured requirements" (Pronko 2019).

A lack of creative writing opportunities for university students in Japan persists, despite the fact that creative writing provides authentic and meaningful language learning for EFL students. Rippey of the University of Shiga Prefecture offers five attributes of creative writing that benefit language learners: opportunity for genuine communication; relevance, with creativity "central to language use"; figurative language, important to "interface with and comprehend the world";

changing the world, via interacting "as collaborative equals"; and big questions, with "the inherent nature of creative writing as a form of ontological inquiry" being "intrinsically motivating for language learners (Rippey 2014). Rossiter, Isobar Press publisher and poet, points out that "creativity and the willingness to experiment and take (reasonable) risks with the language are among the hallmarks of the autonomous learner, and, as the research on what makes a 'good language learner' shows, autonomy on the part of the learner is an important factor in successful language learning" (Rossiter 2003). Based on a survey of ELT professionals, Maley makes a powerful case for creative writing in English-language teaching with seven main arguments; he states that creative writing: 1. aids language development at all levels; 2. fosters playfulness; 3. encourages learners to take risks with the language; 4. puts emphasis on the right side of the brain; 5. increases self-confidence and self-esteem which leads to a corresponding increase in motivation; 6. feeds into more creative reading; and 7. helps improve expository writing, too (Maley 2012).

Poet and Waseda University instructor Karl highlights the exploratory realm of creative writing: "When students are encouraged to think and write creatively, even while learning from existing models, they can shift their focus away from searching for correct answers and move into the territory of exploration … Creative writing can temporarily shift (or destabilize) the authority away from professors and the text, and provide a transformative classroom experience that is student-centered" (Karl 2018: 538).

Further, Hiroe Kobayashi and Carol Rennert, after years of research on L2 writing, assert that "L2 writing is closely interrelated with writing in other languages, and as such is not a separate entity but part of comprehensive multilingual writing competence" (2013: 442). In other words, gaining writing prowess in English will also serve to improve writing prowess in Japanese and other student languages.

Teaching EFL Creative Writing Courses in a Japanese University

The Association of Writers and Writing Programs (AWP "About" 2020) is the largest organization worldwide dedicated to the "making and appreciation of contemporary literature along with the attendant virtues: wisdom, creativity, community, empathy, compassion, solidarity, and joy" (AWP "Values and Mission" 2020). As of this writing, there are nearly 550 college and university member programs, including undergraduate and graduate, residential, low residency and online, offering various degrees including BA, MA, PhD, MFA, BFA, as well as minors and certificates. Member programs are based in the US, UK, Canada, France, Brazil, Italy, Singapore, and Denmark (AWP, *Guide to Writing Programs*). The mission statement of AWP is to "foster literary achievement, advance the art of writing as essential to a good education, and serve the makers, teachers, students, and readers of contemporary writing" (AWP "Values and Mission" 2020). When instructors in Japanese universities do have the rare opportunity to develop undergraduate creative writing courses at Japanese universities, one may ask: are the above guidelines created by the US-based Association of Writers and Writing Programs Associate Writing Programs guidelines relevant to courses offered in L2 programs, and specifically, in Japan?

At YCU, in 2003, as a newly full-time instructor with a graduate degree from the New York University Creative Writing Program (an AWP member), plus experience teaching undergraduate expository, creative, and EFL writing in US universities, I was encouraged to offer, in addition to my academic writing and discussion classes, full semester creative writing courses. Initially, I offered a creative writing semester course combining poetry and fiction writing; from 2005 to 2011, my offerings included separate courses in poetry and fiction; and from 2012 to 2020, only fiction has been offered. These elective courses at YCU are situated within the Division of Arts and Culture in the International College of Liberal Arts, and over the years, registered students for each course have numbered from under ten to over thirty. Students are primarily L1 Japanese speakers writing in L2 English (with an occasional returnee or exchange student with English-language L1, or near L1, proficiency). In recent years, students must have already passed a Practical English program (achieving 500 on the ITP-TOEFL test or 650 on the TOEIC test) to enroll.

Within this Japanese university setting, logistical challenges for teaching creative writing include the following: course time constraints, since 90-minute classes meet only once per week for fifteen weeks; student absences, since officially students are required to attend only ten of fifteen classes per term to pass; heavy course loads, since Japanese university students often take a minimum of fourteen classes per semester, meaning students spend just a few hours per week on homework per course (in 2013, MEXT reported that "Japanese university students' average study time of 4.6 hours per day is very short compared with other countries"); student time constraints, since students work part-time jobs, are active in club activities, and may have long commutes; limited technology, since Wi-Fi is poor or unavailable except on faculty laptops in the classrooms, and while most students own smart phones, few bring a tablet or laptop to class, and some lack computer access in their place of residence.

In a fifteen-week, 22.5-class-hour L2 introductory course in creative writing, then, meeting AWP goals in their entirety is impossible. However, AWP goals can serve as helpful guidelines to instructors when developing creative writing courses in Japan. AWP's nine goals in teaching creative writing to undergraduates are as follows: 1. An overview of literature, 2. Expertise in critical analysis, 3. Understanding of the elements of a writer's craft, 4. Intellectual discipline, 5. Understanding of diverse cultural values, 6. Creativity, 7. A strong command of grammar, 8. Persuasive communication skills, and 9. An understanding of new media technology ("AWP Recommendations" 2020). Creative writing courses that meet these nine AWP goals in Japan, if they existed, would likely occur within English-language university programs, such as Temple University Japan, where semester creative writing courses have met for 45 class hours, rather than the Japanese university standard of 22.5, or they would be found within Japanese-language courses of study, such as the above-mentioned program at Tokai University.

At YCU, another EFL course I teach, Literature in English, serves to complement my EFL creative writing course, Elements of Fiction, by training students in AWP goals 1, 2, 3, 4 and 5—literature study, critical analysis, elements of writer's craft, intellectual discipline and diverse cultural values. Literature in English employs literature circle approaches adapted for short stories, novels and poetry, drawing on the literature circles work of former YCU colleague Furr on Literature in the EFL classroom (2003). EFL literature circles provide ideal scaffolding, and as Maher notes, offer well structured "opportunity for students to collaboratively acquire language, cultural awareness, critical thinking skills, increased comprehension for larger reading passages, and overall story and language meaning" (2015: 12).

Ideally, all of my Elements of Fiction creative writing students would also enroll in the Literature in English course. Due to the limited number of class hours, students in Elements of Fiction, by necessity, are asked to read fewer stories during the semester, and focus most on AWP goals 3, 4, 5, 6, 7 and 8—writer's craft, intellectual discipline, diverse cultural values, creativity, strong grammar, and persuasive communication skills. New media technology receives limited attention in my courses, other than to introduce online literary magazines, resources such as Purdue University's Online Writing Lab (Purdue OWL), and hybrid creative forms such as poetry videos (Moving Poems; Motionpoems).

AWP also provides a comprehensive list of twelve instruction methods and general advice for grading and developing curricula: 1. Extensive and diverse reading requirements, 2. Study of literary terminology, 3. Study of critical approaches, 4. Practice in critical reading, 5. Memorization (for the study of poetry), 6. Practice in critical writing, 7. Practice in the writer's craft, 8. Peer review or workshops, 9. Written comments from the instructor, 10. Practice in revision, 11. Grading, testing and evaluation, and 12. Hands-on experience with new media technology ("AWP Recommendations" 2020). With adaptation for cultural context, these methods also provide guidance to instructors building EFL creative writing courses for Japanese university students. In my poetry courses, method 5—memorization of poetry—has been substituted with reading aloud and watching poetry read or performed by poets online.

Scaffolded EFL Creative Portfolio Model

Over the years, adapting to the Japanese university system and to L2 student needs, while, as a North American-trained creative writing instructor, aiming to follow general AWP guidelines, I have cultivated a system of Creative Portfolios for my fifteen-week creative writing courses. These courses include the following main components.

Literary and craft discussions

In the creative writing classes, I strive to introduce students to a diverse range of authors within a limited amount of time. For fiction, authors include May-lee Chai, Sagit Emet, Wandeka Gayle, Sandra Cisneros, Edwidge Danticat, Toni Cade Bambara, Hisaye Yamamoto, Francisco Jimenez, Tim Tingle and others. In poetry, I share poems by Ross Gay, Naomi Shihab Nye, Lucille Clifton, May Swenson, Li-Young Lee, Carolyn Forché, Gary Soto, Richard Blanco, Linda Sue Park, Mary Oliver and many others. Diversity is critical, since students in Japan have been exposed primarily to celebrated (often white) writers that their professors studied, or *Harry Potter*, or graded readers (stories written or retold for English learners), leaving them with a limited and skewed vision of English-language literature. Despite years of English study, most Japanese university students have read little authentic English-language literature. Thus, while students may be unable to read extensively during a Japanese university course of just 22.5 class hours, instructors can and should ensure that students are exposed to many literary styles and voices.

Depending on class size and scaffolding needs, I adapt and employ literature circles to structure literature discussions, giving students areas of focus and assigned roles. As an alternative to literature circles, I present question sets particular to the story or poem packet for discussion. After literary and craft discussions, I segue into writing via prompts. In fiction, prompts might include writing a story in which an object plays a role, a story involving an encounter, a story centered on a disagreement, or a story of an adventure or journey. In poetry, the poem packet might be a set of narrative poems, news poems, action poems, or other category, with prompts derived from poem category, title, form, structure or other feature.

Modeling and scaffolding

With limited experience in English-language writing, Japanese university students benefit from modeling and scaffolding. As students brainstorm and draft, I also draft on the blackboard or on my laptop, projecting my page onto a screen. Modeling the writing process helps demystify the creative process, establishes the exploratory tone of the course, and demonstrates both the level of rigor expected and the range of creative possibilities. I model pre-writing, drafting, revision and editing.

For scaffolding in fiction, I employ a system of story starts, in which students write five story openings during the first ten weeks of the course before selecting one story start for full development into a complete short story, followed by revision, then editing for publication. I also provide scaffolding via exercises on paragraphing, dialog style, increasing tension, managing verb tenses, and building specificity. As an example, using selected lines from student drafts, students were instructed to collaboratively improve sentence specificity and originality. The statement "She is beautiful," through collaborative revision became "She is beautiful like a flashlight, blinding, and everyone who sees her stops breathing. Her posture is like the Tokyo Sky Tree. Her eyes are the ocean." Meanwhile, "A boy is kicking a ball against a wall," became "A Korean-Japanese mixed-race boy who was rejected from a soccer club kicks a worn-out ball against a wall mural of children from around the world smiling and holding hands" (YCU Elements of Fiction Class Work 2017). Poetry courses include similar scaffolding exercises with line breaks; writing collaborative chain poems; placing time words in narrative poetry; and practicing figurative language.

Peer feedback and instructor feedback

Students meet in groups to workshop, reading each other's drafts, writing comments, offering verbal feedback and discussing further development of the work. Formative instructor feedback consists of written comments about what the work seems to be communicating and what aspects are effective, plus questions for the writer to consider in further development. Comments are largely focused on content, and surface error comments are intentionally limited, to be addressed instead with the whole class. Drafts are marked √ if acceptable, √+ if unusually strong and revealing of significant effort, or R (rewrite) if of insufficient quality or content. During in-class writing sessions, I hold one-to-one conversations with students to address questions and concerns. I encourage students to engage in writing their own authentic stories and being true to themselves, while remaining aware of placing their unique voices out in the world.

Summative assessment is saved for final portfolios containing all the work for the semester. The assessment rubric (Table 1) shared with students in advance (double-sided for self-evaluation on one side, and instructor evaluation on the other), gives significantly more weight to higher order over lower order writing concerns.

Table 1 Final Portfolio Assessment Rubric Elements of Fiction at Yokohama City University.

Final Portfolio Assessment

Criteria	Points Possible	Score	Comments
Does the portfolio contain 1 final complete short story, 1 earlier version of the complete story, 1 peer evaluation, 4 story starts, and 1 story of an hour? Is the final story an original, thoughtful work of fiction?	50		
Does the final story show significant revision and editing work from the second draft to the final?	50		
Does the final story contain strong fiction elements (characters, setting, plot, point of view, etc.)? Is the story fully developed?	50		
Does the writing in the final story follow common grammar and style rules? Does the story have an interesting title properly centered?	50		
Total:	200		

This rubric grading approach encourages risk taking, allowing students to experiment and grow as writers over the semester, and enables instructor comments to focus more on content than mechanics. Fiction portfolios include five short story starts; one full draft of the story selected for completion; peer feedback papers; the revised complete short story; and the rubric. The poetry portfolio is similar, except that revised versions of all eight poems are included. After portfolios are submitted for summative assessment, students edit their work for literary magazine publication.

Audience and purpose through publication and reading

Each creative writing course includes an end-goal project—in fiction, a full-length short story publish-ready for the literary magazine; in poetry, individual collections from which students read several poems during a class or open reading. In 2005 I initiated a simple print-form YCU literary magazine, *Footprints,* that has been distributed in class and on campus. Online editions of the 2018 and 2019 issues were introduced in a March 2020 blogpost (Thompson, "YCU Footprints Literary Magazine").

Toward Including More Creative Writing in Japanese Universities

In the 2017 MEXT White Paper, among the thirteen aims of the Trends and Development in Education, Culture, Sports, Science and Technology Policies section are "Creating a Lifelong Learning Society," "Improving Higher Education," "Cultivating Nation Based on Culture and the Arts" and "Improving International Exchange and Cooperation" (MEXT White Paper 2017). The Basic Act on Culture and the Arts is designed to "comprehensively and systematically promote policies related to culture and the arts" (Section 1-1 2017), and the Visions of the Policies on Culture and the Arts include "A Creative and Vibrant Society" in which "investments are made in culture and the arts" and "A Spiritually Affluent and Diverse Society" in which "everyone participates in society through culture and the arts, which spreads mutual understanding and creates a spiritually affluent society where diverse values are respected" (Section 1-2-(2) 2017). Creative writing practice clearly serves a number of these aims. One can hope that MEXT will recognize that creative writing, when combined with literature study and workshops, plays an important role in encouraging innovation and understanding a diverse range of values. MEXT now also encourages "active learning," as opposed to passive lecture style learning. Ito, in 'Rethinking Active Learning in the Context of Higher Learning,' explains that collaborative learning and project-based learning methods have recently been encouraged in higher education in Japan as active learning (AL) to develop critical thinking, analysis and problem solving that "serve to develop employability" (Ito 2017: 2), but contends that a more fitting term for the type of learning universities should be aiming for is engagement through "proactive learning" (1–10) as a pedagogical methodology as opposed to a collection of methods. Ito points out that "Introducing the concept of proactive may help university instructors understand AL and become aware that they are now expected to create proactive graduates with innovation skills who are able to make changes through actions" (9). Creative writing and writing workshops employ both active and proactive learning involving a range of methodologies and offering students opportunities to engage in literary craft as innovators.

Holloway, of the UK's University of Bolton, notes that creative writing is not just about gaining skills, craft and technique, but:

> also about encouraging students to play, to move beyond their normal styles and subjects of writing, beyond their use of traditional structural, narrative and poetic forms—and to ask them to see what happens. In this sense university is a place for play … If students are not actively encouraged to play then we are simply encouraging them to remain as static as they were when they entered higher education—even if they are more adept at using "writerly" skills and techniques.
>
> Holloway (2016)

My students have spoken to the value of practicing creativity in their end-of-term course questionnaire; one student responded, "Although I had read some stories in English, I never had tried to write. So writing was really difficult for me first, but it made me realize I can create something if I try!" and another wrote, "I really enjoyed both reading and writing fiction in this course. It was fun because you are both discovering and creating new things" (YCU Elements of Fiction Feedback 2016). The combination of discovering literature and creating literature is a natural pairing and an especially effective language acquisition motivator in EFL classrooms. Students appreciate the chance to "play" by writing creatively. One student noted, "I think the assignments provided various different ideas (especially as we read and discussed examples before the assignments were given), while at the same time leaving us with enough creative freedom to develop our own original stories" (YCU Elements of Fiction Feedback 2017).

Creative writing, and particularly poetry writing, enables L2 students to consider complex events, process emotions and reflect on the world as they develop language skills. Smith of Aichi Gakuin University found that "The active exploration of emotions in L2 is well suited to fiction and poetry writing ... Finding an emotional voice in the second language appears to be part of mastering that language" (2013: 15). Smith also values offering students the chance to practice writing associative and figurative language in their L2: "Both the form (e.g. similes with *like, as* etc.) and the purpose (the impact of showing/comparing rather than literally re-telling) of such techniques can be taught and practiced through encouraging students to write literary-style pieces" (17). Meanwhile Hanauer, through extensive studies of L2 poets and poetry, asserts that "second language poetry writers are fully capable of using sound patterns, figurative language and imagery in their writings" in *Poetry as Research: Exploring Second Language Poetry Writing* (2010: 52).

Another advantage of creative writing is that university students may gain mental health benefits from the opportunity to process complex emotions through a safe space of crafting fiction and poetry amid supportive peers. Iida of Gunma University analysed 773 poems written by seventy-eight Japanese EFL university students concerning the 2011 Great East Japan Earthquake. The study provided evidence that "low-intermediate EFL students can handle the expression of their personal life experiences through poetry and suggests that L2 poetry writing can be used to explore traumatic events" (Iida 2016:132) and, in fact, "clarifies that low-intermediate L2 writers can express and communicate deeply traumatic experiences in poetry writing" (131).

The creative writing workshop experience—sharing and commenting on each other's work—offers multiple benefits to EFL university classrooms. Roberts postulates that "the workshop format promotes creative and critical thought processes and output, at the student level, and socialization, co-creation, and constructive teamwork at the group level" (2013: 25). One of my fiction students noted, "[The workshop] gives you insight on how you (yourself) think about a certain thing, and in turn you can see the things from the perspective of the other person." Another student commented, "My friends' feedbacks were helpful for improving my stories. They told me the good points and bad points. They think about the details of the characters with me." Another said, "It was such a pleasant time to see other students' work to experience different perspect[ives] of storybuilding and to get honest comments" (YCU Elements of Fiction Feedback 2018). The workshop creates an authentic discussion opportunity for students to acquire and practice the language of literary elements, character growth, dialog, story arc, tension, voice, tone and meaning.

In his article on teaching creative writing in the Sophia University EFL classroom, Kaufman notes, "As students discover the unexpected in their work, their focus grows. They reach for vivid language. They spend time crafting single sentences, hunting for the perfect detail" (2017:136). One of my students commented on such reach for effective language in this way: "At first I felt hard to write in English, but using my imagination was always fun. I had been thinking while waiting trains, taking shower. When I hit upon good stories, I want to express in good way, so I tried to use dictionary. This made my writing skills up" (YCU Elements of Fiction Feedback 2016). Students in my YCU creative writing EFL courses become engaged in meaningful conversation when discussing their own or their peers' stories or poetry, and discover that with sustained effort they produce written works that resonate with their peers. By the end of the course, they are changed by their journey, and there is evident collective pride in their class accomplishments. After receiving the literary magazine, students write comments such as "I feel happy. And I can't wait to read others' stories," and, "The collaboration *Footprints* . . . is really good and I'm happy to get it. I want to know how other classmates grew and the final story of them," and "It gave me a feeling of accomplishment. I'd like to show it to my family!" and "It will be my treasure" (YCU Elements of Fiction Feedback 2018).

For young and new adults, creative writing enables students to probe their own identity and relationship to the world. David Mura, author of *A Stranger's Journey; Race, Identity, and Narrative Craft in Writing,* states in his first chapter, "If writing is a search for language, it is also a search for identity. We write to articulate who we are, to describe our sense of the world" (2018: 11). My students have awed me again and again in their ability to develop lasting stories that move and inspire, and reveal, through deliberate word choice and story craft, aspects of their own identity. At the start of the course students tend to write vague, flat characters in dull, generic situations. By the end of the course they have created unforgettable characters and scenarios. Table 2 presents the openings of three stories published in *Footprints* 2018 (Thompson). These excerpts reveal the prowess students can develop in building setting and character combined with action and change to propel a short story forward—all within a single semester of just 22.5 class hours.

Table 2 Three short story openings from *Footprints 2018*.

1.

Country Life with a Town Girl

by Natsuki Rokudo

When I came home after school on the first day of fall semester, there was a pair of tiny pink sandals behind the door. I had never seen such fashionable shoes in my house. I was wondering who was visiting our house. I walked into the living room and found that my father who should have been working was sitting on a seat cushion and talking to a girl.

"Who's that girl? Why is Papa talking with her? Do they know each other?" I asked Mama standing in the kitchen.

She looked back and said, "Ken, how was school?"

"Mama, school doesn't matter now. Answer my question!"

"Be calm, please. Can you wait for a minute? I need to serve tea now." She poured green tea into 4 cups. Each cup had 4 different patterns and shapes. We did not have a tea set because it hardly ever happened that someone formally visited us. The aroma of the tea spread.

"Ken," Papa called me. "Come here."

I sat down next to him. The girl and I were facing each other. There were 2 big suitcases beside her.

Mama brought cups of tea to the low table in front of us.

"Let me explain." Papa started to talk about what I wanted to know. "She is Rika. She is eleven and in the 5th grade, the same grade as you. She is from Shinjuku, Tokyo. She'll go to elementary school in Tsubetsu to experience country life."

"To experience country life?" I could not understand what he said because I did not know the system called "Sansonryugaku" where urban students can go to school in a mountain village.

"Yes." He continued with what was more unbelievable for me. "She'll live with us for a half year."

2.

The Florist

by Minami Isaka

1

I'm a money collector of NHK. I come to work at nine o'clock in the morning every day, and I start going door to door to collect the money. Today, I have already collected from six apartments, and the next is the last one. It's already 20:30. I run upstairs to the 5th floor of Fuji terrace.

"Ding dong, Ding dong. Hello, Ms. Endo." There is no response.

Only two or three people willingly open the door. Most people don't want to open up. I'm sure they are at home, but they ignore me. They pretend they aren't at home.

The man who looked sleepy and had a bed head. The woman who opened the door cursing because her baby was crying far side of the room. Most people are busy and irritated at me.

I always think about my job, the collector. A pastry chef sells a lot of cakes. The people who eat cakes become happy. A tour operator, like JTB, sells a lot of tours and travel plans. The families who use the JTB tours make a lot of memories. Everyone sells happiness. What am I doing? I get money and time from people. The more I think, the more I am confused.

Meanwhile I have arrived at Mr. Matsushita's apartment. It's on the second floor. He never opens the door, because he is just working every day. I don't know what he is working for. I think the door won't open. I ring the bell.

"Ding dong, Ding dong. Hello, Mr. Matsushita. Ding dong, Ding dong."

Footsteps can be heard from the other side of the door.

3.

The Hour Before the World Ends

by Oyamada Shusei

————the remaining time is 60 minutes

"I regret to announce to you that our world will end after one hour," the TV announcer says with a serious face in the monitor.

In the classroom, we are told that earth will end because of the clash with a big meteorite. It appeared suddenly and world governments realized we can't do anything. After the announcement, everyone runs out without me. I try to call my parents' home, but I fail. Cell phone service has become hopeless. I sigh and go out slowly. I was a child who hardly ever cried, and I am laid-back still now.

————the remaining time is 50 minutes

After walking, I come to the nearest train station. There are a lot of people. They all look very upset.

"Please listen! All trains have stopped! Please spend your last time near here," a station attendant shouts through a loudspeaker.

The sentence by the man doesn't surprise me. To tell the truth, I already feel resigned.

I have nothing to do in particular. So, I decide to go to the mountain that I wanted to visit someday. It stands between our apartment and school. Some minutes' walk will take me to the mountain. I start to walk slowly.

————the remaining time is 43 minutes

The street is filled with silence like all people had died. I am the only person walking outside. Other people may be spending their last time in the house with their loved ones.

By chance, I see a drowning dog in the river. It is struggling and looks old.

"It will be a waste of time. Even if I help the dog, he will die an hour later," my reason says to myself.

But I have already jumped into the river after taking off my T-shirt and jeans when I realize that.

————the remaining time is 36 minutes

"Fuh......I'm the most tired in my life," I complain to no one in particular.

The old dog that I saved shakes his body and licks my face happily. And he points toward a direction as if he wants to bring me somewhere. I am free, so, carrying my clothes, I follow the dog. I pray that I won't be caught by a policeman because I am in my underwear.

————the remaining time is 30 minutes

The dog stops after a few minutes' walk. There is a wooden house looks so old that it may collapse before the world ends. The signboard of it tells me it is a penny candy store. The dog enters into the shop with no hesitation.

"Oh. . . . . .! Bes! Welcome back. . . . . ." An old lady shows up and she hugs the dog without caring her kappogi apron gets wet. The dog called Bes closes his eyes happily. I finger my hair because I have nothing to do.

Then the old lady notices me and guesses I helped the dog by my wet body. "Please use this towel, and thank you for helping my family," she says handing me a fluffy bath towel.

Course feedback from my YCU creative writing students has been consistently positive over the years. Given MEXT's initiatives including its impetus to develop thirty universities as centers for internationalization ("Higher Education in Japan" 2012), and considering the recent emphasis on AL in Japan, the aim to realize a lifelong learning society "based on the three principles of independence, collaboration, and creativity" ("Trends and Development Pt. 2" 2017), as well as the steady demand for creativity in new media and the elevated importance of communication in every field in this twenty-first-century interconnected world, creative writing courses deserve to be a feature of all Japanese universities. The AWP suggested goals and methods will, if adapted to context and circumstances, provide meaningful guidance to instructors developing these courses.

Alongside the opportunity to read and study literature, students deserve the opportunity to *create* literature in the university. May we dare to hope that one day all students in Japanese universities will have access to both undergraduate and graduate programs in creative writing, in Japanese and in English.

References

AWP "About." Association of Writers and Writing Programs. Available online: https://www.awpwriter.org/guide/guide_writing_programs (accessed November 2, 2020).

"AWP Recommendations on the Teaching of Creative Writing to Undergraduate Students." AWP Board of Trustees, *Guide to Writing Programs*, Association of Writers and Writing Programs. Available online: https://www.awpwriter.org/guide/directors_handbook_recommendations_on_the_teaching_of_creative_writing_to_undergraduates (accessed November 2, 2020).

AWP "Values and Mission." Association of Writers and Writing Programs. Available online: https://www.awpwriter.org/about/mission (accessed November 2, 2020).

"An Introduction to Publishing in Japan, 2017–2018." Japan Booksellers Association, 8. Available online: http://www.jbpa.or.jp/en/ (accessed August 21, 2019).

CROP, Meiji Gakuin University English Department Creative Journal. Available online: http://www.mgucrop.com/ (accessed October 19, 2019).

Footprints 2018: Holly Thompson's 2018 Elements of Fiction Class at Yokohama City University. Unpublished literary magazine, edited by Holly Thompson, Yokohama City University. 2018.

Furr, M. (2003), "Literature circles for the EFL Classroom," *Proceedings of the 2003 TESOL Arabia Conference.* Dubai: TESOL Arabia (in press version). Available online: https://bit.ly/2VSyOpi (accessed October 18, 2019).

Hanauer, D. I. (2010) *Poetry as Research: Exploring Second Language Poetry Writing,* John Benjamins Publishing Company, 2010. ProQuest Ebook Central. Available online: http://ebookcentral.proquest.com/lib/berkeley-ebooks/detail. action?docID=623392 Created from berkeley-ebooks on August 28, 2019, 52.

Holloway, S. (2016), "Why the Teaching of Creative Writing Matters," *The Conversation.* November 9. Available online: http://theconversation.com/why-the-teaching-of-creative-writing-matters-67659 (accessed August 27, 2019).

Iida, A. (2016), "Exploring Earthquake Experiences: A Study of Second Language Learners' Ability to Express and Communicate Deeply Traumatic Events in Poetic Form," *System,* 57, 120–33.

Ito, H. (2017), "Rethinking Active Learning in the Context of Japanese Higher Education," *Cogent Education,* 4: 1298187, 2. Available online: (https://doi.org/10.108 0/2331186X.2017.1298187 accessed October 18, 2019).

"JALT Chapters and SIGs," (2019), The Japan Association for Language Teaching. Available online: https://jalt.org/main/groups (accessed August 21, 2019).

Kamata, S. and Dierk G. (2014), "Fundamentals of Creative Writing for Japanese University Students," in N. Sonda and A. Krause (eds), JALT 2013 Conference Proceedings. Tokyo: JALT, 521–8.

Karl, S. (2018), "The Intersection of Creative Writing and Active Learning for Non-Native Writers—Writing Beyond the Mother Tongue," *Waseda Rilas Journal,* No. 6, October, 533–8.

Kaufman, M. (2017), "Narrative Surprise and the Challenges of Teaching Creative Writing in the EFL Classroom," *Bulletin of the Faculty of Foreign Studies,* Sophia University, No. 52, 127–37.

Kimura, D. and Madoka T. (2017), "Advancing 21st Century Competencies in Japan," *Asia Society Center for Global Education, Global Incubation x Fostering Talents* (GiFT), February. https://asiasociety.org/files/21st-century-competencies-japan.pdf accessed August 29, 2019.

Kitagawa, M. M. (1982), "Expressive Writing in Japanese Elementary Schools," *Language Arts,* Vol. 59, No. 1, Reaching Out, January, 18–22.

Kobayashi, H. and Carol R. (2013), "Second Language Writing: Is It a Separate Entity?" *Journal of Second Language Writing,* 22, 442–3.

Maher, K. (2015), "English Language Literature Circles: Collaboratively Acquiring Language and Meaning," *The Language Teacher,* Vol. 39, Number 4, July/August, 12.

Japan Association of Language Teachers. https://jalt-publications.org/sites/default /files/pdf-article/39.4tlt-art2.pdf accessed October 18. 2019.

Maley, A. (2012). "Creative writing for students and teachers," *Humanising Language Teaching*, 14(3), June 2012. http://www.hltmag. co.uk/jun12/mart01.htm accessed March 24, 2020.

Maloney, I. (2019), "The Place of Creative Writing in an EFL University Curriculum," 名古屋外国語大学論集　第4号　2019年2月. B-NUFS04_17.pdf accessed March 20, 2020.

"MEXT 2017 White Paper on Education, Culture, Sports, Science and Technology," Ministry of Education, Culture, Sports, Science and Technology-Japan. 2017. http://www.mext.go.jp/b_menu/hakusho/html/hpab201701/1417254.htm accessed August 21, 2019.

"MEXT Courses of Study, Elementary School," MEXT Improvement of Academic Abilities. Ministry of Education, Culture, Sports, Science and Technology-Japan. 2011. http://www.mext.go.jp/en/policy/education/elsec/title02/detail02/1373859. htm accessed August 26, 2019.

"MEXT Courses of Study, Lower Secondary School—Foreign Languages," MEXT Improvement of Academic Abilities. Ministry of Education, Culture, Sports, Science and Technology-Japan. 2011. http://www.mext.go.jp/component/english/__icsFiles /afieldfile/2011/03/17/1303755_013.pdf accessed August 26, 2019

"MEXT Current Status and Issues of Education in Japan," in "The Second Basic Plan for the Promotion of Education." 2013. http://www.mext.go.jp/en/policy/education /lawandplan/title01/detail01/sdetail01/1373809.htm accessed August 28, 2019.

"MEXT Higher Education in Japan," Ministry of Education, Culture, Sports, Science and Technology-Japan. 2012. http://www.mext.go.jp/en/policy/education/highered/ title03/detail03/__icsFiles/afieldfile/2012/06/19/1302653_1.pdf accessed September 11, 2019.

"MEXT Trends and Development in Education, Culture, Sports, Science and Technology Policies," Part 2. 2017. http://www.mext.go.jp/b_menu/hakusho/html /hpab201701/detail/1418107.htm accessed October 19, 2019.

Miyawaki, H. (2002), "Colonial Language Policies and Their Effects," Lecture, World Congress on Language Policies, Barcelona, April 16–20. http://www.linguapax.org/ wp-content/uploads/2015/07/CMPL2002_T1_MHiroyuki.pdf accessed August 21, 2019.

Mizumura, M. (2017), translated by Mari Yoshihara and Juliet Winters Carpenter, *The Fall of Language in the Age of English,* Columbia University Press.

Motionpoems. http://motionpoems.org/ accessed August 27, 2019.

Moving Poems. http://movingpoems.com/ accessed August 27, 2019.

Mulvey, B. (2016), "What is Being Taught in Japanese High Schools, Why, and Why It Matters," *The Language Teacher* 40.3, May/June, 3–8.

Mura, David (2018), *A Stranger's Journey: Race, Identity, and Narrative Craft in Writing,* University of Georgia Press.

National Institute for Japanese Language and Linguistics. "Endangered Languages and Dialects in Japan." https://www.ninjal.ac.jp/english/research/project-3/institute/endangered-languages/ accessed September 10, 2019.

New York University Writing Center. "Writing Center." http://cas.nyu.edu/ewp/writing-center.html accessed October 17, 2019.

Pronko, M. (2019), "The First Crop." *CROP*, Vol. 1, Meiji Gakuin University English Department. http://www.mgucrop.com/works/ accessed, October 5, 2019.

Purdue University Online Writing Lab. "Purdue Online Writing Lab." https://owl.purdue.edu/owl/purdue_owl.html accessed October 17, 2019.

Rippey, J. (2014), "Creative Writing in EFL in Japan: A Spirit of Inclusion," *Lit Matters: The Liberlit Journal of Teaching Literature,* Issue 1/Journals. http://www.liberlit.com/litmatters/teaching-eighteenth-century-english-literature-in-japan-purposes-curricula-and-syllabi/ accessed August 23, 2019.

Roberts, J. W. (2013), "Theorizing on the Advantages of the Fiction Writing Workshop in the EFL Classroom, Part I." *The Journal of Literature in Language Teaching*, December, 19–26.

Rossiter, P. (2003), translated into Japanese by Kubota Yuusuke. *Kyoshitsu no nakadeno gengo, bungaku, souzousei* (Language, literature and creativity in the classroom), in Y. Saito (ed.), *Eigo no oshie-kata manabi-kata*, Tokyo: University of Tokyo Press: 131–70.

Smith, C. (2013) "Creative Writing as an Important Tool in Second Language Acquisition and Practice." *The Journal of Language and Literature in Language Teaching*. Vol. 2 (1), May, 11–18.

Spence, L. and Yuriko K. (2018), "Beliefs and Practices of Writing Instruction in Japanese Elementary Schools," *Language, Culture and Curriculum,* 31:1, 56–69.

Stiller, S. (2013), "Raising Critical Consciousness via Creative Writing in the EFL Classroom," *TESOL Journal* 4.1 March, 164–74. TESOL International Association.

Thompson, Holly. (2020), "YCU Footprints Literary Magazine," *Hatbooks: Holly Thompson's Blog,* accessed March 20, 2020.

Tokai University "文芸創作学科" (Department of Creative Writing). Tokai University. https://www.u-tokai.ac.jp/academics/undergraduate/letters/creative_writing/ accessed August 20, 2019.

Waseda University, "Creative Writing and Criticism," Waseda University School of Culture, Media and Society. https://www.waseda.jp/flas/cms/en/about/theoretical/cwc/ accessed August 21, 2019.

Williams, C. H. (2017), "Writing English in the East Asian Classroom," in *Teaching English in East Asia: A Teacher's Guide to Chinese, Japanese and Korean Learners* (Springer Texts in Education, 2017) 147–66, accessed August 21.

Yokohama City University Elements of Fiction Class Work. Unpublished student collaborative blackboard writing in Holly Thompson's Elements of Fiction course, Yokohama City University. November 17, 2017.

Yokohama City University Elements of Fiction Class Feedback. Unpublished
  anonymous responses to end-of-term questionnaire, Fall 2016.
Yokohama City University Elements of Fiction Class Feedback. Unpublished
  anonymous responses to end-of-term questionnaire, Fall 2017.
Yokohama City University Elements of Fiction Class Feedback. Unpublished
  anonymous responses to end-of-term questionnaire, Fall 2018.
Yokohama City University Practical English Writing Center. "PEC Writing Center User
  Guidelines for Students." https://www.yokohama-cu.ac.jp/pec/resource/rc/vocab.
  html accessed October 17, 2019.

9

Through the Looking Glass and Back Again: Writing Reflectively in Creative Writing

Maria Taylor

De Montfort University

Of course the first thing to do was to make a grand survey of the country she was going to travel through. "It's something very like learning geography," thought Alice, *as she stood on tiptoe in hopes of being able to see a little further. "Principal rivers – there are none. Principal mountains – I'm on the only one, but I don't think it's got any name.*

Carroll (1998:145)

In Lewis Carroll's *Through the Looking Glass*, Alice must pause before she navigates a reflection of a familiar but very different world—a world shaped by an author's imagination. As Alice does here, students of creative writing will be expected to reflect—albeit on their writing, rather than unusual terrain. In one way, however, reflection is a way of understanding the "geography" of personal writing practices. Reflective writing offers students a platform where they can assimilate their writing practice and diversity of experience, while assessing their progress. From this wider perspective, reflective writing also "demands" that students have the freedom to exercise "cross-cultural communication," which allows for broader thought about identity and cultural influence in relation to their writing (Hunt and Sampson 1998: 141). Reflective writing is a common requirement for assessment at all levels of university study, from undergraduate to postgraduate level and beyond. For some students, the practice of reflective writing may initially seem like a very odd thing to do. Surely students have chosen to undertake creative writing, not to write *reflectively*, but to write *creatively*? In this essay I will consider how reflective writing is a key part of the writing process. Reflective writing is a common requirement for assessment at all levels of university study and it can enable students to become better practitioners of writing.

The Writer as Daydreamer

Writing is often viewed as an unconscious act, a mysterious process, which has more in common with daydreaming than conscious thought. The Romantic poet William Wordsworth described his poetry and those of others, as a "spontaneous overflow of powerful feelings" (Wordsworth 1984: 598). Reflective writing, by contrast, requires that students delve deep into the *how* and *why* of their own work. Perhaps it is a good starting point to try and reflect consciously on the role of daydreaming, spontaneity and the unconscious in creative writing. Daydreaming, or the creative impulse, is often the beginning for creative writing. In his poem "The Instrument," the Australian Poet Les Murray considers the mysterious process behind creativity and writing, and also, albeit unconsciously, how the body itself actually responds to writing:

> Why write Poetry? For the weird unemployment.
> For the painless headaches, that must be tapped to strike
> down your writing arm at the accumulated moment.
> For the adjustments after, aligning facets in a verb
> before the trance leaves you. For working always beyond
>
> your own intelligence.
>
> Murray (2012: 202)

The feeling of being in a "trance" while working is experienced by many writers. In this state, it is hard to pin down exactly what is happening as a person is writing; the most important thing here is that the person *is* writing.

At this stage it may seem that the need for self-reflection is redundant, yet it is important that reflection tries to grapple with these trance-like stages if students are able to fully understand their writing practices. During that "trance" stage, it may feel as if the writer isn't fully aware of themselves and writing enables a different, less conscious self to emerge. David Morley writes that "many creative writers experience the sensation that somebody other *in* them is at work" (Morley 2007: 149); the "other" self is perhaps the twin I in the mirror, or the twin world that Carroll's Alice surveys. Reflective writing allows for engaging with that mysterious mirror-image figure, and gives the writer fresh insights into the practice of their own writing. It is the creative writing tutor's role to help students engage with both their unconscious and conscious writing practices. By "unconscious" writing practices I am thinking of aspects stemming from personal identity, subjective preferences and how wider influences can affect writing. Reflective writing can focus on these aspects of creativity as well as the mechanical nuts and bolts of editing and research.

In his essay "Creative Writers and Daydreaming" (1908), Freud defines the writer primarily as a daydreamer, or indeed a *phantasist*. According to Freud, a creative writer's habits appear to have much in common with a sense of play and imagination which is intrinsic to childhood development rather than a feature of adulthood. Indeed, many creative writing workshops will use methods which involve some element of play to access these hidden stores of imagination within writers. Freud wrote that "the imaginative writer" may be viewed as the "dreamer in broad daylight" (Freud 1908: 149). Students need to engage with their mirror selves in creative writing.

We tend not to analyse our quotidian daydreams in a more critical, conscious way, unless we are indeed examining a case study for individual psychoanalysis. In creative writing, however, we partly have to analyse ourselves through reflection, as indeed, did Freud himself. The reflective process inevitably leads to some investigation of our unconscious thought—primarily by the writer themselves unraveling the mystery of their own work. Freud describes how these daydreams and their "motivating wishes vary according to the sex, character and circumstances of the person who is having the phantasy" (Freud 1908: 423). Writing is a highly individual activity and it may be shaped by many different influences, such as identity, class, gender, race, and ethnicity. Reflective writing allows students to address these issues directly, and/or provide a platform for exploring elements which are unique to their own writing identities. Yet from this foundation we may also create a fictional self; as Celia Hunt and Fiona Sampson state, "when we write we also create a narrative self on the page" (Hunt and Sampson 2006: 174).

The Reflected Self

Students must be encouraged to take that brave first step through the looking glass into themselves in order to understand their motives and processes as writers, as Morley writes: "Critical self-reflection is a means to develop some self-understanding, and to create and evolve" (Morley 2007: 37). To see yourself anew as a writer through reflection is a way of understanding your processes and subsequently being able to build on them. To a greater extent, reflective writing demands that the writer should cultivate some distance from the creative work. Addressing her comments to hopeful fledging writers, Dorothea Brande writes:

"What, on the whole, *do* you write, when you set down the first things that occur to you? Try to read, now, as though you had the work of a stranger in your hands, and to discover there what the tastes and talents of this alien writer may be" (Brande 1934: 84). How can it be possible that a writer can alienate themselves from something as personal as their own writing? There are various time-honored methods which produce good starting points, such as putting work away for a while before re-assessment; asking peers for opinions; or looking back at notes and drafts for future guidance. A student may see their writing differently during this process. Helpfully, a student may notice errors in certain aspects of their writing which they could not initially see because they were too close to the work.

Self-reflection allows students to compare their practices with other writers. Many established authors have been interviewed about their writing habits and motivations and these sources can provide invaluable insight. Students may notice crucial patterns in their own work that are common to other writers when they research particular elements in their own work. Francine Prose writes: "A work of art can start you thinking about some aesthetic or philosophical problem; it can suggest some new method, some fresh approach to fiction" (Prose 2012: 9). This can be a more empowering aspect of the reflective process.

In the same way there is a certain pleasure derived from reading poetry or prose fiction, students can also develop a love of craft through reading. This allows the student to develop a sense of engagement with the writing world and also feel as if they are actively offering something by participating in this world:

> … many writers in the real world like to explain themselves, as a form of setting up their stall, and for creating an audience that understands their approach and purpose. They often do so vicariously when writing about, or reviewing, the creative writing of other authors. They discuss their working processes; they advocate and opinionate; they make no secret of their influences, enthusiasms or motivations. You must practice at this mirror. You reflect on the aims of your writing and the process – for example, of drafting – by which it arrived at its final form. You also give critical attention to your own writing – for example the affinities you may feel it has with the work of other authors – and by placing your work in any intellectual, aesthetic, social or other context you feel it should be seen in.
>
> Morley (2007: 37)

The student therefore is participating in a form of dialog with other writers through reflective writing. Students should review and think of authors' work more critically, and not simply read for escapism if they are serious about developing their craft. Established or favored writers provide real-world models for students to learn from, usually with the intention of eventually adding more layers to their own writing. It is also helpful here to consider what is entailed by reflection.

Elements of Reflective Writing

Most reflective writing appears to address two elements:

1. The process of writing: this includes initial ideas, editing, drafting and so on. It may also extend to an investigation of linguistic and stylistic features. Students may work with passages and quotations from their own writing to reach conclusions. This is the side of reflective writing that relates to the student's personal practices.

2. Research and wider reading: this involves not only reading the work of other writers, but other forms of research. This will most likely involve critical or theoretical practice. This is the side of reflective writing that relates to how a student interacts with the practices of others. This adds some authority to the reflective process, by bringing the *world* to the learner's writing.

For some learners, reflective writing may feel like a very self-conscious activity, perhaps even a "narcissistic" act (Morley 2007: 37). Reflective writing is not about ego; the focus must always be how *creativity* is shaped rather than *self*.

Spontaneity or Conscious Method?

Earlier I mentioned Wordsworth's view of poetry as a "spontaneous overflow of feeling" (Wordsworth 1984: 598). In his *Preface to the Lyrical Ballads* (1800), William Wordsworth describes the best and purest forms of writing poetry in this way. This Romantic view of writing still persists today, and is one which suggests creativity *apparently* materializes from nowhere. Wordsworth did, however, also acknowledge that writers must inevitably think "long and deeply" (Wordsworth 1984: 598) about their work. Wordsworth goes on to write: "For our continued influxes of feeling are modified and directed by our thoughts, which are indeed the representatives of all our past feelings" (ibid.). This suggests that for Wordsworth, reflection is an inevitable part of the creative process.

Wordsworth employs a clear rationale behind his reasons for writing. This makes the preface to the *Lyrical Ballads* a kind of prototype piece of reflective writing. Using such a text as a guide, it may be worthwhile to ask students to summarize reasons that guide their own writing practices. A sense of personal manifesto can shape a clearer sense of self-identity as a writer for students.

Reflective Writing and Self-identity

Creative writing tutors know that the students in their classrooms come from very different and diverse backgrounds. Some may have had more privileged upbringings and others may not have been so lucky. In most instances, creative writing tutors have to teach a cross-section of both home and overseas students who come to the subject with different expectations. For instance, some students are not writing in their mother tongue, which makes them exophonic writers. Exophonic writers may have very different challenges to their fellow students writing in their first language. This may mean their having to internalize a different system of grammar and style. This has an impact on their own writing which they may feel obliged to discuss in their reflective commentaries. Students may explore identity in a more sensory way through reflective writing, rather than stylistically. Gloria Anzaldùa writes:

> There are more subtle ways that we internalize identification, especially in the forms of images and emotions. For me food and certain smells are tied to my identity, to my homeland.
>
> Adsit (2019: 176)

Reflective writing isn't simply about the mechanics of grammar and style; instead it can open up a subjective range of enquiry when looking at politics and identity—with issues of class, gender, and ethnicity.

Immediate Exercises for Self-reflection

A common writing exercise often utilized in creative writing classrooms is the practice of automatic writing. I should say, however, this is not of the occult variety famously employed by the poet W. B. Yeats! Automatic writing can be used as an initial warm-up activity in order to generate a freer piece of stream of conscious writing. A good opener for instance, might be "It was winter and . . .";

this allows for very free writing and invites students to use their "daydreaming" skills. Students will then be asked to write on from this opening phrase without over thinking the content of this writing. This exercise guarantees that no two students will write the same piece, although there may be obvious thematic similarities between them. This is where we can introduce an immediate reflective task. Students are asked to reflect on their pieces, and make notes of patterns, such as recurring images or themes the writing exposes. They may allow students to explore *why* their writing was formed in such a way unique to themselves. This is very similar to what Kathleen Blake Yancey labels "Reflection in Action," which is defined as "the process of reviewing and projecting and revising, which takes place within a composing event, and the associated texts." (Yancey 2016: 4) Yancey also underlines that it is necessary to have a more conscious awareness of process at this early stage of reflection, as it forms a central introduction to the formal assessment associated with reflective writing, from undergraduate level to beyond. In her pioneering work on the evolution of creative writing teaching, Yancey noted that in the 1990s "reflection was playing a major role in assessment" (5) and now it is a vital part of assessment practices. Yancey also defined two other key areas which follow "Reflection in Action"; firstly "Constructive Reflection," which refers to reflection practices by students between, as stated earlier, "composing events," and finally "Reflection in Presentation," when students articulate "relationships between and among the multiple variables of writing and the writer in a specific context for a specific audience." (4) This stage, I would suggest, is what many Creative Writing practitioners would want their students to aim for in a final assessment piece. It seems, however, that without embedding the initial stage of "Reflection in Action" into seminars, students might find it more of a challenge to marry all three stages of Yancey's Reflective framework.

Quick exercises, such as automatic writing, can generate an initial discussion as to how students engage with writing—how does the same exercise create output which differs from writer to writer? In either large or small groups, key elements of writing such as voice, style, and structure, among others can be discussed. Peer discussion allows for students to begin articulating ideas on the reflective process even at the drafting stage.

These more "instant" exercises can be developed to incorporate poetry and prose written by published authors to generate fresh work from students. In one exercise I select two pieces of creative writing by different authors, in this case two poems which are thematically linked. Both poems are about shops, but the two poets who have written then come from different times and cultures. The first poem, "My Grandmother," is by the English poet Elizabeth Jennings and was published in the 1960s. On the surface, this is a poem about the antique shop kept by the speaker's grandmother, but within the poem Jennings' is exploring tense family relationships; the grandmother has a more active relationship with her shop than her own family. To complement the poem I also use a more recent poem, "Artisan du Chocolat, Borough Market," by Hannah Lowe, a poet of Chinese-Jamaican origin who was raised in London. The poem is set in a cafe and explores the pain of partings and subsequent loneliness. Having read the two poems, with some brief class discussion, students are asked to write a piece set in a shop or cafe they are or were familiar with in their lives. Once the piece is initially drafted students are asked questions they can answer on paper without sharing. These questions may consist of:

a)   what is your involvement with that location?
b)   how did you structure the piece and why do you think you chose that approach?
c)   a more linguistic question—are there more static or active verbs present in your piece? Can you underline verbs which you feel are working harder than others?

These questions are examples and of course can be tailored to the moment. I keep the number of questions limited. Students then share their very early draft with a peer. The peer student is asked to isolate three things they like and one thing they might change. The other student meanwhile will do the same for their peer. Everyone will be asked to re-draft their poem in their own time and bring the more revised draft to class where we will consider their changes, preferably with the same peer. Of course, as a group, we would love to hear their work too as this is part of the enjoyment of creative writing! The exercise provides a model for thinking about a range of areas that may be tackled in a later reflective piece. Students are expected to keep all their drafts and notes on the process, as this will support their formal reflective writing.

Reading as a Writer

A useful exercise for study outside the classroom might be to set a reading task, for example a short story or a sequence of poems by a single author and then ask students to isolate examples in the writing which show strengths and weaknesses. This supports students developing the important skill of reading as a writer in their own time. This should involve a consideration of the mechanics of the writing itself, and not be based on interpreting theme or character, unless students are discussing how these elements are presented by an author (or possibly not in their opinion). This research can be presented in class and students can compare findings. A useful question here which takes the emphasis away from a literary focus is *why should we enjoy the work of a particular author?* These debates and skills, when developed, often appear in successful reflective writing commentaries, especially when balanced with well-chosen quotations from texts. The initial exercise of reading as a writer allows students to model skills they will use in their own reflective writing. As Tara Mokhtari writes, "reflective writing is as much about the input of existing knowledge as it is about the output of newly synthesized knowledge. The reflective writer is simultaneously recording information and finding new depths of meaning within that information." (Mokhtari 2019: 48).

Wider Reading

Good reflective writing relies on careful choices made in terms of wider reading. Which authors should a student choose from the near-infinite numbers of authors both living and dead? This is a major challenge in terms of guiding students through the process of reading as a writer. A tutor may offer suggestions and attempt to enrich a students' appetite for reading. Tutors may select extracts, poems, or whole texts which may be taught in classes in order to highlight certain skills and illustrate techniques that benefit their students' practices. Of course, this can only ever be the tip of the iceberg, where reading is concerned. Traditional literary courses might offer a compulsory reading menu of work produced by dead, white males for the most part, but creative writers should spread their nets far and wide and read across genres, timescales, and cultures. This reading should be underpinned with a specific emphasis on contemporary writing—after all, the student is writing for a contemporary audience.

The tutor of creative writing therefore has an obligation to introduce students to a range of writing styles written by a diverse range of authors and themselves be up to date with a good sense of contemporary writing and publishing. Suggested reading might include Shakespeare or Dickens, but also Zadie Smith or Claudia Rankine. Isaac Ginsberg Miller writes: "The cannon is evolving, expanding and changing. This is something to be celebrated, not bemoaned" (Adsit 2019: 111). Students of creative writing must also be discerning readers who are guided by a personal internal compass when it comes to exploring and developing their tastes and styles. Reflective writing can serve as a record of an individual journey through a range of texts and sources that have captured the imagination. As Porochista Khakpour writes:

> I often think of the great Jean Rhys quote "reading makes immigrants of us all," and the many temporary homes I've found in all the books from around the world that I've loved. In that way, we writers are the creators of entirely unique homes. "Every time you write," I tell my students, "you reinvent the universe." No two worlds are identical to any two writers.
>
> Adsit (2019: 104)

Reflective Writing Throughout the Teaching Year

There are various stages throughout the course of an academic year that yield different possibilities for reflective writing and offering vantage points for students to assess their development.

1. At the beginning of the year students might be asked to write down their hopes and expectations for their own writing. What do they wish to achieve? Rather than general comments, such as "to write more," tutors may ask students to focus on three specific areas. The more specific these are, the more results might be. A personal aim could be something quite straightforward, such as "experiment more with poetic form by writing a sestina." To some extent this informs the writing before the student begins in earnest. Rather than being prescriptive, however, it may open different avenues of experimentation and interest to students and offer a frame for their subsequent writing.

2. During the academic year students may isolate how they have built on the areas addressed above and use the reflective writing as a focal point for how they're meeting their goals and aims.

3. At the end of year, students can look back on their work in a formal reflective commentary. This might also be undertaken creatively. A good end of first-year creative reflective exercise is to ask students to write a letter addressed to their former selves twelve months earlier, before they started their course. In these letters they will be expected to offer hints and advice on the writing experience. Another light-hearted exercise may be to ask students to write an imaginary blurb for a potential book, or a review

of a short story or poem they've written. If there is a good working dynamic in the group this can be done as a peer activity. Such exercises can lead to fresher insights. A creative approach to reflective writing can potentially be extended into a longer final assessment.

The Big Picture and the Small Details

Good reflective writing can switch between looking at writing with a macroscopic as well as a microscopic focus. The student can discuss overarching areas, such as narration; their general progress over a stretch of time; a particular style or genre they are trying to emulate or ideas and influences that informed their ideas at the start. The microscopic focus is just as important. This can include looking at the writing at sentence level or word level. I encourage students to use short quotations from their own work when making points. It is also handy for students to quote passages, lines or even individual words from earlier drafts and compare them with the final draft of a project. Drafts should be kept so students can refer to them later in reflective commentaries when the changes are evident. I tell students to keep all their drafts safe.

Meanwhile, many students feel secure writing in a more formal essay style. They may structure their ideas chronologically according to the time they wrote the piece/s, or write focused paragraphs on key areas such as drafting, narration, or imagery. It is good practice to underpin points with short quotations from their own work, as well as quotations from writers or theorists.

Of course some students choose more creative approaches to reflective writing. It is always a pleasure and a joy to read successful imaginative reflective commentaries. A range of forms could be employed, depending on the student's ability to execute a plausible style. This could be a "mock" interview structure; the work being discovered in the future by a curious reader (the epilogue of *The Handmaid's Tale* by Margaret Atwood may provide a model for this), or a critic commenting on a student's work. One example I remember with great admiration was by a student who wrote a mock trial of her writing, where the poets Sylvia Plath, Adrienne Rich, and Anne Sexton were called as witnesses. Plath's, Rich's and Sexton's responses all consisted of things they had said or written in their lifetimes. The entire project was a compelling and excellently researched piece of imaginative reflective writing. Reflective writing can succeed when framed in a creative way, as Roland Barthes writes, "Let the commentary itself be a text" (Barthes 1981: 44).

Signposting Writing and Editing Stages

To enliven research, students may be encouraged to take themselves on a creative field trip. On undergraduate courses, I have asked students to visit local historic locations. Students are encouraged to conduct recorded discussions with experts, such as historians or curators. This is also to take the research aspect away from simply browsing the Internet. They will be asked to write a short creative piece, either poetry or prose, which is connected to their visit. Students can also revisit locations and readdress their writing in the light of new research they've gained on the second trip. These potentially multiple visits serve as markers when students consider how their writing has developed over a time period. It allows for editing stages which are more actively signposted. Also, with the addition of a well-kept notebook, there should be a good store of information which is readily available during the reflective writing period.

This is quite literally an active quest-like approach, and a geographical model of reflective writing in order to navigate the strange territory of creative writing. It offers a more concrete focus when the time for writing reflectively comes and keeps writing and research methods fresh and varied. The method can also be beneficial for less confident students, who can use notes and observations they have made to shape their ideas for writing. Students might write about geographical features having an impact on their creative work, and this widens the scope of the commentary. Take for example this reflective extract from a student discussing her visits to the UK town of Rugby as a location for her writing:

> Rugby's central location has created a commuter town, a substitute for unaffordable London housing. Rugby's Poverty and homelessness is one of the most extreme per capita in the UK, and exists in plain sight of one of the most famous and affluent boarding schools in the world ... [the] hospital has closed; all major theatres and thus all emergencies are redirected to University Hospital in Coventry. In terms of Psychogeography, all character's experiences are a direct result of these [changes] ... and [this] colonizes the characters' psychological space.
>
> Litten (2019: 67)

During the reflective period the student becomes aware of geographical research directly shaping the interior presentation of her characters. With this awareness, she can begin to explore her writing practices more explicitly.

Stepping Out of the Looking Glass

The reflective writing process is not simply an "add-on" to creative writing teaching and learning. It is an integral part of the writing process which shapes and informs a creative writer's future writing as well as offering fresh perspectives on their past experiences and achievements. Reflective writing offers an opportunity for dialog with that shadow twin in the looking glass; the other self who dreams and writes unconsciously. Reflective writing is a way of engaging with the child-like figure within ourselves who makes discoveries through play, accident, and experiment. It may even be a genre of writing in itself, that allows for a different kind of creative freedom, as Robert Graham et al. write:

> A finished piece of writing is arguably creative writing in its own right.
>
> Graham et al. (2005: 83)

References

Adsit, J. (2019), *Critical Creative Writing*, London and New York: Bloomsbury Press.

Barthes, R. (1981), *Untying the Text: A Post-Structuralist Reader*, ed. Robert Young, Boston: Routledge & Kegan Paul.

Brande, D. (1990), *Becoming a Writer*, United States: Harcourt, Brace and Company 1934. Reprinted London: Papermac Macmillan.

Carroll L. (1998), *Alice's Adventures in Wonderland and Through the Looking Glass*, London: Penguin.

Freud, S. (2001), *The Standard Edition of the Complete Psychological Works of Sigmund Freud: Volume IX: 1906-1908*, London: Vintage.

Graham, R., Newall H., Leach, H. and Singleton, J. E. (2005), *The Road to Somewhere: A Creative Writing Companion*, Hampshire and New York: Palgrave Macmillan.

Hunt, C. and Sampson, F. eds (1998), *The Self on the Page: Theory and Practice of Creative Writing in Personal Development*, London: Jessica Kingsley.

Jennings, E. (2012), *The Complete Poems*, Manchester: Carcanet Press.

Litten, J. (2019), *Blindspot*, De Montfort University, undergraduate reflective writing project, with permission by author.

Lowe, H. (2013), *Chick*, Tarset: Bloodaxe Books.

Mokhtari, T. (2019), *The Bloomsbury Introduction to Creative Writing*, London: Bloomsbury Press.

Morley, D. (2007), *The Cambridge Introduction to Creative Writing*, Cambridge, Cambridge University Press.

Murray, L. (2012), "The Instrument", from *New Selected Poems*, Manchester: Carcanet.

Prose, F. (2012), *Reading Like a Writer*, London: Union Books.

Wordsworth, W. (1984) *The Major Works*, Oxford: Oxford World's Classics.

Yancey, Kathleen Blake, ed. (2016), *A Rhetoric of Reflection*, Colorado: University of Colorado Press.

10

Teacher Lore and Pedagogy in Creative Writing Courses in Poland

Hanna Sieja-Skrzypulec
Jagiellonian University

Brief History and Practices that Work

From the very beginning, the creator of the first creative writing studies courses in Poland, Gabriela Matuszek, pointed out that it was not based on Western practices, "that it significantly differs from the American models" (2005: 347) and that it offered not only writing workshops but also lectures on literature and culture. This article outlines the history of the first creative writing studies in Poland and presents teaching practices and methodologies from the perspective of twenty-five years of Polish creative writing traditions.

Views

From among the numerous conceptions of the writer, the one shaped by the Romantics remains the most attractive definition that still stimulates our imagination today. Inspiration, creative freedom, but most of all the cult of the exuberant genius are the main associations connected with the figure of the writer. A writer is expected to be an individualist who is strong and original. It is not expected for the world of art to pass through the doors of the egalitarian education system, namely the university. Such a conviction has to a large extent shaped the history of writing in Poland.

Despite the fact that Jan Parandowski, a writer and translator who was twice nominated for the Nobel Prize in Literature (1957 and 1959), had postulated the establishment of the School of the Art of Writing as early as the 1950s, the first studies of this type (Literary-Artistic Studies) were not launched until 1994 at the Jagiellonian University in Krakow. At that time the Romantic conceptions of writers and writing still prevailed in mainstream thought. In the media the initiative was often commented on but was viewed differently. In the Polish weekly *Polityka* (*Politics*) an article positively disposed towards the school appeared, written by Piotr Sarzyński entitled *Wieszczem być* (To be a Bard), in which the journalist noted:

> The lack of tradition for such types of education in Poland encourages comments that one either has talent or does not, and therefore this is not the correct path to educate a contemporary Shakespeare. (1994)

The initiators of this field of study spoke with reserve about it and underlined that "it is not about breeding geniuses." The art of writing in Poland has for many years been treated as a way of spending free time rather than an artistic craft. The conviction that a person can be educated to become a writer or simply someone who can write well was a rare thing indeed. As a consequence, despite the growing popularity of curricula aimed at improving writing skills, there is a lack of creative writing institutes and faculties at Polish universities.

Beginnings

Until 2015, when I defended the first PhD thesis on the topic of creative writing, there was only one Polish-language work devoted to this concept (Dąbała 2012). Looking at its history, I found that the first lectures on the subject of the writer's workshop were given by Jan Parandowski. Immediately after the war, Parandowski went to Lublin, where he became the head of the Department of Ancient Culture and then Comparative Literature. He lectured at the Catholic University of Lublin until 1950, then moved to Warsaw. He began a series of lectures devoted to the subject which he described in *Alchemia słowa* (The Alchemy of the Word), and later shared his experiences in the introduction to his book:

> Every question, which in the book was only touched upon, sometimes in very few words, grew during a lecture; details multiplied, bringing new aspects to light; that which was unclear became visible; that which required more attention apparent; and certain problems returned in discussion during the seminar.
>
> Parandowski (1986: 8)

Jan Parandowski not only conducted lectures, but also talked with students regarding the crucial aspects of his book. In a nutshell, during his time at the

Catholic University of Lublin there were classes concerning literary creation. It is important to note that the Polish history of creative writing began with lectures. We can conclude that their subject was the psychology of literary creation, the process of writing and the writer's workshop with a broad historical and literary context. Lectures on the theory and history of literature are still of great significance in the education of writers and they constitute an important element of numerous creative writing curricula.

In order for the Polish history of creative writing to officially commence it was necessary to put the content presented in the lectures and seminars into effect—namely, through workshop practice. Parandowski was well aware of this fact, since he had previously desired to establish an institute known as the School of the Art of Writing, however "Protests opposed to such a coup against the inborn freedom of the development of future writers came from all directions" (1986: 133). It seems that it was not yet the time to implement such breakthrough ideas. Just how unprepared we were for these types of changes is confirmed by the words of another writer, Melchior Wańkowicz, remembering his visit to a New York school of journalists:

> Visiting a journalist school at Columbia University in New York prior to the war, I felt a certain anxiety. I was unable to communicate with its professors with my slight Polish megalomania expecting that all writing must be colored with genius and the fact that in Poland it is 'to each his own'. I thought of them as routinists. They were polite, attempted to answer my questions thoroughly, but I suspect that they were shocked by my synthesizing chaos of thought. Now, after a close inspection of American journalism schools, I believe that they were probably right.
>
> (1981: 779)

The idea of literature as a medium of Romantic and Modernist patterns plays an important role in the discussion of the subject of creative writing. This is confirmed by the opinions of a number of Polish writers, who had the opportunity to participate in The International Writing Program in Iowa:

> The idea of the poetry program in Iowa City was very useful, but as everything in America somewhat surprising to a foreigner. Every year, approximately thirty poets, novelists, dramatists, and translators from all continents were invited. From the so-called people's democracies there were only Poles and two Romanians, where one observed the other and they avoided contact with other members of the program.
>
> Skwarnicki (2011:175)

Many writers shared their memories from Iowa in the pages of journals, letters, and interviews. They are filled with skepticism and doubt. Marek Nowakowski wrote the following:

> Paul Engle is a poet of these very plains, a descendant of farmers. Indeed, he is one of the faculty of creative writing at the local university. There they teach the creation of literature. It is not so much the fact that it is a risky idea. Writers are not created at universities ... Perhaps such studies can aid young people with a literary talent? (2014)

Nowakowski recalls the beginnings of the workshops and the moment when Poland was invited to take part in the program:

> Engle's ambition was to broaden this multi-lingual community with writers from the Eastern Bloc in Europe. He started with Yugoslavia and Romania, the Communist states which conducted more independent politics. Then he turned towards Poland. After long negotiations he received consent to host two guests in Iowa. The conflict concerned the selection of candidates. (2014)

At the very last moment, the outstanding writer Tadeusz Różewicz resigned from participation in the workshop, "stating that he will not learn English ('I love you' is sufficient enough for him), and he will not waste time on the Program as he had wanted to take his son along. All this he said with a mocking grin on his face" (Szczepański 2013).

Today opinions regarding creative writing are no longer so extreme. It must be assumed that criticism of the subject is temporary and is a result of the development of the discipline. A similar argument is put forth by David Galef, describing its development in Great Britain. He recalls that still in the middle of the nineteenth century it was unthinkable that one would occupy oneself with the study of novels or romantic poetry, since the study of literature was based on the analysis of classical texts: Horatian monuments, he noted, being far more enduring than bronze (Galef 2013: 3).

Independence

The beginnings of the first field of study educating writers occurred during a period of regeneration in Polish literary life. The first half of the 1990s saw the disappearance of a cultural center, and the simultaneous appearance of a popular conviction on the necessity of freeing art from national responsibilities, from political entanglements and from all non-artistic duties.

In 1994, at the initiative of Gabriela Matuszek, who was still then a doctor, the Literary-Artistic Studies (LAS) was launched. The initiator of this undertaking was also the author of a curriculum, which as was highlighted at the time, was not created based on Western models. Instead, the author noted that "various forms of *creative writing* education are present at American universities, but our Institute significantly differs from the American models" (in Matuszek 2005: 347). What exactly did that mean? Bronisław Maj, who was asked this question, responded:

> In the United States these schools have a much wider range and they are not a type of separate institute. Creative writing programs are a part of general studies. They are geared up for students to acquire purely professional writing, journalistic and publishing skills. The classes are quite a bit more formalized.
>
> (in Nowak [1998: 35])

In another interview conducted by Katarzyna Kwiecień, Matuszek developed this topic further:

> The LAS curriculum encompasses not only a broad spectrum of workshop classes (poetry, prose, drama, translation, and publishing workshops, as well as literary criticism, screenplay, and reportage), but also 'theoretical' classes (in modern literature, contemporary drama and theatre, film, lectures in aesthetics, copyright law, the culture of language, theory of the creative process, and analysis of literary texts)."
>
> (2005: 6–7)

The heavy emphasis placed on independence had numerous causes. One of these was the fact that the idea of the literary workshops done in the fashion of the American ones enjoyed very little popularity, while Polish models of literary education were practically nonexistent. A new idea was needed which would change the Polish unwillingness to teach writing and the existing way of thinking.

A program was developed in such a way so that the writing courses at the Jagiellonian University would be treated as an academic discipline. Strong emphasis was placed on the analysis of literary masterpieces while the most outstanding writers were employed to conduct the workshops (including Nobel Prize winners such as Czesław Miłosz, Nobel in 1980 and Wisława Szymborska, Nobel 1996), as well as critics, scientists, and experts in other fields like Andrzej Wajda, who in the year 2000 received an honorary Oscar at the Academy Awards.

The program was filled with lectures known from other humanistic fields of study. The school was to become an elite facility, for those who exhibited the most literary talent. The simultaneous lectures and workshops were to aid the growth of talents. From this perspective, one opinion that seems very interesting is that of Katarzyna Jakubiak, a first-year student, who is now an Associate Professor of English at Millersville University, where she conducts workshops in creative writing:

> During my Ph.D., for two semesters I attended prose workshops at Illinois State University in the United States open to all graduate students ... The classes themselves concerned 'discussions' on selected texts in a rather democratic manner ... These 'civilized' discussions were very often in contrast to the 'drama' that played out right in front of our eyes in the LAS.... I enjoyed their objectivism and optimism, as well as the philosophy in which they were grounded, that every text can be improved, while the weaknesses of its early versions do not automatically mean that their author is worthless. This is what I was missing in the LAS ... Of course through their 'politeness' the American classes were perhaps a bit more boring than those in the LAS. They lacked the great, charismatic personalities, whom I met among the staff and students of the Krakow-based school of writing. Furthermore there was a lack of a strong bond between students, which developed in the LAS thanks to joint work in the editorial room in the Institute
>
> (Survey for LAS lecturers and graduates, 2014).

Gabriela Matuszek adds that each lecturer implemented his or her own signature syllabus, based more on imagination and intuition than experience and the mastery of didactic and writing principles and techniques. In her opinion, the strength of the workshops was based on inspiration, brainstorming, pulling others into the whirlpool of your own experiences, and sometimes sharp criticism, bereft of "political correctness"—"Because in truth we were after real literature, not the teaching of the skills of creative writing. It was about the authentic, strong experience on the border of existence and art, not teaching the elementary techniques of writing" (Matuszek 2015: 7–9).

The opinions expressed by participants in surveys after the first academy year varied greatly. Generally they valued the lecturers writing about the work and methods of "great luminaries," and presentation of important and interesting content, but there were also critical opinions: "I would advise a more systematized and competent way of conducting classes, especially prose workshops"; "lack of decisive personal evaluation of our creativity"; "very often the classes were improvised, they seldom concerned a specific topic. There were also a few very interesting conversations and statements of Mr. Słomczyński. A noticeable lack of preparation, too much learning together"; "good organization but little money".

How did the lecturers perceive it? For Michał Zabłocki, a poet and text writer who began working at the LAS in 2009, its most important characteristics, which developed the Krakow-based writing studies, were cultural awareness and the approach to teaching:

> I did not expect anything great, although in my opinion it is possible to learn a lot both during lectures as well as exercise classes. However, for the teaching to be effective, the lecturer must be a person who is well-organized, systematic and methodical. In Poland these features are very rare.
>
> (Survey for LAS lecturers and graduates, 2014)

In Search of Teacher Lore and Pedagogy: Blazing New Trails

The uniqueness of this program of study is most of all due to collaboration with various lecturers, who conduct their own signature classes. As a result, it is difficult to speak of a uniform curriculum over the years. The formula was thought of as open, and the shape of each series of workshops was unpredictable, although agreed upon and approved by JU authorities. The subject matter discussed during classes, recommended books, the course of the workshops, and the stories told in the process, are a direct result of the literary interests of the teacher and their experiences. The tenth anniversary of the establishment of LAS provided the opportunity for its initiator Gabriela Matuszek to recall:

> Ewa Lipska is very attentive to what young people have to say, she shows keen interest in the new sensitiveness, and has a different way of perceiving the world. Classes are conducted in a still different manner by Izabela Filipiak. She deals with that which interests her the most. However, she is not concerned with forcing her own way of perceiving the world upon the students, but with activating the deeply hidden, personal feelings, which the students subject to sublimation. Olga Tokarczuk is a psychologist by education; therefore she willingly uses role-play, entering the deep areas of the psyche where subconscious regions. Stanisław Lem enjoys meeting our students, but he always uses the most cunning strategies to encourage them to write. Every year he begins his classes stating that 'Ladies and gentlemen, give up, writing cannot be learned, while literature really serves no purpose.' Everyone accepts this game, listen, discuss and . . . write.
>
> (Survey for LAS lecturers and graduates, 2014)

Through the years, attempts were made to get in touch with the most outstanding creators in each individual field. Apart from them, classes were conducted by academics. The decisions made regarding the main assumptions of this program of study influenced the fact that, in the LAS, the dominant form of teaching is based on the relationship between mentor and student. Is it possible that a cohesive pedagogy of the subject can come from such a curriculum? Twenty-five years of practice in class shows that several conditions must be fulfilled.

I believe that it is possible to say that, for the history of creative writing in Poland, the actions of women played a key role.[1] There would be no creative writing workshops had it not been for "the idea of an energetic blonde."[2] Although the University does not keep any statistics in this matter, women constitute the greater part of the academic staff as well as graduates and students. (The work devoted to graduates published for the twenty-fifth anniversary of the field of study includes twelve texts written by men and forty-six texts written by women.) When it comes to manuals on creative writing it is the same. The first of these, *Twórcze pisanie dla młodych panien* (Creative Writing for Young Ladies), and one of the most original, was written by a woman for women.[3] Let us devote some time to it, since the assumptions presented within show an approach which both the author, as well as some of the lecturers, presented during their classes. The teaching of writing is only a pretext to discuss problems which are more important than the ability to wield words. This is another characteristic feature of the first creative writing program of study in Poland. Besides a rich theoretical background, teachers initially place a lot of emphasis on such issues as stimulating the imagination, and inspiring and provoking the thought process, rather than on presenting specific workshop tools. Thanks to such an approach, an honest relationship can be established between the teacher and the student. This is well described by Filipiak in her manual: "But I did not want my voice, which is part of this book, to be a voice which gives out orders" (1999). Creating an atmosphere of openness and shortening the distance between workshop participants is one

---

[1] The notion of schools of writing as an inherently female concept is extremely inspiring. As early as the Middle Ages, in his *Dialogue of Authors*, probably from the beginning of the eleventh century, Conrad of Hirsau defines *poetria* (the theory of poetry) as a "woman practicing poetry." Conrad of Hirsau, *Dialogue on Authors,* in M. Brożek, *Źródła do średniowiecznej teorii wykładu literatury* (Sources to the Medieval Theory of Literature Lectures), Warsaw 1989, 123.

[2] The title of an article by G. Łęcka regarding the beginnings of the JU Polish Literary-Artistic Studies. cf. G. Łęcka *Pomysł energicznej blondynki* (The Idea of an Energetic Blonde) *Polityka* (*Politics*) no. 5 (2126), January 31, 1998, 48–9.

[3] Although, as the author herself admits, the form of a manual which she had chosen does not mean that it is addressed exclusively to women. I. Filipiak, *Twórcze pisanie dla młodych panien* (Creative Writing for Young Ladies), Warsaw 1999.

of the leading ideas which was implemented since the inception of this program of study. This was contributed to by small-size classes and the possibility of individual consultations with the instructor.

LAS was always addressed to those who were "talented in literature." This can create some doubts and questions, whatever the teachers and initiators of this program of study may themselves believe, over whether writing can be taught. Based on research carried out by Stephanie Vanderslice, this would not be an isolated case (2011: 60). Nevertheless, enrolling only the most talented students, often those who had already written a book, explains why during the workshop the emphasis moved from presenting writing strategies to searching for writing inspirations.

It is also worth mentioning yet another teaching method. It can be called rejection, namely in the encouragement to question all authorities, and also to not fall into a trap of blind imitation. Filipiak goes on to say: "Forget everything that you think you know about writing and art, especially about what 'real art' and 'proper text' should look like." One of the most basic tasks of a writer is believed to be challenging and questioning. This is not in opposition to building an atmosphere of openness and dialog. Extreme differences (in views, or in approaches to the writer's workshop) allow us to verify our attitudes, and allow for a deeper look within ourselves, and as a result writing becomes more conscious and mature: "Question everything I say, this is what I want. I am a foreign country and you are my foreigner" (Filipiak 1999: 201).

Two Teaching Models

It is symptomatic that when talking about the very first universities such as Plato's Academy, Aristoteles's Lyceum and the Alexandrian School, we mention the name of the mentor. The statues of the papal legate Robert de Courçon from 1214 stated: "*Nullus sit scolaris, qui certum magistrum non habet*" (Nobody can be a student if he does not have a mentor). Apart from knowing Latin and possessing elementary knowledge from parish school, this was one of the conditions of enrollment at a university. The relationship between teacher and student is fundamental for the education process and therefore for the university itself, and it lies at the basis of its origin. Teachers speak to us "face to face" in lecture halls, from pages kept on library shelves, and sometimes, even though they have been gone a long time, they live on in academic anecdotes passed from student to student. They inspire, force us to review our current attitudes, and provoke us to protest. Michał P. Markowski often brings up a differentiation championed by Umberto Eco, who divided mentors into two types. The first of these requires the student who follows in their footsteps, to verify their hypotheses in order to improve them or prove them false. The second type, making their students come face to face with the impossible, necessary and unfulfilled imitation, cause anxiety—"working with mentors of the second kind, one always becomes a heretic and it would be impossible not to be one" (Markowski 2001:17).

Taking part in creative writing classes at Polish universities and analysing syllabi, it is hard not to notice that two tendencies are dominant in teaching, around which didactic methods are focused. The first of these is based on sharing one's own experience and telling of one's own creative practice—the mentor model. The second, on the other hand, is based on the presentation of methods and strategies stemming from formalistic and structuralist thought and narrative grammar, thorough analyses of popular literature and current trends prevalent in publishing markets—a model which is common for literary instructors. Let us take a closer look at both of them.

The first method of teaching can take on a form of a lecture, a story about one's life, or a presentation of self-created strategies or workshop discoveries. Non-standard solutions often appear in these kinds of workshops. At the basis of this method lies the conviction that one cannot talk objectively about creativity and, sometimes, that writing cannot be learned. One can only show one's own creative path. That is the reason why personal works are used, which are analysed during classes, since these are the only texts about whose technique the author can speak responsibly. Not understanding the assumption at the basis of classes based on experience can create misunderstandings and objections from students. In a survey evaluating classes during the 1994/95 academic year at LAS, one of the participants had this to say about classes with Maciej Słomczyński:

> Too concentrated on his own works. Constant questions about the obvious and previously agreed upon. Despite this fact, the best up to now analysis of our texts, valuable pointers, individual conversations, openness, help, always possible to visit him at home.

Although the above evaluation is rather contradictory, it contains several valuable insights. Our attention is specifically drawn to the final words. In my opinion, the way of teaching to write based on personal experience is exactly that—visiting the writer in his home, the master in his workshop. A teacher who treats writing as an integral part of his or her own life invites students and lets them enter their "kingdom."

It seems that this way of teaching is reserved for great figures, writers who have achieved success. Definitely it is a method which carries with it a high degree of risk. The student must put in a lot of effort, in order to creatively ponder the teacher's experience and use it in their own practice. In addition, a distinctive personality and literary achievements alone are not sufficient to impart knowledge in an appropriate way. It can also happen that the writer dominates the space, which should serve the purpose of mutual education, or that classes would be conducted by writers who believe that they have a monopoly on good writing. A fascinating writer always makes a good lecturer. In one of the surveys of the LAS we can read: "I understand that these are famous people, but the things they say are of no interest to me, they cannot even arise my curiosity, but perhaps it is my frailty." A student is not always able to comprehend the point of view of the lecturer and then such opinions as that written about Antoni Libera appear: "The biggest egoist whom we have met during classes, more than four hours of talking about how great I am. Sure the book is quite good, but is should be able to defend itself."

The second method of conducting writing classes is taken up by writers who like to talk about themselves as craftsmen and text writers. The teacher does not hide, does not cut themselves off from their experiences, however they are focused on presenting useful strategies—therefore they says something like "there are such and such tools," or "these are the methods of maintaining suspense in a criminal story," rather than saying "I understood that by writing in such a way I have lost my current readers while obtaining brand new ones." The presented methods can intertwine to a certain degree; however, I have observed that one of them is always more dominant. The "experience" method derived from the teacher themselves accentuates that which is personal, while the second "craftsman" method focuses on the workshop. That is why the former contributes to the creation of fine literature, while the latter to the creation of popular literature. Each of them has its limitations and it is up to the teacher to break through these and allow the student to grow creatively. In one of the surveys, Izabela Zubko, a graduate of LAS writes: "Such a relationship is possible and recommended. We should pattern ourselves after the best but at the same time not forget about our own values, personality and message."

Workshops can be a place of birth: both of a community and of trust. I trust you, since I am showing you my texts which are still imperfect. Sometimes I am showing you that which I am ashamed of, so I am trusting you not to judge me based on my texts, and to criticize them in a sincere manner. I trust you to allow me to grow creatively at my own pace. This is the significance of the role of the lecturer—watching over and making sure that the trust which was bestowed by the student will not be broken. The creative relationship is always individual and unpredictable. The university can employ the best-prepared academic staff, however, establishing such a relationship in which the student will discover their own personal authority cannot be predicted. Even more fascinating is the fact that, if such a relationship develops, it is not only students who might grow and develop as a result.

There is Only That Which is Biography

The philosopher Stanisław Brzozowski wrote that whatever is not biography does not exist (Markowski 2001:13). During the creative writing workshops, the discussion of problems and issues allows students to understand that identity has both a narrative and an interpretational structure. The mentor is therefore tasked with not only developing the creative potential of the students, but also with showing them the best way to get to know and understand themselves. Dramatic writing workshops present a good opportunity to achieve this goal. Creating a story about oneself, through both "reading" oneself and "writing" oneself, constitutes an integral part of learning how to write. It is within writing and reading that the biography plays out. Speaking about personal experience, as well as interpreting it, gives it meaning and is something that the students seemed to desire:

> What I really wanted was a Mentor. Not a pragmatic . . . At that time, working on my writing and working on myself was more or less the same thing to me. I wanted a Mentor who understood that, who understood what I was up to and could show me how to keep going.
>
> Cain (2007: 28)

According to Karol Maliszewski, a significant problem is the diversity of the auditorium. He recalls that the workshops are attended by both enthusiasts as well as those who simply want to obtain course credit. That is why individualizing classes is important. "Separating the enthusiasts from the mediocre. Establishing individual contact with the former, suggesting an individual path of development". Among the first category he noticed a distinct division into "impressionists" and "professionals." An impressionist is anyone who sketches the fragments necessary to achieve subsequent thresholds of self-awareness and self-development. Here writing might appear as the chiseling in a journal, or a personal report. It is difficult to find ready recipes for such writers. Teaching them must focus on empathy and the direct, sincere sharing of personal experiences, divulging views and attitudes on all possible subjects. "Professionals are no less sensitive and talented but they do not search for a private confessor or psychotherapist, but rather a mentor" (Maliszewski 2015: 88). Styles of teaching are to a large extent dependent on the audience and the specificity of each individual meeting.

Breaking Boundaries

When the first School of Writers was established in Poland, students regularly filled out evaluation surveys on their classes, evaluating their usefulness, as well as speaking about the writers who lectured there. This is a rich source of information on the subject of the relations between teachers and adepts of writing formed within the framework of this exceptional field of study.

From analysis of the surveys we can conclude that building the mentor-student relationship was one of the goals along with a new kind of didactic method. However, a certain doubt arises here. The popularity of this field of study was preceded by stories about being in the master's workshop, of how learning might occur in the same way that in the past knowledge was imparted to artists-craftsmen. Thus, the idea of what should happen during classes could have already been rooted in the students' minds. The school was compared to a sixteenth-century painting workshop: "we read the poems of various poets and ponder how they were written. This is necessary and inspiring, as it teaches patient reading. Even observing the master at his work is learning" (Nowak 1998: 35).

In order for an authentic relationship between the teacher and the student to develop, they should be given the chance to remain themselves. Ewa Sonnenberg, a poet who both graduated among the first cohort of LAS and later conducted workshops there herself, said in one interview that meeting with people such as Szymborska, Miłosz, Kornhauser, Słomczyński, and Maj changed her approach to literature, since "The border between mentor and student no longer exists" (Łęcka 1998: 49). In building relationships it is also important for the hierarchy to break down, for the distance between each party to decrease. In creative writing classes, it turns out that this is possible to implement since all the parties present in the room are on the same journey known, namely that of developing their writing. They have different goals, find themselves at different stages of this journey, and take different paths to get to their destination. However, they sometimes meet and stop for a while to chat. One of the graduates of LAS would write "I did not feel the distance appropriate for the relationship between Mentor and Student. Despite the name 'literary', the institute was characterized by discipline which had a beneficial influence on our work." In the previously mentioned anthology of graduates, apart from literary texts, we will find memoirs regarding the field of study. The most interesting and most characteristic theme which can be found there is human relations (between students and between students and lecturers). They are described in various ways but always with a bit of nostalgia. "It was something more than a mentor-student relationship, it was a human-human relationship, magnificent, direct," recalls Małgorzata Oczak, a former student (Graboś 2019: 287). On the other hand, Ewa Szawul had this to say "In time the borders of intimacy freely moved, building among us almost family-like relations, which helped both in writing and in life itself" (395).

Conclusion

In my article I focused on the description of the Krakow-based LAS, because of its distinctive approach to teaching. Workshops do not always concentrate on creating. Many of them are devoted to analysis and interpretation. Writing studies can, paradoxically, turn out to be a place where writing is not always in the center and is not always the most important element.

In 2007, Paul Dawson postulated introducing classes on literary theory to the curriculum, as well as agreeing on a theoretical canon which could be read at writing workshops. According to Dawson, using such an approach can be one of the ways to "demystify the workshops" (2007:80) and reform pedagogical practice, under the condition that a balance would be maintained where lecturers would not treat them as a place to impart knowledge, which would annex these workshops. In Poland, this need was immediately noticed. In retrospect this experiment can be deemed as successful.

Rooting a subject in a schedule filled with theoretical classes, especially on literary theory and the philosophy of literature, helps students acquire some distance and look critically upon classes—even those taught by the most famous "literary celebrities." Diversity is also important. The LAS workshops are a place where relationships are established between people who would otherwise never meet. They are completely different from one another as far as education, place of birth, age, and experience are concerned. They also come to the school with different expectations. Some want to develop poetically, while others dream of writing a bestseller. The fact that the same subject can be undertaken by various writers allows the students to hear different voices and as a consequence find their own voice. Twenty-five years of the LAS shows that it is possible to develop an effective compromise between typical university education and creative meetings. Courses conducted by outstanding writers can be based on the mutual exchange of experiences. The joint attempt to respond to the most important questions, questions about individual voice and therefore also about identity, can lead to the disappearance of the mentor-student division and to the creation of an authentic relationship based on trust.

The experience of teachers, the stories told by them, and sharing details from their own writing life—especially concerning their personal struggles—are all reasons why creative writing studies arouse interest. The opportunity to come face to face with a person whom one considers to be an authority opens up new perspectives. However, it is not simply about learning from the master. It is about learning together with the master. The twenty-five-year history of the LAS can also be viewed as the Polish story of the contemporary search for effective methods of teaching how to write. It is thus a story of many, various narrations, out of which none (although they could easily have done so) became the dominant narrative.

References

Cain, M. A. (2007), *Charming Tyrants and Faceless Facilitators. The Lore of Teaching Identities in Creative Writing*, in *Can It Really be Taught? Resisting Lore in Creative Writing Pedagogy*, ed. by K. Ritter and S. Vanderslice, Portsmouth, NH.

Conrad of Hirsau, (1989), *Dialogue on Authors,* M. Brożek, Źródła do średniowiecznej teorii wykładu literatury (Sources to the Medieval Theory of Literature Lectures), Warsaw.

Dawson, P. (2007), *The Future of Creative Writing*, in *The Handbook of Creative Writing*, ed. by S. Earnshaw, Edinburgh.

Dąbała, J. (2012), *Mystery and Suspense in Creative Writing*, International Studies Hermeneutics and Phenomenology, Volume 7, ed. by Prof. Andrzej Wierciński, Ph.D., Zürich-Berlin.

Filipiak, I. (1999), *Twórcze pisanie dla młodych panien* (Creative Writing for Young Ladies), Warsaw.

Galef, D. (2013), "But Is It Art.? Creative Writing Workshops in the U.S.," *Journal of American & Canadian Studies*, 26/2008.

Graboś, J., Czarnecka, K., Skucha M., Matuszek, G., eds (2019), *SLApidarium. Antologia utworów absolwentów studiów Literacko-Artystycznych UJ, na 25-lecie* (Anthology devoted to graduates published for the 25th anniversary of the LAS UJ).

Łęcka, G. (1998), *Pomysł energicznej blondynki* (The Idea of an Energetic Blonde), *Polityka, (Politics)* no. 5 (2126).

Maliszewski, K. (2015), "Z doświadczeń praktyka. Od warsztatów poetyckich do zajęć z creative writing," in *Twórcze pisanie w teorii i praktyce* (The Experiences of a Practitioner. From Poetry Workshops to Creative Writing Classes), G. Matuszek, H. Sieja-Skrzypulec (eds), Creative Writing in Theory.

Markowski, M. P. (2001), *Występek. Eseje o pisaniu i czytaniu* (Transgression. Essays on Writing and Reading), Krakow.

Matuszek, G., ed. (2005), *Talent i nauka* (Talent and Learning). An interview with Gabriela Matuszek Ph.D., by Tadeusz Kornaś, *Literatura wobec nowej rzeczywistości* (Literature in Face of a New Reality), Krakow: Sic!.

Nowak, K. T. (1998), "Podpatrywanie mistrza" (Observing the Master), *Przekrój* (*Overview*) no. 30 (2770).

Nowakowski, M. (2014), *Tak zapamiętałem Paul Engle z Iowa City* (This is how I Remembered Paul Engle from Iowa City). Available online: http://gpcodziennie. pl/20826-tak-zapamietalem.html#.VO2rffmG9ng

Parandowski, J. (1986), *Alchemia słowa* (The Alchemy of the Word), Warsa : Czytelnik:

Piechniczech, M. M., ed. (2003). *Studium Literacko-Artystyczne* (Literary-Artistic Studies), Krakow.

Sarzyński, P. (1994), "Wieszczem być" (To be a Bard), *Polityka* (*Politics*), no. 44 (1956), VI.

Szczepański, J.J. (2013) *Dziennik*, Tom III, 1964-1972, (Journal, Vol. III, 1964-1972), Krakow.

Skwarnicki, M. (2011), "Hejnał mariacki (9)" (The Marian Bugle-Call) (9), *Kwartalnik Artystyczny (Artistic Quarterly)* 3 (71).

"Trampolina do sukcesu. Z prof. Gabrielą Matuszek rozmawia Katarzyna Kwiecień" (Trampoline towards success. An interview with Professor Gabrielą Matuszek conducted by Katarzyna Kwiecień), *Krakow*, 2005, no. 6–7.

Wańkowicz, M. (1981), *Karafka La Fontaine'a, Tom II* (La Fontaine's Carafe, Vol II), Krakow.

Vanderslice, S. M. (2011), *Rethinking Creative Writing in Higher Education: Programs and Practices that Work,* Wicken: The Professional and Higher Partnership Ltd.

11

The Long Shadow of the Local Canon: Historical and Pedagogical Influences on Creative Writing in Greece

Triantafyllos H. Kotopoulos, Sophie Iakovidou, Iordanis Koumasidis
*University of Western Macedonia, Democritus University of Thrace,
National Kapodistrian University of Athens*

Introduction

Creative writing is a fairly recent addition to Greek academia, yet a very vibrant one. Though some informal aspects of it that were already being practiced, such as creative writing workshops and courses offered by notable writers, it has only been institutionalized during the last fifteen years: first and foremost by the establishment of an MA program at the University of Western Macedonia and then via a joint-degree program between the University of Western Macedonia and the Hellenic Open University. These two postgraduate programs are still the only ones in Greece. Nonetheless, its relative newness may appear misleading given the accumulation of its lore and the depth of penetration in Greek academia and society.

In order to give the subject the necessary academic breadth and objectivity, this chapter covers three main areas: the history and pedagogy of creative writing, the cultural context of Greek literature in the twentieth century which academic creative writing draws upon, and the particularities of open and distance learning in these contexts. Without those three interlinked aspects, it would be impossible to grasp the current state of creative writing in Greece, nor its inner logic and dynamics. We would like to stress the fact that the very concept of lore is quite different in Greek, as the comparative term *paràdosi* covers two different, yet coexistent meanings: 1) the tradition of written texts, which comprises the canon of a certain national literature; and 2) what is being taught in a classroom (a selected part of the canon). This chapter develops those aspects in order to offer a comprehensive analysis of creative writing lore in contemporary Greece.

History of Writing Cultures in Greece

In Greece, the term "creative writing" can be ambiguous, which causes confusion and awkwardness not only because of the multiple possible interpretations of this title but also because of their evaluative connotations (Κωτόπουλος 2012, Κωτόπουλος, Βακάλη, Ζωγράφου 2013: 13). Today, more than ten years since creative writing was institutionalized in two postgraduate degree programs, and two years since it was included in elementary and secondary education, academic teachers and writers agree that the term is used in a twofold way. It denotes an analytical approach to language that works simultaneously in two complementary fields: the act of (creatively) writing and the act of thinking critically about the process of writing and its effects. Moreover, creative writing remains distinct from other disciplines and their teaching in universities due to the fact that it refers to an activity, or a set of actions, and at the same time encompasses an analysis and cerebration of that activity and the results produced (Κωτόπουλος 2011).

The formation of this distinction is attributed to the philosopher Aristotle (384–322 BC). Many current professors and historians of creative writing claim, fairly in our opinion, that the roots of academic creative writing may be traced to Aristotle's *Poetics*: that is to say, the interpretative review of those practices the philosopher had collected and studied, and which in the meantime had been accepted and been applied for many years. Aristotle began his own works by studying and analysing the tragedies of three of the great theatrical writers of the fifth century BCE: Aeschylus, Euripides, and Sophocles (Κωτόπουλος 2012). In his work, he then goes on to instruct his students what to look for and what to avoid in the composition of their own poetic dramas; the result they should aim for in that genre of text; the means that will help them master this; how achieving goals defines and delineates the form of dramatic text; and what deficiencies can lead a dramatist to failure. Creative writing's lore, therefore, starts long before the two postgraduate degree programs that were established in the early twenty-first century, and thus requires more thorough and substantive research. Indeed, the results indicate that Greek culture has had a profound impact on the concept and practice of creative writing.

This has no doubt aided its cultural reach, so that nowadays creative writing is internationally subsumed in the fields of liberal arts (literary writing, art of writing, literary theory of reading), in the field of pedagogy (experiential education methods), the field of psychology (therapeutic methods), and the fields of graphic design and advertising, among others. One comprehensive history of creative writing to date is the work of D. G. Myers, *The Elephants Teach: Creative Writing Since 1880* (2006). In modern Western culture, creative writing's methods and reasoning now support, in the most systematic way, an experiential approach to language and its abilities to be reconstructed, leading to the production of new texts. In the educational environment, this familiarity with language and exploration of its capabilities is combined with a creative "game" and experimentation in various literary genres without the fear of right or wrong (Morley 2007: 6), while at the same time an emphasis is given to the creative activity, to self-revelation through language, and to the imaginative exploitation of personal experiences and feelings (Protherough 1983: 56).

The Historical and Cultural Context of Greek Literature in the Twentieth Century

In order to understand the broader context of literary production in Greece, it is important to emphasize the meaning of the word "lore" in Greek, because it defines much of the work and core beliefs that underly the Greek educational system. Ultimately, it is worth taking a closer look at the meaning of the word "lore" in Greek [*paràdosi*] in order to (re)evaluate both social and political centripetal reactions towards it, namely those that lead us back to the established and traditional way of doing things; and the centrifugal reactions, namely those that insist upon a new or modern way of approaching creative writing. Starting from the original meaning of the word as "transfer, concession," its meaning, especially in the field of education, is focused on: 1. transmission of writing culture, and 2. teaching in a real or virtual class, classroom, or broader educational context.

The newly inaugurated postgraduate creative writing program at the Hellenic Open University combines these two meanings of lore, as well as the two above-mentioned reactions to it, in a systematic, functional, and playful way. The large attendance of students (composed of various age groups, and coming from both educational and professional backgrounds), attests to the program's response to the growing societal appetite for such creative explorations. Over the last decade, as Greece has experienced intensified conditions of financial and sociopolitical instability and crisis, the interest in creative writing has significantly intensified. It should be noted that such an occurrence is broadly comparable to what has occurred in other countries that have gone through conditions of general austerity or supervision from international institutions like the International Monetary Fund, such as Argentina. There too, as in Greece, many members of society searched for alternative ways of escape, self-expression, and personal empowerment, which increased the interest in creative writing and its potentials. Through such an engagement, the new creative writers themselves often discovered an alternative way of living and interacting with various social strata.

Combining lore on one hand as transmission of the local or general writing culture, and on the other hand as an original, playful, and functional way of teaching, is dependent on the systematic structure in which it is transmitted. In the program at the Hellenic Open University this is achieved through a structured program which gradually evolves and develops in terms of course offerings every semester, allowing students to choose their own modules and pace of completion, while also providing the opportunity for live group meetings as well as online ones.

Traditional teaching methods, such as those employed at conventional public or private university, for example, where programs are more or less institutionally structured, can be enriched through the combination of theoretical training and literary knowledge with creative writing. In this way, multifaceted learning can be achieved without arbitrarily focusing on one single subject. Instead of avoiding basic academic concepts and knowledge, instructors can focus on aiding student understanding and processing of these through original creative texts and exercises. These activities can be updated on the teaching platform so that they do not become tired or predictable with overuse.

The material used for study follows the lore, since courses examine the historical evolution of literature, its genres and aesthetic schools or movements (including a special course on European literature). Particular emphasis is given to the nineteenth and twentieth century, while the trends of the current century are also covered, especially in creative activities. In this way, the program can avoid the (frequent) dedication of students solely to their personal genre or period preferences or, even worse, to those preferred by their instructor. While the present time is emphatically present, the partiality of focusing only on the immediate is avoided and so the program is distanced from another danger that can afflict creative workshops: namely the tendency to focus on the theme of crisis and refugees, to take two common examples, thus ignoring other potential subjects or possible perspectives.

Courses on Modern Greek prose and poetry introduce students to different styles of managing historical and cultural time, in line with the major historical events that have troubled Modern Greek life. For instance, from the Second World War onwards, students can examine trends in prose that cohere around the idea of a literary responsibility for recording and processing recent historical events, in order to identify why things have ended up this way. Unlike other European countries, which in the postwar era experienced a period of growth and prosperity, a further war followed in Greece, the fratricidal Civil War (1946–9), as well as a second dictatorship (after that of I. Metaxas before the war, who was the ideological "ancestor" of the coup d'état of the Colonels during the seven-year period of 1967–74) and the painful partition of Cyprus. This need to record and interpret recent events was mirrored in popularity with the reading public, and a hunger to engage with ideas that was reflected in the ideological-political struggles in which many poets and authors took part, often with severe consequences (such as exile or torture). However, one problem at the time was the contemporary ideological polarization, one which often motivated readers to seek and writers to attempt to bring to light the Truth (a word often capitalized during those times) which would explain everything. This gave rise to the two great narratives of the time: the Truth of the Right and the Truth of the Left (Θαλάσσης 1992: 13–33). Thus, three dominant postwar literary trends emerged: a) the historical-political, which had the most representatives in contemporary literature (in both the prose and poetry of that period); b) the philosophical-existential, with only representative, but nonetheless one of major importance, the only truly international Greek novelist, Nikos Kazantzakis; and c) the micro-narrative, which proved a counterbalance to the great narratives (such as long novels or trilogies) of the time (Τζιόβας 1993: 244–79). As time progressed, there was an increasing tendency towards fragmentation, and a growing popularity of intimate writing expressing the neurosis of the individual in the big cities, with G. Ioannou as its main representative, whose writing still remains popular (Iakovidou 2004).

Of course, this need to process and record the contemporary situation was not new. However, before the twentieth century, poetry was seen as of the highest importance, enjoying a long hegemony over the previous centuries and therefore coming to dominate the canon of Modern Greek literature. The novel may have enjoyed great popularity in the interwar years, for example via novelists such as M. Karagatsis, but the poetry of the renowned 1930s generation was the one to combine a high level of creativity with popular success inside and outside of Greece.

Indeed, the poets of the 1930s generation provided Modern Greek culture with its contemporary classics, from the unique irony and cultural ingenuity of Cavafy to the sarcastic nihilism of Kariotakis, and their success in part depending on being voracious readers and consumers of Greek lore. The two Nobel Prizes won by G. Seferis (1963) and O. Elytis (1979) served to crown the successes of an entire poetic generation, that brought out personalities such as Y. Ritsos and the leading surrealists A. Empirikos and N. Engonopoulos. Such authors were able to combine elements of European modernism with Greek flavors (emphasizing "hellenity" in a similar manner to other European local expressions of ethnicity, such as *hispanidad* or *italianita*), and thereby managed to create a popular literary culture embraced by both experts and audiences. They thus rendered an extremely difficult art popular—which was no doubt helped by the fact that their major works were turned into musical pieces by great musicians such as M. Theodorakis and M. Hatzidakis.

The generation of the 1930s could provide today's writers with a successful example of cultural management in conditions of crisis and general discouragement. Captured in the claws of austerity, now that access to European resources and visions which previously affected or even "spoiled" Greek society has diminished, and faced with the constant request to record and process the current reality, contemporary Greek writers find themselves facing new (and yet uncannily similar) creative challenges. The example of the 1930s generation offer the examples of creative solutions that may well appeal to current Greek writers facing difficult times, for example, in their work to temper their sense of defeat, of shrinking territory, with the promotion of the idea of the excellence of Greece on a spiritual level (Τζιόβας 1989: 55–81). In many ways, then, much of contemporary Greek literature can be seen as either following the lessons of, or reacting against, those models that became prevalent thanks to the 1930s poets. This is how lore and tradition often function: through resemblance and remaking with contemporary differences.

In order to understand the abundance of the range of styles available to potential creative writers, and the pursued writing consciousness, mere writing exercises are not enough. Creative writing programs need to lead students to engage with both texts and the theoretical, critical, and literary lore which surrounds them: this way their writing practices will be reshaped through a theoretical lens (Horton and Freire 1990: 36; Ιακωβίδου 2017). An appreciation of local literary history and lore are thus an integral part of a "critical pedagogy" of (creative) writing. Many of the current trends of Greek poetry and prose, such as the expected theme of crisis or the theme of refugee flows, as well as the turn to local idioms, the flourishing of short fiction, and the resurgence in popularity of crime novels (Tziovas 2017), reflect reactions against (as well as the influences of) the national canon and lore. Creative writing can, and should, thus provide continuity channels between the languages of criticism and those of essential creative practices.

Creative Writing in Contemporary Greece

In Greece, creative writing began as a means of training and preparing aspiring writers, but soon began to widen its focus in order to renew the rigid, narrow approach and teaching of literary and philological studies, and of the humanities in general. Creative writing was taught informally in the late 1980s in Greece via seminars (given by the poet Nikos Fokas and the novelist Stratis Chaviaras). In 1996 it was taught for the first time as a university seminar lesson in the Departments of Foreign Languages in Aristotle University of Thessaloniki and National Kapodistrian University of Athens. Postgraduate courses related to the discipline of creative writing were launched by a peripheral university, however; namely, the pedagogical department of the University of Western Macedonia. Two of the founders, Professor Mimis Souliotis and Professor Triantafyllos H. Kotopoulos, found in this outpost the opportunity to collaborate creatively and launch a new academic strain of creative writing. Assisted by Professor Kotopoulos, Professor Souliotis established the first postgraduate degree program for creative writing in Greece, focused exclusively on the art of writing. Professor Kotopoulos succeeded him at the directorship of the program, when Professor Souliotis passed away in 2012, and started making an effort to broaden the horizons of the academic discipline in Greece. At first he focused the program on two key areas, writing and education, while at the same time he traveled for the next five years with his associates all over Greece offering lectures and seminars to schools of all levels, in order to spread the message that creative writing is valuable not only for those who wish to become professional writers but also to teachers and instructors, as well as to all those who believe that if they become better readers of literary texts, they will become more thoughtful, critical citizens. At the same time, he organized the first international conferences of creative writing in Greece: in Athens in 2013, in Corfu in 2015 and 2017, and in Florina in 2019.

Since that first conference, there have been substantial collaborations with several prominent universities, including Iowa, East Anglia, and Winchester; and with entities and organizations of international range and prestige (such as OuLiPo). The conference has brought numerous poets and novelists to Greece in order to improve and develop the quality of the postgraduate program. Nowadays, the program—in collaboration with the School of Film Studies in the Aristotle University of Thessaloniki—has become intercollegiate, and a third distinctive course of studies (scriptwriting) has been added. For the last three years the University of Western Macedonia has been collaborating with the Hellenic Open University (namely its School of Humanities). This collaboration now offers a Masters in Creative Writing using the distance learning method. In the first three years, enrollment exceeded all expectations and reached a total of 1,300 students. The innovations of the new program consist of using the e-educational platform Moodle to post teaching material as well as to provide feedback from the teaching staff. The program also uses teleconferences to conduct group advisory meetings (Ο.Σ.Σ.) in most student departments. Concerning the organization of the program at the level of the educational material provided, particular emphasis has been given to theoretical foregrounding (a course on the theory of literature and of creative writing has been set up as the opening course), to the history of literature (with two courses on Modern Greek and European literature), as well as on the intended outcome of providing students with practice in as many forms of literary endeavor as possible (novels, poetry, drama, screenplays), and with modern technological tools (particularly digital storytelling and media writing).

We should additionally note the active engagement of novelists, poets, scriptwriters, and film directors in this academic program. The program has had a double impact on the literary culture of the country: on the one hand by attracting students to the modern literary world (by turning them into both consumers and creators of books, magazines, and journals) and on the other hand by integrating creative writing into the education system through the practical experience of prominent teachers and writers. The Director and Academic Director of both programs is still Professor Triantafyllos H. Kotopoulos, who is also the only university professor in Greece to bear the title of Professor of Creative Writing and Modern Greek Literature and was the first instructor to supervise doctoral dissertations in creative writing. The two Masters programs have also developed a number of community interventions, with the most important of those of being the teaching of creative writing in penitentiaries across the country, as well as working alongside with rehabilitation centers (ΚΕΘΕΑ), with disability cultural centers, and with some of the most important libraries of the country (Veria, Koventarios, Municipal Library of Thessaloniki). It is worth mentioning that many senior students and graduates of the two programs have received various awards (for example, a first prize in the national teenage fiction contest and a first prize in the national poetry contest). We are particularly proud of the various initiatives that our students have taken, such as publishing a volume of their texts entitled *What If Buildings Could Talk?* (Kedros Publishers, 2019, under the coordination of the student Yiota Kotsafti), organizing workshops, and their continuous activities in primary and secondary education.

The collaborations of the programs and their associates with all the levels of education has inspired the Institute of Educational Policy to include creative writing exercises in all classes of secondary schools, while it also recommends that teachers and professors make use of elements of creative writing pedagogy and their theoretical framework. The future seems auspicious, but we must note that, despite the fact that undergraduate and postgraduate courses are offered all over the globe, in Greece only the two aforementioned programs currently offer such courses.

"Democratic Writing"

Despite the surge in demand for creative writing,[1] the dispute over whether writing can be taught has never stopped in Greece. These views are framed by old-fashioned skepticism, namely the familiar debate over natural talent versus learned skill. But beside that, it is worth noting that this debate is complicated by the politically troubled recent past of Greece. The country that gave birth to democracy experienced successive dictatorial regimes up until 1974, as well as a globally unprecedented and extended financial crisis since 2009, and this had an effect on its literature. After all, the world of literature, with its associated norms and conventions, and the eventual social impulses which constitute it, are parts of the field of cultural production, as defined by Bourdieu (Μπουρντιέ Πιέρ 2006: 327–46), and the semantic decentralization and indeterminacy of literary texts conforms to and simultaneously expresses the acceptance of the dispersed and scattered nature of power in the modern world. This semantic uncertainty and ambiguity reflects the historical awareness that power cannot be trusted. Internationally, creative writing workshops are part of the field of cultural production, as they critically control both the view of the "sacred particularity" of the literary writing world, as well as the view that celebrates and praises an extremely detailed approach to literature, handing the baton of primacy to

---

[1] Both formal and informal education providers offer a large number of courses and seminars on creative writing in Greek territory, from universities and schools through to public libraries, museums, and ecclesiastical youth centers to bookstores, magazines, and counseling centers.

academics and theorists. In creative writing workshops, at least to those which perceive seriously their synchronic and diachronic role, creative works are always conceptualized through the system of their differences, but the position and the individual contribution of the author are taken under serious consideration (that is, their position in the literary field via their social and geographical origin, their value system, their unique characteristics, and the active or passive engagement in shaping tendencies of literary production). The author who is enriched through workshops is confronted with and asked to take a position in terms of following or even renovating the literary field, at the same time as engaging with the competitive field of the commercial sector. It is often noted that authors and practitioners, apart from "producing" active and regular readers, also create potential producers (poets, novelists, playwrights, and screenwriters), who possess similar qualities and skills, or have the ambition to acquire them. In principle, of course, the literary work will express the conflict of views in society, sometimes even without the conscious intention of the writer. The teachers in creative writing workshops, however, must be concerned about the way that every social structure restricts its members and, as public intellectuals, according to Raymond Williams (1983: 169–71), must not only find a different path to follow on their own, but also tap into a desire to change society with their enlightenment.

In education, until recently in Greece, much pedagogy had relied on traditional practices that considered students passive receivers and asked them to memorize sterile knowledge or, in the case of literature, to accept without question the writer's meaning as it was offered by teachers and/or experts. However, within creative writing programs, students are now encouraged to summon their inventiveness and imagination, to activate all their spiritual, mental, and emotional forces, in order to become authors of a text, not only critical readers-interpreters but also re-creators. Creative writing workshops permit teachers to challenge given rules and norms regarding what is considered logical, reasonable, and rational, and to accept the noncompliance of students with such social compromises. Creative writing workshops, with their experimental status and operation, contribute to the understanding of the relations between education and society, as well as the relations in university and school classes, through a radical pedagogy that contributes to the transformation of both educational and social reality. They can therefore be seen to have a political aspect. The pedagogic overthrow of conservative analytic programs and methods presupposes breaches with both the adversaries of creative writing as an academic discipline and the culture of financial effectiveness in higher education. The educational goals of achieving learning outcomes and developing transferrable skills are strengthened by the fact that literary writing is by its nature a critical procedure, and so helps the discipline to thrive in an interdisciplinary and multidisciplinary context. However, if creative writing studies are altered through being forced to integrate into a field of competing development theories and through pedagogical interaction with other disciplines, their innovative elements are likely to be weakened as a result. In this case, one can imagine not only authors or qualified university teachers being invited to lead workshops, but specialists of any discipline to teach whatever they wish. Creative Writing theorists, indeed, have expressed opposition to the inclusion of students in integrated workshops, arguing that they will thus be turned away from "the poetics of the specific," therefore leading to possible improvements as intellectuals but not necessarily—or at all—as creators (Dawson 2005: 208). The working mode that derives from such a view of "multidisciplinary cultural synergism" eventually ends up manipulative and prescriptive.

Creative writing in Greece has a number of issues to resolve. The aspiration to write in an international and thus easily readable language presupposes the adoption of mainly Western literary models and modes, a fact that may lead to entrapment in Western intellectual processes and ideologies and a preference for those styles over more local variations. Two other problems are the validity of evaluations and the dilemmas of imposing specific views on style, plot, themes, and so on. How is it possible to give instructions without being considered coercive and authoritarian in stating what should and should not be done in "good" writing?

Co-responsibility at workshops offers one possible solution. Evaluation is offered by instructors with many different views, while participants know from the beginning that they will have to contend with each teacher's personal obsessions and preferences in class (Κωτόπουλος 2016). The field of critical pedagogy has repeatedly identified the ironic and cynical paradox that has emerged: that is, at the same time that critical thinking is promoted as a principle of society's development, a democratized education system can often serve only to reinforce skills focused on the needs of global markets (Θεοδωροπούλου 2014: 33–4).

In conclusion, then, the lessons of Greek literary developments and lore suggest that it is advisable to think in terms of local literary contexts and, instead of designing courses and outcomes to respond to the needs of the marketplace, to instead identify the core local literary principles and ideas, not as compelling truths that inductively lead to good writing, but as an attempt to organize courses that might overthrow the reign of the practical, which contradicts the central function of creative and critical work in Greece.

References

Adorno, Th. (2000), Θεωρία της Ημιμόρφωσης (εισ. και μτφρ. Λ. Αναγνώστου), Αθήνα: Αλεξάνδρεια.

Arendt, H. (1978), *The Life of Min-Thinking-Willing*, New York – London: Harvest / HJB Book.

Brophy, K. (2008), "Workshopping the Workshop and Teaching the Unteachable," in *Creative Writing Studies, Practice, Research and Pedagogy*. Great Britain: MPG Books Ltd. 75–87.

Dawson, P. (2005), *Creative Writing and the New Humanities*, London: Routledge.

Deleuze, G. and Guattari, F. (1996), *What is Philosophy?*, New York: Columbia University Press.

Harper, G. (2010), "Several Faces of Creative Writing," *New Writing: The International Journal for the Practice and Theory of Creative Writing* 7 (3), 175–8.

Horton, M., Freire, P. (1990), *We make the road by walking. Conversations on education and social change*, Conversations on education and social change, Bell B., Gaventa, J., Peters, J. (ed.), Philadelphia: Temple University Press.

Iakovidou, S. (2004), *G. Ioannou: le corps de l'oeuvre. Psyché de l'écrivain, sociopoétique de l'œuvre*, Presses Universitaires de Lille, ANTP.

Koumasidis Iordanis (2019), *Crisis and historical/political context in Greek Literature*, (Historical materialism: rethinking crisis, resistance and strategy), May 2–5, Athens, Panteion.

Morley, D. G. (2007), *The Cambridge Introduction to Creative Writing*, Cambridge: Cambridge University Press.

Myers, D. (2006), *The Elephants Teach: Creative Writing Since 1880*, Chicago: University of Chicago Press.

Protherough, R. (1983), *Encourage Writing*, London, New York: Methuen.

Tziovas, D. (ed.) (2017), *Greece in Crisis. The Cultural Politics of Austerity*, London, New York: Tauris.

Williams Raymond, W. (1983), Keywords: A Vocabulary of Culture and Society, New York: Oxford University Press.

Θαλάσσης, Γιώργος, *Η άρνηση του Λόγου στο ελληνικό μυθιστόρημα μετά το 1974*, Αθήνα: Γνώση, 1992.

Ιακωβίδου, Σοφία, «Μεταξύ θεωρίας της λογοτεχνίας και δημιουργικής γραφής», στο Κωτόπουλος Τρ, Νάνου Β. (επιμ.), *Πρακτικά 3ου διεθνούς συνεδρίου δημιουργικής γραφής*, Κέρκυρα, 2017, σ. 278–84.

Θεοδωροπούλου, Ε. (2014), "Φαντασία νεκρή φανταστείτε. . ." το παράδοξο μιας επίκλησης στην εκπαίδευση. *Η δημιουργικότητα στην Εκπαίδευση* (επιμ. Κ. Σαραφίδου), σελ. 181–99.

Καστοριάδης, Κ. (1995), *Η άνοδος της ασημαντότητας*, Αθήνα: Ύψιλον.

Κουμασίδης Ιορδάνης (2014), *Αριστοτέλης και Νίτσε: από την Ποιητική στη γέννηση της τραγωδίας. Ορισμένες εισαγωγικές σκέψεις*, στο *Φιλοσοφείν* τ. 9.

Κωτόπουλος, Η. Τ. (2011), Από την ανάγνωση στη λογοτεχνική ανάγνωση και την παιγνιώδη διάθεση της Δημιουργικής Γραφής. Στο Παπαντωνάκης Γ. and Κωτόπουλος Τ. (επιμ.) *Τα ετεροθαλή*. Αθήνα: Ίων, σελ. 21–36.

Κωτόπουλος, Η. Τ. (2012), Η «νομιμοποίηση» της Δημιουργικής Γραφής, *Κείμενα 15*, ανακτήθηκε Σεπτέμβριος 23, 2012 από το διαδίκτυο. Available online: http://keimena.ece.uth.gr/main/index.php?view=article&catid=59%3Atefxos15&id=257%3A15-kotopoulos&option=com_content&Itemid=95

Κωτόπουλος, Τ., Βακάλη, Ά., and Ζωγράφου, Μ. (2013), *Η δημιουργική γραφή στο Νηπιαγωγείο*, Θεσσαλονίκη: Επίκεντρο.

Κωτόπουλος Η. Τριαντάφυλλος, Πράξη και διδασκαλία της «Δημιουργικής Γραφής» στη σύγχρονη ελληνική πραγματικότητα, *Πρακτικά Ε' Επιστημονικού Συνεδρίου «Συνέχειες, ασυνέχειες, ρήξεις στον ελληνικό κόσμο (1204–2014), οικονομία, κοινωνία, ιστορία, λογοτεχνία»*, Ευρωπαϊκή Εταιρεία Νεοελληνικών Σπουδών (European Society of Modern Greek Studies), 2–5 Οκτωβρίου 2014, Θεσσαλονίκη, Α' τόμος, σελ. 801–22.

Κωτόπουλος Η. Τριαντάφυλλος, στο Από τη ΡόζαΛούξεμπουργκ στο *Τερατώδες Είδωλο της Ευρώπης. Οι παθογένειες του καπιταλιστικού συστήματος* (επιμ. Καλεράντε Ε., Βαμβακίδου Ι., Σολάκη Α.), Τρίκαλα 2016: Εκδόσεις Επέκεινα, σελ. 351–67 Εργαστήριο Δημιουργικής Γραφής: η ποιητική της ανατροπής στη σύγχρονη εκπαιδευτική πράξη ή ένας δομικός εναγκαλισμός με την κουλτούρα της οικονομικής αποτελεσματικότητας της εκπαίδευσης στο σύγχρονο ευρωπαϊκό καπιταλισμό;

Μπουρντιέ Πιέρ (2006), *Οι κανόνες της τέχνης. Γένεση και δομή του Λογοτεχνικού Πεδίου*, Αθήνα: Πατάκης.

Sarup, M. (2006), *Μαρξισμός και Εκπαίδευση*, Θεσσαλονίκη: Επίκεντρο.

Τζιόβας, Δημήτρης, (1989), *Οι μεταμορφώσεις του εθνισμού και το ιδεολόγημα της ελληνικότητας στο μεσοπόλεμο*, Αθήνα: Οδυσσέας.

Τζιόβας, Δημήτρης (1993), *Το παλίμψηστο της ελληνικής αφήγησης*, Αθήνα: Οδυσσέας.

12

An American Walks into a Bar
(with her British Creative Writing Students)

Lania Knight
University of Gloucestershire

I.

In her essay "Sleeping with Proust vs Tinkering Under the Bonnet: The Origins and Consequences of the American and British Approaches to Creative Writing in Higher Education," Stephanie Vanderslice traces the histories of creative writing in the US and the UK, and notes some of the differences in approach to pedagogy. She argues that there is room at the table (discussing US creative writing pedagogy) to allow for "both the Romantic concept of creative writing, involving, as Tim Mayers (2005: 66) describes them, an 'aesthetics of inspiration,' and for a Craftsman model driven by an 'aesthetics of work'" (Vanderslice 2008: 72). In 2015, I moved to the UK from the US and began working as a Senior Lecturer in Creative Writing at the University of Gloucestershire, a post-1992 university. The department was housed within the School of Humanities, with an intake cohort of 30–40 undergraduates a year, 15–20 postgraduates at the MA level, and a handful of PhD students. Prose, poetry, and drama were (and still are) taught at all three levels, no small feat for a small department. In the essay mentioned above, Vanderslice also briefly explains the history of the 'Workshop Method' in the US:

> This innovative practice [of allowing creative MA theses under Norman Foerster] lead to the founding of the Iowa Writer's Workshop, an MFA program that blossomed into a full-fledged American icon under poet Paul Engle ... Once this program began graduating writers who went on to accept university teaching positions, exponential growth ... soon followed as disciples fanned out across the country to form Creative Writing programs in the image of their alma mater.
>
> Vanderslice (2008: 67)

As a lecturer at University of Gloucestershire, for several hours each week I taught prose within a pure workshop setting, as in, Iowa Writers Workshop "workshop method" kind of sessions. We—I and my students—discussed and critiqued the work submitted by students each week, which was the "aesthetics of work" part mentioned above in Vanderslice's observations about creative writing pedagogy. For an additional hour each week, though, the students attended a lecture entitled Prose Fundamentals delivered by one of my colleagues, which was the "aesthetics of inspiration" part of Vanderslice's observations. In my first year, I attended the Prose Fundamentals lectures each week alongside the students, a style of delivery that reminded me of the science and math lectures from my undergraduate days studying botany in the US, which were augmented by hands-on laboratory sessions every week.

Through my first professor Marly Swick at University of Missouri where I received my PhD, I can trace part of my lineage to the Iowa Writers Workshop. She studied at Iowa and went on to write several critically acclaimed novels. Some of the PhD students in that first semester also had MFAs from Iowa, so the workshop method of critique was reinforced by other students in the room. When I began teaching my own workshops, it was inherited lore I leaned on, not the composition pedagogy I was required to study in order to fulfill my duties as a teaching assistant. I came to Creative Writing as an outsider—my undergraduate degree was in Plant Science and Environmental Conservation, and I'd been at home raising children in the ten years between undergraduate and postgraduate studies. Anything that made me feel welcome, that helped me understand what I was writing and how to make it better—those were the ideas and methods I incorporated into my own practice as a workshop facilitator. Luckily for my students, most of those practices also helped them understand their own writing and feel connected to and supported by each other, and by me. But with pedagogy, luck isn't enough. "[I]f we don't understand how or why it works (and with lore, we sometimes don't)," Tim Mayers argues, "or if we do not make some attempt to understand, we are back to square one if at some point in the future, with different students or in a different situation, it stops working" (2017: 14).

Part of understanding how teaching choices work is to look at the goals of the lecturer. Although my PhD is in Literature and Creative Writing, I have always been more interested in how a story works rather than what it means. Or rather, I've always been more interested in discussing and teaching how a story works rather than what it might mean. Literary analysis, in terms of meaning-making, feels, to me, like a private, intuitive process. Additionally, I recognize that others are far better at doing it and teaching it than I am. Reading like a writer though, reading for craft and structure, those are what have always drawn me to creative writing. Books like *Reading Like a Writer* by Francine Prose and *13 Ways of Looking at the Novel* by Jane Smiley felt to me more like points of entry to understanding fiction as opposed to, say, *The Oxford Guide to Literature*. James K. Folsom, professor at Yale in the early 1960s, deduced this about his course based on feedback from a student that his creative writing course was the best course in criticism being offered at the college: the "proper question to ask in the interpretation of literature is not 'What does the story mean?' but rather, 'How does the story work?'" (Mayers 2017:159).

In regard to the old question of whether or not creative writing can be taught, of course I believe that on some level, writing can be taught, or I would feel a charlatan at my job. But, and here I agree with what Norman Foerster—considered the father of creative writing in the US—pronounced for the student trying to learn how to write poetry and fiction—that he would "have the writer go to college" (Myers 2006: 134). Anyone inclined toward writing would benefit from going to college, or, in a broader sense, from experiencing more of the world beyond them. In a second-year module I teach called "Research and Enquiry," the semester opens with a pamphlet written by Henry James in 1884, *The Art of Fiction*, in response to a lecture by Dr Walter Besant in which Besant admonished writers to "write what they know." Henry James' counter to this was, yes, write what you know, but go further than that:

> The power to guess the unseen from the seen, to trace the implication of things, to judge the whole piece by the pattern, the condition of feeling life, in general, so completely that you are well on your way to knowing any particular corner of it—this cluster of gifts may almost be said to constitute experience, and they occur in country and in town, and in the most differing stages of education. If experience consists of impressions, it may be said that impressions are experience, just as (have we not seen it?) they are the very air we breathe. Therefore, if I should certainly say to a novice, "Write from experience, and experience only," I should feel that this was a rather tantalizing monition if I were not careful immediately to add, "Try to be one of the people on whom nothing is lost!"

Experience and observation, learning to read like a writer, exposure to new ideas and geographies and materials, to ways that others have made art—these are what can be taught, and it is up to the student to make sense of it, to write it, and, one hopes, to one day make art of it.

II.

An unquestioned part of my inherited lore in my early days of teaching creative writing was the expectation for student writers to listen to and take in what others were saying in workshop about their creative work. I knew it was important to listen to what others said—why else would we be dedicating all this time to workshop?—but I didn't really understand why, nor what the history behind the workshop method was, nor the possible consequences—such as the "workshop story," a story with all its strange, jagged corners rounded off. As Tim Mayers describes in "Re(Figuring) the Future: Lore, Creative Writing Studies, and Institutional Histories," teachers, of course, bring inherited lore to the classroom. However, it's our unexamined inherited lore that is of concern. "Probably the most significant problem with lore is—and long has been—that the conditions of its emergence tend to make it appear natural and neutral, as though it is purely pragmatic and outside the realms of history, ideology, and culture. Yet lore is never outside such realms, and its perceived naturalness can serve to limit—sometimes severely—our field of vision" (2017: 14). Part of the lore I brought with me to the UK is inherited from my first postgraduate creative writing workshop at University of Missouri. Marly Swick invited us to attend workshop at her house. She encouraged us to relax. There was always wine and cheese. The seating was comfy. Art decorated the walls of her living room, statues and figurines, all sorts of lovely things to look at. Most important though, was that we met off campus, and we were being introduced to new possibilities for locating the writing life, *our* writing lives. Where do we write? Where are we creative? What places do we seek out when we are working on a novel or poem, and where do seek out spaces to meet with other writers in the vulnerable step of opening ourselves to critique?

Another part of my inherited lore had to do with the very nature of storytelling. Short fiction works a lot like a good joke. *A horse walks into a bar. The bartender says, "Why the long face?"* It's funny because of the play on the phrase, "long face". You have the set-up, which, in a short story is the rising action; and then you have the payoff, which, in a short story is the climactic moment. In a joke, of course, the payoff is the punchline. Consider Amy Hempel's story "In the Cemetery Where Al Jolson is Buried". There's the set-up—the dying friend asking the narrator to tell her "things she won't mind forgetting"—and what follows, once she admits she has her audience, are stories and tidbits, odds and sods we ostensibly "won't mind forgetting" (1985: 37). Early on, we (and the dying friend) are told the story about the chimp who, when taught to talk, lied.

As Hempel's story unfolds, it is filled with twists and turns, and, like any good joke, comes with a punchline of an ending. The narrator reveals how awful she is—really, she didn't want to visit her friend in the hospital at all, but, like the chimp who learned to sign—"hands moving with an animal grace: forming again and again the words: Baby, come hug, Baby, come hug, fluent now in the language of grief" (52)—the narrator too finally grieves her friend. As with jokes and with storytelling, my own inherited lore had a set-up, and a payoff, but it took moving to the UK to unpack the various bits and make sense of it all.

So, here's a joke: it's Friday afternoon, West Midlands, UK, a bar called the Frog & Fiddle. It's an American writer's first semester working as a lecturer in the UK. She approaches the bar with her students—they order pints and half-pints of lager, ale, a few sweet and fruity drinks and a few coffees, all at cheap prices. Fliers for live music and trivia night cover the walls. Drink specials fill the board above the array of spirits on the back wall. One of the students asks about a function room—the American writer doesn't even really know what a function room is yet—and they move as a group towards the back. In said function room, students arrange themselves in a semi-circle, fanning out from the writer/lecturer's position on the bench against the wall.

It's 13:30. It's 13:34. It's 13:37, and still no one has spoken.

In the third book of her teaching trilogy, *Teaching Critical Thinking: Practical Wisdom*, bell hooks discusses engaged pedagogy which:

> begins with the assumption that we learn best when there is an interactive relationship between student and teacher. As leaders and facilitators, teachers must discover what the students know, and what they need to know. This discovery happens only if teachers are willing to engage students beyond a surface level. As teachers, we can create a climate for optimal learning if we understand the level of emotional awareness and emotional intelligence in the classroom. That means we need to take time to assess who we are teaching.
>
> hooks (2010: 19)

Engaged pedagogy utilizes empathy—it is a way of approaching teaching where the goal is to understand *who* the students are, *how* they are, so as to better help them learn whatever it is we want to teach them. Back to that scene in the bar: nervous laughter and shy glances, and then finally, those dozen British students begin to talk. Young people who had nothing to say this time last week when they were all sitting in a blue-carpeted room on campus are now smiling, giving eye contact, sitting up a little straighter or slumping a little more relaxed in their seats. And sipping their drinks. The American writer/lecturer leads discussion of the first piece of student work, and every one of the students has something to say. The lecturer nods. She encourages. She sips at her half-pint slowly as she's not much of a drinker, and finally, her shoulders begin to relax, the tension draining as she realizes yes, this was the right thing to do.

> Engaged pedagogy emphasizes mutual participation because it is the movement of ideas, exchanged by everyone, that forges a meaningful working relationship between everyone in the classroom. This process helps establish the integrity of the teacher, while simultaneously encouraging students to work with integrity . . . The root meaning of the word 'integrity' is wholeness. Hence, engaged pedagogy makes the classroom a place where wholeness is welcomed and students can be honest, even radically open.
>
> hooks 2010:21)

The writer/lecturer at the Frog & Fiddle is, of course, me. And, because I practice engaged pedagogy, I realized early on that the classroom was not the place for this particular group of British first-year creative writing students to critique fellow students' short story submissions. Does is matter where we go to talk about creative writing? By bringing my British students to a bar, I certainly sidestepped Norman Foerster's admonition that he would "have the writer go to college" (Myers 2006: 134). But sometimes, campus is not the place to stimulate discussion, or at least, it wasn't for these students. I had similar issues with students in the year just ahead of them—I was told by creative writing colleagues that during those students' first year, only a dozen turned up regularly for lectures, and of those few, only a handful would contribute to discussion. One of my tasks with those second years was to try to pull them together as a cohort. I called on colleagues across the university to help me, and they responded, including eco-linguist Arran Stibbe, who, in less than an hour, had the students giving three-minute presentations about their hometowns to the rest of the class.

But for this first-year creative writing workshop, I decided to go it alone and to play my card as an American outsider. I was just beginning to recognize the ins and outs of drinking culture in the UK. This was 2015, and my students were only eleven years on from the "Peak Booze Year" of 2004 (Giles 2015), a year when Brits were drinking on average the equivalent of 100 bottles of wine a year. I was also noticing the importance of local pubs, like The Bayshill or The Railway near my campus, where colleagues meet regularly to have a drink and vent about the week's frustrations. As observers noted in the 1930s—and still seemed true to me since arriving to the UK—"One of the basic institutions in British work life is the pub" (Mass Observation: iii).

Many things are remarkably different about the scene with the students in Frog & Fiddle than what a creative writing undergraduate workshop looked like when I taught in the US. Because the drinking age is twenty-one in the United States, most undergraduates are too young to legally drink. In the UK, young people are legal adults at sixteen, can leave school and enter apprenticeships, and can legally drink at eighteen. As in the US, drinking in the UK actually happens earlier than at the legal drinking age, but unlike in the United States, the young people here work out some of the kinks of drinking *before* they get to university rather than *while* they're at university. As I did with American students when I taught undergraduate workshops in the US, I was searching for a way to reach out to my UK students by acknowledging the "self" of each of them as an individual writer. Leahy argues, "The self is always already there in the creative writing classrooms, in the process of writing creative work, and in the products of [their] efforts. The self – the individual wrier – cannot be ignored" (2017: 44). By acknowledging the "self" of my students, namely their anxiety at being asked to contribute to discussion of fellow students' work, I found a way to reach them and help them feel more comfortable, more able to speak out loud. Going off campus to a pub or bar—an environment they associated with being sociable and with which they were already familiar—helped release them from the expectations of being a "student" on campus.

At the beginning of each semester, one of the first things I share with my students about myself is why I like to teach creative writing. I tell them I'm fascinated by how different we are from each other, how differently we each glow and glitter on the inside, and it's my goal to help them find a way to communicate that uniqueness on the page. What I'm talking about is originality. I'm not only interested in the inherent originality of each student, though—I'm also interested in their ability to continue to see the world in an original way throughout their lives, and to communicate this "way of seeing" in their fiction and essays. In his book *On Creativity*, physicist David Bohm examines and attempts to define originality:

> One prerequisite for originality is clearly that a person ... must be able to learn something new, even if this means that the ideas and notions that are comfortable or dear to him may be overturned ... [R]eal perception that is capable of seeing something new and unfamiliar requires that one be attentive, alert, aware, and sensitive. In this frame of mine, one *does* something (perhaps only to move the body or handle an object), and then one notes the difference between what actually happens and what is inferred from previous knowledge. From this difference, one is led to a new perception or a new idea that accounts for the difference. And this process can go on indefinitely without beginning or end, in any field whatsoever.
>
> Bohm (2006: 4–5)

To get to that state of "real perception," students must overcome so many obstacles. As an outsider in the UK, I could see that the politeness, the reticence cultivated in these young British students was also hindering them from taking risks with each other during critique sessions, and with their own writing. They were trying to get it right, but they didn't want to be too unkind. Anne Lamott, in her humorous guide to writing, *Bird by Bird*, says perfectionism is no friend of the writer. "I think that perfectionism is based on the obsessive belief that if you run carefully enough, hitting each stepping-stone just right, you won't have to die ... [P]erfectionism will ruin your writing, blocking inventiveness and playfulness" (1995: 28). As a long-time facilitator of workshops, the last thing I want to promote is a rounded-corners, "written-by-committee" workshop-style of short story. Rather, I want original stories. It's Lamott's "inventiveness and playfulness," and the "real perception" Bohm mentions, which lead to original stories, those that come closest to revealing the quirky, singular and quite possibly odd ways student writers see the world. And to get to those original stories, sometimes, the workshop needs to move off campus.

III.

In the United States, I would have never considered meeting with undergraduates in a bar. American undergraduate students never seemed like adults in the way UK students do. I can see now, with time, this has had a knock-on effect to my teaching strategies. I treat my UK students more like adults—I see them more as writers just a few years behind me and less like teenagers away from home for the first time. This makes it easier to accomplish what US writer Jane Smiley says is one of the aims in much of teaching creative writing: it's about "showing students how to become teachable, that is, how to listen to what others are saying about their stories, and how not to resist but to receive" (Leahy 2017: 46). I treat my UK students as writers, as adults, and I am clear about my expectation that part of being a writer is learning how to receive what others say about your creative work. Perhaps in this case, though, I am still playing my "American outsider" card—I'm asking students to fulfill *my* expectations of being a writer. And who am I, you might ask? An American, contributing to—unwittingly at the time when I first arrived—as Conchitina Cruz explains, "the 'positive effects' of American imperialism repackaged via cultural diplomacy in the arena of institutionalized creative writing" (2017: 12). When my UK students first hear my voice, they go a bit starry-eyed, which I have since realized is because they see me as an extension of the iconic pop culture milieu transmitted to the UK via US films, TV, and online series. I've seen how other foreigners are treated by Brits in general, especially Eastern Europeans and Asians, how they have become scapegoats for Brexit rhetoric. I feel lucky to be on the "good guy" foreigner list, while at the same time realizing my placement on this list is entirely beyond my control. Once I realized the political implications of my presence here—that I contributed further to positive associations with the US, including "widespread consumption of American cultural commodities" (Cruz 2017: 12)—I began talking with students about politics relevant to the US, including Brexit. I told students my stance on the differences between trade negotiations with the EU and those with the US that would be instated after Brexit, how the balance of power would shift in a detrimental way for the UK as one of the outcomes of the leave vote. It was not my students, however, that needed convincing. Few of them voted to leave. Later that first year, when the US primary results came in, my students were as stunned as I was. It was a strange time to walk the line of being an unwilling diplomat of the US at a time when US politics looked, from across the pond, completely out of control.

In the function room at Frog & Fiddle, I was aware, as I listened to my students begin to talk about each other's work over pints of beer, that I held enormous privilege. I brought not only my inherited lore via the way I structured workshop, but I also had more power than they realized. One basic example was my tendency to encourage them to write more complex characters. Many of my students aspire to write fantasy—they often list *Harry Potter*, *Lord of the Rings*, and *Game of Thrones* as their favorite books. And there is a great deal of privilege and power in, say, the many ways I encouraged them to revise their high fantasy chapters so their characters were more complex. Matthew Salesses describes in "Pure Craft is a Lie": "The 'literary' writer enjoys a lot of privilege in this lesson. The rich get richer . . . The fantasy writer has to learn a whole 'culture' before she can start learning the craft the instructor is teaching. And she has to learn a whole 'culture' and its craft before she can apply that craft or not to the context of high fantasy" (2019: 6). Years before in the US, I received a crash course in my own privilege when I was asked to teach a pre-composition module for first-generation college students, students for whom recent changes in government funding was offering access to university for the first time. I asked them to write about a family dinner. Most of them were from inner-city Chicago. They told me they didn't have family dinners. They rarely sat at a table to eat a meal with family members. They rarely sat at a table to eat a meal, full stop. By the end of the semester, when I explained to them about "code-switching," I admitted that I felt awkward for being the one who knew how to speak and write in an academic way, and that by accident of birth and background, they did not. And I am aware more recently that I invoke my privilege when I ask students to use more concrete description and less abstraction. As Tim Mayers argues, "There is nothing natural or neutral about an aesthetic preference for concreteness over abstraction (just as there would be nothing neutral or natural about an aesthetic preference for abstraction over concreteness)" (2017: 14). There is nothing natural or neutral about anything I ask of my students.

Because I have moved across the Atlantic, I have had the rare opportunity to question what I'm asking of my students and why. I try to walk the line of being "a citizen of the world"—despite Teresa May's attempt at sullying that phrase— by questioning my motives as a lecturer, by examining my cultural assumptions, my privilege, and still holding fast to what I consider essential to creative writing pedagogy.

So, about that joke, about that American who walks into a bar with her students— what's our punchline? If we examine the story for the elements of a joke according to Jeremy Corley, we've got character, setting, plot, conflict, and theme. Character: a lecturer and her creative writing students. Setting: the Frog & Fiddle, a most unusual location for a creative writing workshop. Plot: students won't speak up in class, teacher assesses "emotional awareness and emotional intelligence" of students, teacher walks with them to an environment where they'll feel relaxed, and students in the end share their critique. They, as hooks says, "discover together that [they] can be vulnerable in the space of shared learning, that [they] can take risks" (2010: 21). Conflict: how does one get shy, polite British students to speak up in a group workshop? Theme: pedagogy and cultural awareness. The punchline is, the American walks into the bar with her students, but a) she never leaves because they drink her under the table, and b) they never leave because they don't want anyone to find out they got their tutor pissed. That's the funny version. The insightful version is that she is aware, as she listens to her students discuss stories over pints of beer, how very far she's come in traversing the Atlantic, that "seeing something new and unfamiliar requires that one be attentive, alert, aware, and sensitive." If she is to be original, if she is to help her students write original stories, if she, again quoting Bohm, "*does* something (perhaps only to move the body or handle an object), and then . . . notes the difference between what actually happens and what is inferred from previous knowledge . . . she is led to a new perception or a new idea" (2006). And that new idea is this: it looks like she's just having drinks with her students, but if you look closer under the bonnet, you'll see she's gone and moved shop, she's made the bar a classroom, "a place where wholeness is welcomed and students can be honest, even radically open" (hooks 2010).

References

Bohm, D. (2006), *On Creativity*, Routledge Classics.

Corley, J. (n.d.), "How to Write a Joke". Available online: https://www.standupcomedyclinic.com/how-to-write-a-joke-2/ (accessed October 28, 2019).

Cruz, C. (2017), "The (Mis)Education of the Filipino Writer: The Tiempo Age and Institutionalized Creative Writing in the Philippines," *Kritika Kultura* 28.

Giles, C. (2015), "Why do Brits Drink So Much?" Available online: http://www.bbc.com/future/story/20151102-why-do-the-british-drink-so-much (accessed September 10, 2019).

Hempel, A. (1985), "In the Cemetery Where Al Jolson is Buried," *Reasons to Live*. Harper Collins: New York: 37–52.

hooks, b. (2010), *Teaching Critical Thinking: Practical Wisdom*, Routledge.

James, H. (1884), "The Art of Fiction," *Longman's Magazine* 4. Available online: https://public.wsu.edu/~campbelld/amlit/artfiction.html (accessed September 13, 2019).

Lamott, A. (1995), *Bird by Bird: Some Instructions on Writing and Life*, Anchor.

Leahy, A. (2017) "It's Such a Good Feeling: Self-Esteem, the Growth Mindset and Creative Writing," in *Can Creative Writing Really Be Taught?* 10th Anniversary Edition. Stephanie Vanderslice and Rebecca Mannery (eds). London: Bloomsbury Academic.

Mass Observation, *The Pub and the People*, a Worktown Study. Faber Finds.

May, T. (2016), "May's Conference Speech in Full," *The Telegraph*. October 5, 2016. Available online: https://www.telegraph.co.uk/news/2016/10/05/theresa-mays-conference-speech-in-full/ (accessed September 16, 2019).

Mayers, T. (2017) "(Re)Figuring the Future: Lore, Creative Writing Studies, and Institutional Histories," in *Can Creative Writing Really Be Taught?* 10th Anniversary Edition. Stephanie Vanderslice and Rebecca Mannery (eds). London: Bloomsbury Academic.

Myers, D. G. (2006), *The Elephants Teach: Creative Writing Since 1880*, Chicago: University of Chicago Press.

Prose, F. (2006), *Reading Like a Writer: A Guide for People Who Love Books and for Those Who Want to Write Them*, New York: Harper Perennial.

Salesses, M. (2019), "Pure Craft is a Lie," in *Critical Creative Writing: Essential Readings on the Writer's Craft*. London: Bloomsbury Academic.

Smiley, J. (2006), *13 Ways of Looking at the Novel*, New York: Penguin Random House.

Vanderslice, S. (2008) "Sleeping with Proust vs. Tinkering Under the Bonnet: The Origins and Consequences of the American and British Approaches to Creative Writing in Higher Education," in *Creative Writing Studies: Practice, Research and Pedagogy*, Graeme Harper and Jeri Kroll, eds, Clevedon: Multilingual Matters Ltd.

13

Teaching Chinese-Language Creative Writing in Hong Kong: Three Case Studies

James Shea
Hong Kong Baptist University

Introduction: Three Conceptual Models of the Creative Writing Workshop

A great deal of scholarship on English-language creative writing pedagogy exists in Anglophone countries, where creative writing has been an established academic discipline for decades (Myers 1996; Dawson 2005; Harper 2006; 2012; McGurl 2009; Bennett 2015). Chinese-language creative writing pedagogy, however, is relatively new and unsettled, and there is comparatively little research on this subject, either in English or Chinese. Taiwan has the longest history of offering Chinese creative writing courses, going back at least to the early 1960s (Neih 2011).[1] Recently, leading universities in mainland China have begun to offer the equivalent of a Master in Fine Arts degree in Chinese creative writing, starting with Fudan University in 2009 (Zhao 2009). Other universities followed with their own graduate programs in creative writing, such as Shanghai University (Shen 2011), Peking University (2014), and Tongji University (2016).[2] In Hong Kong, Chinese creative writing courses at the university level date to the 1980s, when The Chinese University of Hong Kong (CUHK) offered a two-semester course in prose and poetry, and some final exam questions from the early 1970s at CUHK included creative writing prompts.

---

[1] Neih Hualing recalls being the first fiction writing teacher in Taiwan: "In 1962, Mr Tai [Ching-lung] invited me in person to teach fiction writing at the Department of Chinese, National Taiwan University, where he was the Chair. It was the first program of its kind in Taiwan" (Neih 2011: 237).

[2] For more background on English and Chinese creative writing programs in mainland China, see Dai (2015; 2011) and Jose (2015).

Individual creative writing courses in Chinese and English are now a fixture at numerous Hong Kong universities and among various departments.[3] The author's home institution Hong Kong Baptist University, for example, offers creative writing courses in Chinese in the Department of Humanities and Creative Writing, Department of Chinese Language and Literature, Language Centre, and the School of Continuing Education. Despite the proliferation of creative writing courses, there is little consensus about what constitutes a writing workshop. Whether in Chinese or English, academic research on creative writing pedagogy in Hong Kong remains limited, and this article is one of the first efforts in English to document Chinese-language creative writing pedagogy in Hong Kong's tertiary institutions.[4]

A review of literature on various frameworks for teaching creative writing suggests at least three conceptual models of the creative writing workshop. The first model posits workshops primarily as sites of "mentoring or apprenticeship" to foster creativity and self-expression (Leahy 2012: 76). Marilynne Robinson, a professor at the Iowa Writers' Workshop, signaled this model when she noted, "The workshop idea does, after all, depend on the willingness of a group of people to pay careful attention to a piece of written work, to criticize it thoughtfully and constructively, and to learn from criticism in their turn" (Robinson 2011). This "Iowa model" is the most common way of framing creative writing instruction today. The second model largely regards creative writing as a "skill" that can lead to employment. Grigorenko and Tan articulated this view in their proposed framework for teaching creativity in Singaporean schools. Defining creativity as a "demand-led competency," they emphasized the primacy of the job market:

> Such a pragmatic approach to teaching creativity reflects the capability of diverse labor markets to merge and blend . . . under the pressure of changing economies, educators can and should develop ways to teach creativity.
>
> Grigorenko and Tan (2008: 24)

Grigorenko and Tan advocated the use of "proficiency scales for assessing creativity" and suggested, "each level can be decomposed into a set of teachable and exercisable skills that can be developed while acquiring specific content areas within particular academic domains" (Grigorenko and Tan 2008: 22–3).

---

[3] For more on the history and development of English-language creative writing pedagogy in Hong Kong, see Lim (2001), Tay and Leung (2011) and Tay (2014).

[4] Chinese-language research on creative writing pedagogy in Hong Kong include Kwok, Chan and Ko (2011a, b).

The third model, informed by critical theory, considers creative writing classrooms as spaces for social criticism that can explore power structures in society. Rather than view creative writing workshops as a community to foster creativity or as a training ground for the workforce, these critics, such as Morton and Zavarzadeh, argue for a creative writing pedagogy that emphasizes the instruction of "radical theory." The premise of such critiques is that the workshop "is not a 'neutral' place where insights are developed, ideas/advice freely exchanged and skills honed. It is a site of ideology: a place in which a particular view of reading/writing texts is put forth and through this view support is given to the dominant social order" (Morton and Zavarzadeh 1988: 161). Critical theory can be used to examine accepted values in creative writing pedagogy, such as the emphasis on voice, characterization, and realism in typical fiction writing workshops, and it can encourage the teaching of experimental writing that "intervenes" in students' understanding of the social construction of reality (168). Morton and Zavarzadeh argue that the workshop should be the "pedagogical space" that posits "theory as resistance" to an entrenched and unquestioned hierarchy (173). This model can be viewed as an extension of arguments espoused by Henry Giroux and others for a "critical pedagogy" in the classroom (Giroux 1983; 1988).

To what degree are Chinese-language creative writing courses in Hong Kong regarded as a means of self-expression, a vehicle for improving skills for the workplace, a tool for social criticism, an admixture of these models, or something altogether different? As the findings from these case studies suggest, instructors' pedagogical values include the fostering of self-expression by way of mentorship. Their pedagogy also entails implicit social criticism based on the practice and concept of defamiliarization.

Methodology

My data source included semi-structured, hour-long interviews with three instructors of undergraduate creative writing courses at three different universities in Hong Kong and course documents, such as syllabi and handouts. Due to the limited number of Chinese-language creative writing courses and the lack of uniform design and course goals across creative writing curricula in Hong Kong's tertiary institutions, it is a challenge to conduct a valid comparative study of the course structures, in terms of finding equivalent class sizes, offering departments, assignments, etc. Consequently, I employed a grounded analysis of the instructors' interview responses by coding for key terms, practices, and attitudes in order to understand the instructors' pedagogical values (Creswell 2013). Interview questions focused on the instructors' formation as creative writing instructors, their philosophy of teaching creative writing, their practices in class and how they regard creative writing within the university system.[5] Hon Lai-chu represented a full-time writer who is relatively new to teaching creative writing; Mary Wong Shuk-han is primarily a scholar who has been teaching creative writing over the past few years; Wong Leung-wo is a writer and teacher with the most years of experience in teaching creative writing.[6] The instructors in this study consented to the use of their real names.

Findings

Hon Lai-chu: "Writing is the only exit"

Hon Lai-chu (韓麗珠) is a part-time lecturer in the Department of Chinese Language and Literature at The Chinese University of Hong Kong. One of Hong Kong's most celebrated authors, she has written numerous books and is the recipient of multiple awards, including the Hong Kong Biennial Award for Chinese Literature for fiction, Taiwan's *Unitas* New Writer's Novella first prize, and the Hong Kong Book Prize. In 2010, she was a resident at the University of Iowa's International Writing Program (Hon 2017). In an interview with the author, Hon reported that she never took a formal creative writing class. She majored in translation at City University of Hong Kong, and during her sophomore year, she published her first book of fiction. She earned an MA in cultural studies at Lingnan University and worked for a local newspaper as a

---

[5] Sample interview questions included: "Did you ever take a creative writing class as a student? Who were your mentors as a young writer? Which writers and texts do you teach the most, and why? Do your students sit in a circle and critique each other's writing? How often does your class discuss (workshop) writing by the students? How has the creative writing by your students evolved, such as the content or style? What is the most important advice you give to creative writing students? What would you like to see changed in terms of creative writing pedagogy in Hong Kong?" The interviews with Hon Lai-chu (May 27, 2015) and Mary Wong Shuk-han (May 12, 2016) were conducted in English, and the interview with Wong Leung-wo (December 19, 2016) was conducted in Cantonese. My research assistant, Nicolette Wong, interpreted our exchange and translated the transcript into English. All translations of Chinese-language materials in this publication were by my research assistant and validated by colleagues at Hong Kong Baptist University.

[6] This article renders Chinese names with the family name first. To differentiate Mary Wong Shuk-han from Wong Leung-wo, however, I refer to Mary Wong Shuk-han by her English name, "Mary."

reporter and later as an editor. She resigned from her position at the age of twenty-five to become a full-time writer, but she still had to find work. After her first book appeared in 2004, she was invited by a student group at Lingnan University to lead an informal creative writing class. In 2014, Hon began to teach as a part-time instructor at CUHK, but in the past, she has taught for the YMCA, where she would often experiment with new teaching methods. She also teaches for The House of Hong Kong Literature, a nonprofit organization that promotes literary appreciation and creation. CUHK is her first and only experience teaching a university-level class.

Hon teaches a two-credit hour general writing course for first-year majors in CUHK's Department of Chinese Language and Literature called "Writing" (寫作訓練) that she tailored as a creative writing class. Her class sessions consist of three parts: 1) discussion of model works; 2) in-class writing activities; and 3) discussion of student writing. She teaches mainly the works of Hong Kong writers, such as Liu Yichang (劉以鬯), Xi Xi (西西), Leung Ping-kwan (Ye Si) (也斯), Dung Kai-cheung (董啟章), Wu Xubin (吳煦斌), Tse Hiu Hung (謝曉虹), and Chan Chi-tak (陳智德), and some Taiwanese writers, such as Xia Yu (夏宇). One reading she gives to students on the first day is Xi Xi's short story "Drawer" because, as she put it, the story raises the question, "What is the self?" Hon doesn't usually teach international writers, except for an occasional work by Italo Calvino. Students are allowed to pick their own genre for writing assignments, although Hon begins the term with short essays and poems, and, later, introduces short stories. In class discussion, she encourages students to connect the assigned readings to their own lives.[7]

During the term we spoke, Hon's two-hour class session had roughly twenty students (although the quota can be up to twenty-four students) and was held once a week. The in-class writing activity, which takes about thirty minutes, might include asking students to pick an object in the room and imagine a special relationship between themselves and the object: how does it represent you? If you were this object, how would you feel? What would you do? Then she asks students to write a short essay from the point of view of the object. She usually plays meditative music in the background while they are writing, and she may ask them to do yoga for a few minutes, before they begin. Hon described her aim to make her creative writing classroom into a "special" atmosphere, different from the typical university class. She asks students to sit in a circle, for example,

---

[7] Hon's discussion questions for an assigned reading include the following: "What do you think about this reading? What's your understanding of this reading? What do you think about the relationship between this reading and your own life?"

or on occasion, she takes them to a grassy area on campus where she invites them to take off their shoes to feel the grass, take in the air and trees, and write.

When students share their work, they often read aloud their in-class writing and provide immediate feedback on each other's work, discussing which pieces they liked the most. Hon offers her remarks throughout the entire discussion. Most of the students' writing is done mainly in class, with students finishing or polishing their work at home. One of her five writing assignments asks students to select a family member and mimic his or her actions for an evening, and then write a story from that person's point of view. For homework, students must finish or revise their in-class writing and do a reading assignment. The final exam (required by the university) is in three sections: 1) response to a creative writing prompt; 2) response to an assigned reading; 3) response to a second creative writing prompt. For Hon, revision is optional and not assessed. When asked how she grades assignments, she responded that she asks herself "if it can touch me." If a student describes a tree, for example, the writing should avoid clichés and move her. When she first started teaching, she had fewer in-class activities and more lectures on theory, including PowerPoint presentations, but she found eventually that they were not necessary.

Her teaching philosophy is based on her aim "to free [the students]." She described the education system in Hong Kong as a "prison" and that "writing is the only exit." She wants to "try to persuade the students to believe in themselves' and "to dig into themselves." Later in our interview, she returned to her main point: "We don't have freedom in our city" and "freedom is decreasing." She observed that the Hong Kong government views creativity like an app that can be downloaded into people's brains and activated when it's needed. The central government posits creativity as concrete, practical, and related to the world of commerce and goods, rather than as a way of life. For Hon, creativity is more abstract in that it expresses the imagination, freedom, a sense of hope and a "taste of living" or aesthetic sense. She connects this tension to the 2014 Umbrella Movement, which she considered as expressing great creativity on the part of student activists, and yet the government opposed the movement. For Hon, it's a central example of how the government compartmentalizes creativity in society—it wants creativity to occur here and there (in creativity institutes and creativity centers), but it does not want imaginative thinking spreading too far into society. She continues to believe that engagement with creative writing can help students to "build up a better self," a "better life" and, in turn, a "better world."

Mary Wong Shuk-han: "Defamiliarize" the classroom

Mary Wong Shuk-han (黃淑嫻) is an Associate Professor in the Department of Chinese at Lingnan University, where she teaches "Creative Writing in Chinese" (中文文學創作), an elective course for third- and fourth-year Chinese majors. Although Mary has published short stories and non-fiction, she self-identifies primarily as a scholar of comparative literature and film. Her course is Lingnan's main creative writing class in Chinese, whereas other writing courses cover journalism, travel writing, children's literature, etc. She co-taught the course with the Hong Kong poet and scholar Leung Ping-kwan (Ye Si) until he died in 2013. Leung had moved to Lingnan University from The University of Hong Kong in 1997, and began a writer-in-residence program in 2003 (Leung 2008).

Mary reported that her teaching goal is "not producing great writers, but trying to help students to present their ideas through fictional ways." She teaches mainly short stories, and when there is a writer-in-residence, the visiting writer gives lectures, and she teaches some of the tutorials. During the semester we spoke, her class had about forty-five students who met for thirteen weekly lectures (one and a half hours), and they broke into three tutorials (one and a half hours) of fifteen students each. These separate tutorials are workshops in which students sit in a circle and discuss their stories. Rather than use writing exercises, Mary provides "thinking exercises" in which students are asked, for example, to describe verbally how a character might behave based on a given backstory. Students share their stories by email at least one day before their assigned workshop, and their classmates refer to the stories on their phones during discussion.

Mary stressed that students are not required to follow her verbal comments on their revisions for the final portfolios, which includes three writing assignments. She wants them to reflect for themselves on how best to revise their work. Her reasoning is based on the stressful atmosphere found in secondary schools, where students must revise their writing based directly on their teachers' corrections. She faults secondary school education for the lack of risk taking in her students. Unlike in her other courses, such as "Literature and Cinema," "Introduction to Literature," and "Popular Culture: 1950s to 1960s," Mary avoids PowerPoint, because, in her words, she wants to "defamiliarize" the classroom experience, so that her students feel the writing class is different from a typical university class and they will pay deeper attention to their work. "Defamiliarization" refers to Victor Shklovsky's theory that art should make us see the world anew by waking us from the "automatism of perception," and in the case of her pedagogy, Mary encourages students to experience writing and literature afresh by differentiating the learning experience from her students' normal Chinese literature courses, in which lectures generally take precedence over discussion, and from their previous writing courses in secondary school (Shklovsky 1965: 13).

Mary provides verbal feedback on her students' writing, because of her large class size. She focuses less on grammar and more on creative uses of language, structure, character, and plausibility, within the world set by each story. She wants her students to focus on emotion, asking students, for instance, "What made you feel happy or angry this week?" She also emphasizes close observation and attention. She takes into consideration the revisions made between students' first drafts and their final portfolios, when she's grading. She changes her readings every semester, but for the term during which we spoke, her reading list included Hong Kong writers, mainland Chinese writers, such as Su Tong (蘇童), Wang An Yi (王安憶), and Yan Lianke (閻連科), and international writers, such as Mario Benedetti. Asked to reflect on how her students have changed in recent years, she gave three specific examples:

1. Over 90 percent of her students now write about social problems, such as suicides among young people or government policies, whereas in the past, students wrote more about personal relationships.
2. Students tend to write more speculative fiction, such as setting their stories in an alternative or fantastical world.
3. Students are using more Cantonese in their writing, especially for dialogs, whereas the narration generally remains written in literary Chinese.

Wong Leung-wo: "Fermentation of feelings"

Wong Leung-wo (王良和) is an Associate Professor in the Department of Literature and Cultural Studies at The Education University of Hong Kong (EdUHK). A prolific writer, Wong has received numerous literary awards, including the Hong Kong Arts Development Council's first award for literary arts. He has published over a dozen books of poetry, essays, and fiction, and he has co-edited a series of books on teaching literature in primary and secondary schools. During the late 1980s, Wong began teaching creative writing in secondary schools, and in 1996, he joined EdUHK (formally known as the Hong Kong Institute of Education), where he has taught creative writing for over two decades. In 1999, he formed the "Passing the Torch Literary Society" (薪傳文社), a student literary organization that he describes as having "nurtured generations" of new writers in Hong Kong (The Education University of Hong Kong 2016).

As for his own formation as a writer, Wong cited a secondary school teacher who encouraged him to submit his writing to a newspaper. As an undergraduate student, Wong took a creative writing course at CUHK in 1985. The course was taught by Yu Guangzhong (余光中), a Taiwanese poet, and Wong Wai-leung (黃維樑), a Hong Kong writer and scholar. Wong described his experience in the course this way:

> Both professors would tell us to submit our works, and then we'd all discuss the works. They didn't look at the work of any famous writers. We were told to just write. There wasn't any topic or limit. It was the same every session. They didn't really have any teaching pedagogies. No theory. Just writing.

Wong's class "Creative Writing" (文學創作) is a required course for students majoring in Education in Chinese, and it is an elective for other majors at EdUHK. Most of his students will become primary and secondary school teachers in Hong Kong, and the course is intended to make them more comfortable teaching language arts. The class seats up to forty-five students, meets for thirteen weeks (in one three-hour session per week), and is divided equally into three genres: poetry, prose (essay), and fiction. The final assignment is a poem, an essay, and a short story. He does not use class time to workshop student writing. Rather, each week he conducts an in-class activity that illustrates a point about the writing process and he leads the class in a discussion of the assigned readings.

One activity is an observation exercise Wong does on the first day of class. He empties two large bags of different objects on a table, such as flowers in a vase, cans, small bronze statues and other curiosities, and small groups of students take turns coming forward to observe the objects and describe them in writing. He doesn't explain what their observations should entail and he doesn't answer their questions directly.[8] At the end of the activity, Wong explains that good observation entails "sensory perception," so they should use all of their senses to experience an object and it's best if they pick an object in which they have a strong interest, as their close affinity with the object will help them to write a better passage. He describes this process as the "fermentation of feelings," in that one's feelings should brew or strengthen before writing. Wong's activity

---

[8] If a student asks, for example, if he or she may touch an object, Wong responds by saying, "If you think observation includes touching, then it's up to you."

emphasizes an emotion-centered approach to writing, one that privileges affect. Rather than framing observation as an objective or emotionally-neutral exercise, he encourages students to consider how an object can be charged with feeling, and how that can enhance one's own writing. Although Wong is not explicit about defamiliarization, his teaching practices center on weekly activities that are dissimilar from the typical teaching methods of most university courses.

Instead of workshopping in class, he requires students to find peer reviewers to receive feedback on their writing outside of class time. They may have up to five peer reviewers and if they find the maximum, then their grade on an assignment can improve. He also advises them to keep their poems to fourteen lines or less, because he said they can't handle longer poems. He teaches mainly Hong Kong authors, although he includes poems by Rainer Maria Rilke and Jacques Prévert, and short stories by Ryūnosuke Akutagawa. When asked if his students write more speculative fiction these days, he responded by saying that they don't do so, because they know that their teacher prefers realism. Like Mary, he agrees that students are using more Cantonese in their writing, and he attributes the rise of Cantonese partly to "localism." Localism refers to "a political movement centred on the defence of Hong Kong's identity and autonomy" in opposition to mainland China's rising influence (Kwong 2016: 68). Localism may account for the increase in Cantonese as way to signal Hong Kong identity, especially given that the number of Hong Kong people who identify as "Hong Kongers" has "doubled since July 2012" (Lao 2016).

Conclusion: Self-Expression as Social Critique

The three case studies above differ widely in terms of the instructors' training, background, and experience, as well as in terms of the target students and course goals. Wong's course, for instance, is intended to educate students who will teach language arts in Hong Kong's secondary schools, whereas Mary's course is for upper-level Chinese majors, and Hon's course is for first-year Chinese majors. Yet based on a grounded analysis of their interview responses, their self-reported pedagogies demonstrate striking similarities in relation to the three conceptual models of creative writing workshops. The instructors follow mainly the model of apprenticeship to cultivate self-expression, and although they do not prioritize skills-based teaching, they include, to varying degrees, critiques of Hong Kong society in the form of their teaching practices. This social criticism is often not explicit, but is, rather, embedded in the perception of these courses as a reprieve from students' traditional learning experiences, given the context of Hong Kong's education system.

Despite their differences, the three instructors overlap in their pedagogies in various ways. Examples are as follows:

1. Assign at least three take-home writing assignments (Hon: 5; Mary: 3; Wong: 3).
2. Generally do not provide written comments on students' drafts.
3. Generally do not prioritize revision.
4. Have writing classes that are not genre specific (Hon allows students to pick their own genre; Mary teaches mainly fiction, although the Master syllabus allows for other genres, such as essays, poetry, book reviews, film reviews, and cultural criticism (Lingnan); and Wong covers three genres equally: essay, poetry, and fiction).
5. Assemble their own reading materials, rather than use textbooks or anthologies.
6. Teach works by primarily Chinese authors, including Hong Kong writers.
7. Use experiential learning methods, such as mimicking a family member (Hon), thinking exercises (Mary) or an observation activity (Wong).
8. Present their courses as different from typical Hong Kong courses, and they take care to create, as Hon puts it, a "special" atmosphere in the classroom.
9. Emphasize affect in their pedagogy: If you were an object, how would you feel? (Hon), How did you feel this week? (Mary), the fermentation of feelings (Wong).

The instructors regard self-expression as the primary goal of their writing workshops, as evidenced by their multiple creative writing assignments and the valuing of personal feelings in the writing process. The minor emphasis on revision suggests that the model of writing workshops as opportunities to teach creative writing as a skill for the workforce is not a priority among these instructors. It is also likely that the large class sizes for Mary and Wong make individual written comments onerous. Their practices do not frame creative writing as practical training for employment, in terms of the assignments or the instructors' rhetoric. Even in the case of Wong's class, which is intended for students who will become school teachers, his teaching strategy is to encourage students to think of themselves as potential authors by engaging in writing.

Although the instructors do not emphasize critical theory, social criticism is present in their pedagogy, albeit indirectly. First, the teaching of Hong Kong literature privileges Hong Kong writers in a way that is uncommon in primary and secondary schools, because their curriculum involves teaching mainly classical and modern Chinese writers and contemporary mainland Chinese and Taiwanese writers. The subject of Hong Kong Literature is offered only as an optional course within the elective called Chinese Literature, a non-compulsory concentration for secondary school students (Education Bureau of Hong Kong 2010: 4). In other words, the study of Hong Kong literature and even literature itself is optional in Hong Kong's secondary schools, and, so, the instructors' use of local writers as literary models invites a reflection on Hong Kong identity and the role of power to define it. Second, the very encouragement of self-expression and the discourse of affect are an implicit social critique of the dominant practices in Hong Kong's secondary schools which prioritize the memorization of model answers (McNaught 2012).[9] Third, the differentiation of creative writing courses from typical university courses implies a critique of the status quo in Hong Kong's tertiary education system, implicitly questioning its values. Defamiliarizing strategies—such as playing meditative music, sitting in a circle, not using PowerPoint, leading large-scale in-class activities and welcoming Cantonese in student writing—create a space for alternative educational practices and a reprieve from conventional assessment measures (Zuba 2016; Thomas 2005).

Hong Kong's "cultural and creative industries" continue to expand as an important source of employment, and it is likely that creative writing courses will remain popular with students (Census and Statistics Department 2016).[10] These courses also reflect Hong Kong's recent turn toward the liberal arts. In 2012, Hong Kong's University Grants Committee (UGC), the governmental body that oversees Hong Kong's tertiary institutions, changed undergraduate education from a three-year to a four-year program with an emphasis on the liberal arts and general education courses. Undergraduate education in the United States was the "explicit model for Hong Kong's liberal-education campaign" with the goal of promoting "creative thinking" for the workforce (Wildavsky 2016). Whereas the UGC may envision creative writing as a means for skills-based instruction for cultural and

---

[9] Some university teachers in Hong Kong report that their students are not accustomed to expressing their own opinions: "Students who grow up in Hong Kong, however, are generally frightened as they are so used to having model answers given to them in their secondary school training" (Lo in Kember and McNaught 2007: 40 quoted in McNaught 2012: 2).

[10] Although "cultural and creative industries" (CCI) do not constitute a large share of Hong Kong's gross domestic product, they are an expanding part of Hong Kong's future: "During 2005 to 2014, the value added of CCI in nominal terms increased at an average annual rate of 8.6%, significantly faster than the average annual growth rate of the nominal GDP of Hong Kong, at 5.4%" (Census and Statistics Department 2016).

creative industries, the instructors in these case studies clearly value self-expression and, implicitly, social critique as pedagogical objectives. Framing creative writing as a skill with instrumentalist purposes may have profound consequences. B. B. Tye described what is lost due to the commodification of education:

> First of all, it deprives young people of the feeling that what they are doing *now* is important. All the rewards seem to be somewhere in the future. Secondly, it deprives society of the understanding that learning has value in itself and not just as a saleable commodity (Tye 1985: 337–8 quoted in Elliott and Phuong-Mai 2008: 42).

It remains to be seen whether creative writing pedagogy in Hong Kong will embrace an instrumentalist vision of "creative thinking," or if these courses may engender a new way of approaching university education in Hong Kong.

References

Bennett, E. (2015), *Workshops of Empire: Stegner, Engle, and American Creative Writing During the Cold War*, Iowa City: University of Iowa Press.

Census and Statistics Department, Hong Kong Special Administrative Region (2016), "Hong Kong Monthly Digest of Statistics June 2016." Available online: http://www.statistics.gov.hk/pub/B10100022016MM06B0100.pdf (accessed April 21, 2017).

Creswell, J. W. (2013), *Qualitative, Quantitative, and Mixed Methods Approaches*, Thousand Oaks: Sage.

Dai, F. (2011), "Writing, Sharing and Growing: Creative Writing in English at a Mainland Chinese University," *TEXT*, 10 (April): 1–13.

Dai, F. (2015), "Teaching Creative Writing in English in the Chinese Context," *World Englishes*, 34: 247–59.

Dawson, P. (2005), *Creative Writing and the New Humanities*, Oxford: Routledge.

Education Bureau of Hong Kong (2010), 教育局課程發展處 (Curriculum Development): 中國文學 (Chinese Literature). Available online: http://www.edb.gov.hk/attachment/tc/curriculum-development/kla/chi-edu/D03_chi_lit_v3.pdf (accessed April 25, 2017).

Elliott, J. G. and N. Phuong-Mai. (2008), "Western Influences on the East, Eastern Influences on the West: Lessons for the East and West," in O. S. Tan, D. M. McInerney, G. A. D. Liem and A.-G. Tan (eds), *What the West Can Learn from the East: Asian Perspectives on the Psychology of Learning and Motivation*, 31–58, Charlotte: Information Age Publishing.

Giroux, H. (1983), *Theory and Resistance in Education: A Pedagogy for the Opposition*, London: Heinemann Educational Books.

Giroux, H. (1988), *Teachers as Intellectuals: Toward a Critical Pedagogy of Learning*, Granby: Bergin and Garvey Publishers.

Grigorenko, E. L. and M. Tan (2008), "Teaching Creativity as a Demand-led Competency," in O. S. Tan, D. M. McInerney, G. A. D. Liem and A.-G. Tan (eds), *What the West Can Learn from the East: Asian Perspectives on the Psychology of Learning and Motivation*, 11–30, Charlotte: Information Age Publishing.

Harper, G. (ed.) (2006), *Teaching Creative Writing*, New York: Continuum.

Harper, G. (2012), "A Short History of Creative Writing in British Universities," in H. Beck (ed.), *Teaching Creative Writing*, 9–16, Basingstoke: Palgrave Macmillan.

Hon, L. (2017), "About the Author," Muse: East Slope Publishing Limited. Available online: http://www.musemag.hk/books/the-kite-family (accessed April 25, 2017).

Jose, N. (2015), "Creative Writing in China," *The China Story* (1 February). Available online: https://www.thechinastory.org/2015/02/creative-writing-in-china/ (accessed April 25, 2017).

Kember, D. and C. McNaught. (2007), *Enhancing University Teaching: Lessons from Research into Award Winning Teachers*, Abingdon, Oxfordshire: Routledge.

Kwok, S., Z. Chan and C. Ko (eds) (2011a), *Shùxià zāi huā: Xiězuò jiàoyù jīngyàn tán* 《樹下栽花：寫作教育經驗談》 (Growing Flowers Under a Tree: Experiences in Creative Writing Education). Hong Kong: Spicy Fish Cultural Production Limited.

Kwok, S., Z. Chan and C. Ko (eds) (2011b), *Yúnshàng bōzhòng: Gěi xiězuò dǎoshī de shí táng kè* 《雲上播種：給寫作導師的十堂課》 (Cloud Seeding: Ten Lessons for Creative Writing Teachers). Hong Kong: Spicy Fish Cultural Production Limited.

Kwong, Y. (2016), "The Growth of 'Localism' in Hong Kong: A New Path for the Democracy Movement?" *China Perspectives*, 3: 63–8. Available online: https://chinaperspectives.revues.org/7057?file=1 (accessed April 25, 2017).

Lao, S. (2016), "Why Hong Kong Independence, Localism, Nativism and Recolonisation Worry Mainland China," *South China Morning Post*, 22 July. Available online: http://www.scmp.com/news/hong kong/politics/article/1993405/why-hong-kong-independence-localism-nativism-and# (accessed April 25, 2017).

Leahy, A. (2012), "Undergraduate Creative Writing in the United States: Buying In Isn't Selling Out," in H. Beck (ed.), *Teaching Creative Writing*, 73–9, Basingstoke: Palgrave Macmillan.

Leung, P. (2008), "Introduction," in P. Leung, P. Lam and C. Cheung (eds), 梁秉鈞： 〈序〉，《跟白先勇一起創作》。梁秉鈞策劃； 梁秉鈞、林佩華、張頌賢合編 (Creative Writing with Pai Hsien-yung), 4–6, Hong Kong: Centre for Humanities Research.

Lim, S. G. (2001), "English-Language Creative Writing in Hong Kong: Colonial Stereotype and Process," *Pedagogy: Critical Approaches to Teaching Literature, Language, Composition, and Culture*, 1 (1): 178–84.

Lingnan University (undated), "Creative Writing in Chinese." Available online: https://www.ln.edu.hk/chi/ug/course/CHI3219.pdf (accessed April 25, 2017).

McGurl, M. (2009), *The Program Era: Postwar Fiction and the Rise of Creative Writing*. Boston: Harvard University Press.

McNaught, C. (2012), "SoTL at Cultural Interfaces: Exploring Nuance in Learning Designs at a Chinese University," *International Journal for the Scholarship of Teaching and Learning*, 6 (2). Available online: https://doi.org/10.20429/ijsotl.2012.060203 (accessed April 25, 2017).

Morton, D. and M. Zavarzadeh (1988–9), "The Cultural Politics of the Fiction Workshop," *Cultural Critique*, 11 (Winter): 155–73.

Myers, D. G. (1996), *The Elephants Teach: Creative Writing Since 1880*, Englewood Cliffs: Prentice-Hall.

Neih, H. (2011), *Sān Bèi Zì* 《三輩子》 (Three Lives), Taipei: Linking Publishing.

Peking University (2014), *Běijīng dàxué 2014 nián chuàngyì xiězuò fāngxiàng shuòshì xuéwèi zhuānyè yánjiūshēng zhāoshēng jiǎn zhāng*, 北京大學2014年創意寫作方向碩士專業學位研究生招生簡章 (Brief Admissions Rules for Peking University 2014 MFA in Creative Writing), Department of Chinese Language and Literature, Peking University Graduate Admissions Office. Available online: http://chinese.pku.edu.cn/bxgg/4692.htm (accessed April 25, 2017).

Robinson, M. (2011), "The Workshop as Phenomenon" [speech], Iowa Writers' Workshop, Iowa City, 9 June. Available online: https://www.youtube.com/watch?v=QfDDXhn_iXU (accessed April 25, 2017).

Shen, L. (2011), "Can Writing Be Taught?" *Global Times*, December 8. Available online: http://www.globaltimes.cn/content/687754.shtml (accessed April 25, 2017).

Shklovsky, V. (1965), "Art as Technique," in L. T. Lemon and J. R. Marion (trans.), *Russian Formalist Criticism: Four Essays*, 3–24, Lincoln: University of Nebraska Press.

Tay, E. (2014), "Curriculum as Cultural Critique: Creative Writing Pedagogy in Hong Kong," in D. Disney (ed), *Exploring Second Language Creative Writing: Beyond Babel*, 103–18, Philadelphia: John Benjamins Publishing Company.

Tay, E. and E. Leung (2011), "On Learning, Teaching and the Pursuit of Creative Writing in Singapore and Hong Kong," *New Writing: The International Journal for the Practice and Theory of Creative Writing*, 8 (2): 103–13.

The Education University of Hong Kong (2016), "Dr Wong Leung-wo: Passing on the Passion for Literature," August 5. Available online: https://www.eduhk.hk/main/features/FeatureBanner_20160805_095436 (accessed April 25, 2017).

Tongji University (2016), *(Xuéwèi shuòshì) Tóngjì dàxué MFA (chuàngyì xiězuò fāngxiàng shuòshì) 2016 nián lóng zhòng zhāo sheng*, 【學位碩士】同濟大學MFA (創意寫作方向碩士) 2016年隆重招生 (Master's Degree MFA (Creative Writing) 2016 Admissions Open). Available online: http://sal.tongji.edu.cn/index.php?classid=4536&newsid=6043&t=show (accessed April 25, 2017).

Thomas, C. (2005), "Moments of Productive Bafflement, or Defamiliarizing Graduate Studies in English," *Pedagogy*, 5 (1): 19–35. Available online: https://muse.jhu.edu/article/177783 (accessed September 25, 2017).

Tye, B. B. (1985), *Multiple Realities: A Study of 13 American High School*s, Lanham, MD: University Press of America.

Wildavsky, B. (2016), "The Rise of Liberal Arts in Hong Kong," *The Atlantic Monthly*, March 20. Available online: https://www.theatlantic.com/education/archive/2016/03/the-rise-of-liberal-arts-in-china/474291/ (accessed April 25, 2017).

Zhao, X. (2009), "New Hope for Writers Blocked by Lack of Education," CNN, December 28. Available online: http://travel.cnn.com/shanghai/play/look-mom-im-going-be-writer-093134/ (accessed April 25, 2017).

Zuba, C. (2016), "Monstrosity and the Majority: Defamiliarizing Race in the University Classroom," *Pedagogy*, 16 (2): 356–67. Available online: http://pedagogy.dukejournals.org/content/16/2/356.full.pdf+html (accessed September 25, 2017).

14

Playing Catch-Up: Finding a Voice for Creative Writing in Brazil

Bernardo Bueno

Pontifical Catholic University of Rio Grande do Sul

Introduction

Creative writing is a new field in Brazil. Even though writing workshops have been popular for quite some time, it was not until 2006 that they became part of our academic ecosystem, with the Pontifical Catholic University of Rio Grande do Sul (PUCRS) offering MA students within the Literary Theory concentration the possibility to write a creative piece as part of their dissertation. Following that, creative writing classes became part of Literature undergraduate curricula in 2007. In 2012, it became an official concentration in MA and PhD courses and, finally, the first undergraduate course started in 2016.

PUCRS programs were inspired by their American and British counterparts: every creative piece is accompanied by a critical essay, there are workshops, seminars, lectures, graded papers, and supervision meetings. Writers, who now encompass both students and teachers, have to play the academia game: publish or perish, attend conferences, write reports and evaluations; meanwhile there are meetings about attracting new students, allocating budgets and scholarships. There are rules: suddenly, writing is not as free as it was before—but that is a good thing; it allows us to encourage those who want to write and need the structure that only a place with grades, supervisors, and deadlines can offer.

All that happened recently, starting thirteen years ago, at a time when even the term itself was rare: people were still getting used to the idea of "Creative Writing" as something different to regular writing. So far, the effort has been fruitful, attracting a good number of students even during times of economic and political crisis. However, I believe mimicking foreign programs is not enough: it is time to start thinking about the Brazilian context. What does it mean to teach creative writing in Brazil? Are we just trying to keep up with countries with older literary traditions, or have we found our own voice?

Brazil has a readership problem and a challenging publishing market, as well as a unique literary history, allied to a strong desire for international recognition. At PUCRS, we teach creative writing classes in Portuguese and, in some cases, in English (in an effort towards internationalization). The field is striving, with new programs beginning to appear in different states around the country. Students applying to creative writing classes tend to have an interdisciplinary background: roughly 50 percent of MA students are not Literature majors (they come instead from Communication Studies, Journalism, Psychology, Law, and Visual Arts). However, students, despite being eager and enthusiastic, sometimes comment on feeling as though we lag "behind" other countries; they find it hard to keep up with foreign programs and literary markets; they fear we will never be as successful as "them" (or "you," depending on who is reading). I worry about all that too. We will only be able to solve those issues if we look at our country, our voices, and our history, and find our value and place without the constant need for comparison or playing catch-up.

What follows is my personal take on the process of finding uniqueness in creative writing in a developing country such as Brazil. The examples given are real, but names or titles were changed or omitted to preserve the privacy of those involved. Since this chapter is based on my experience as a student, writer, teacher and, more recently, Undergraduate Creative Writing Director, it is important to note that any mistakes are my own.

Find Your Voice

Today, PUCRS has a range of Creative Writing courses on offer: at least four elective undergraduate classes every semester, a year-long writing workshop, distance learning classes, an undergraduate course, and a graduate program (MA and PhD). Elective classes and workshops focus on writing exercises and constructive criticism, while undergraduate and graduate programs look at a wide range of topics and genres and demand the writing of both an essay and a creative piece, under the close supervision of faculty members.

While this system was inspired mostly by American and British programs, PUCRS also looked at other international models, such as workshops and classes in France, Spain, Portugal, Uruguay, and Argentina, for example. The rationale behind our classes and programs is that writers need a place to learn and practice their craft; that writers should not rely on inspiration alone; that a certain level of academic structure is helpful, and that, above all, the exchange of experiences between students, as well as faculty members, helps build a "literary ecosystem" that fosters creativity.

Creative writing has its share of mantras: sayings that we repeat to each other to offer encouragement, things we say to our students to guide them, clichés that are equal parts cringeworthy and true. Show, don´t tell. Write what you know. Find your voice. My proposition is therefore that, just like the students who frequent them, creative writing programs have their own voices too.

From all the advice, clichés, and motivational quotes I read (and they are always fun to read, because they inspire you, make you feel less lonely, show you that you are on the right path but are, ultimately, useless unless you simply sit down and write until you finish something), my favorite is *find you voice*. It's my favorite piece of lore because it can mean a lot of things: the style of your writing, your confidence when writing, the genre you write on or even your place in the world.

As noted by Mark McGurl in *The Program Era*, "voice" is a loaded term, and finding one's own is not a simple task. On a personal level, writers both struggle to find their places in the literary system, and struggle to figure out how best to express their ideas. In addition, voice goes even further, suggesting relationship to history and place, and revealing much about identity and power. Moreover, in an unequal society and an unequal world, some voices are heard more frequently and more easily than others. This is the case both when we talk about postcolonial writing (Brazil became independent in 1822) and when we talk about Brazilian writing programs in the twenty-first century.

Creative writing programs have their own voices. Some focus on teaching and research; others are famous for their writing workshops; some have a reputation for giving birth to prize-winning authors; others are connected to the Humanities, Literature or Language departments or, sometimes, to the Arts. Every program has their own group of writer-teachers, or teacher-writers, each with their own voice and experience, and, collectively, all these elements (the university, department or program ethos, the library, the program history, the alumni and their reputations, and so on) give each program their unique identity.

The danger that new writing programs face, when they are built on foreign experiences, and when they are offered for the first time in countries without an academic creative writing tradition, is this: trying to follow someone else's experience, copying and pasting from other institutions, won't be enough to sustain a program after the novelty of something new wears off. At first, it might be fun to be part of the club: *look, we can do what they do too.* But, ultimately, we need to face the question: what are we doing that is uniquely ours? What does it mean to teach creative writing here? What is our voice?

The Value of Our Culture

Brazil has long struggled as a developing country. When I was in school, I remember classes when the teachers would talk about poverty, and explain about being a third-world country and part of the Global South. I remember watching lines of cars stretch for blocks just before the gas prices were adjusted. People would buy groceries for an entire month because inflation was so rampant that price tags changed every day. When I was a child I was consumed by a sense of dread about my country. Meanwhile, in our collective imagination, the United States seemed like paradise: a place where everything worked, everything was better and everyone was rich.

Then the economy changed. The Brazilian real was introduced as the currency and it equaled the American dollar. I was fourteen in 1997 and went on a trip with my friends to Walt Disney World in Orlando. I come from a privileged family; we were not rich, but we had enough to live comfortably. I remember learning in high school that less than 2 percent of Brazilians at the time went on to get higher education degrees. Walt Disney World was a lot of fun, but also consolidated my feeling that Brazil would never be as organized and beautiful as the USA. I didn't understand at the time that Walt Disney World should not be mistaken for the real world, just as Middle Earth should not be mistaken for the Middle Ages.

In 2006, I was a new student in the PUCRS Graduate Program in Letters. That year, four students, myself included, were able to submit a creative piece as part of their dissertation, accompanied by an essay on a topic of their choosing. This sort of thing had been done before in Brazil, but not officially. There had been reports and rumors of people who managed to negotiate the possibility of handing in a creative piece as their dissertation or thesis, but now the idea was proposed by the program. Professor Luiz Antonio de Assis Brasil had been conducting a Writing Workshop at PUCRS since 1985 and, together with other faculty members, convinced the university that submitting a creative piece should be allowed for graduate students.

A few years later, in 2012, Creative Writing became an official concentration in the program. This process took many years, meetings, and proposals before finally being granted authorization from the Ministry of Education. The Graduate Program in Letters understood that Creative Writing would interest current and future students and that is was time for a university as big as PUCRS to encourage the development of this field within Brazilian academia.

It is now 2019, and I know a student who is writing a book. She was born and raised in Porto Alegre, and though she has never been abroad, she grew up with a constant exposure to American and English culture: from translated books, radio stations that played music mostly in English, theaters that only showed Hollywood movies, and American sitcoms repeated on television. Most importantly, she grew up with the Internet, making a clear contrast to my own generation (I was fourteen when I got my first computer, and fifteen when I got online for the first time). She writes in Portuguese.

This student is a promising writer. She showed me a chapter of her work-in-progress, from an urban fantasy novel in which characters from a world similar to ours interact with creatures from myth and legend. It has action, a good balance between showing and telling, a strong rhythm, and an epic plot. The only thing that bothers me is the setting and the names. Why New York? Why James, Connor, Alexa, Johnny, and Phoebe — especially considering she is Brazilian and is writing in her native language?

It is also common to meet students who dream of writing in English. I also felt that way in the past; after all, setting a story in Brazil wouldn't be as cool, right? Orcs, trolls, and mermaids are cooler than *curupiras*, *boi tatás*, and *iaras*, creatures from Brazilian folklore.[1] On one hand, it is good to have an international sensibility. But on the other, shouldn't we place a little more value in our own culture, myths, folklore, and history?[2]

The same can be said about reading lists. Few people question the value of Ernest Hemingway, Virginia Woolf, and Edgar Allan Poe but, at the same time, we need to include contemporary Brazilian writers and our own classics. In that sense, curricula in schools and universities are more varied that before, and we read more widely: Machado de Assis, Clarice Lispector, Fernando Pessoa, Jorge Luis Borges, Adelia Prado. However, the question of diversity and representation remains, and it is clear that we need to read more women, more people of color, and more LGBTQ+ authors.

---

[1] Forest spirits that protect nature from those who seek to harm it. The *curupira* is a humanoid spirit with red hair and feet that point backwards to confuse hunters; *boi tatá* is a giant fire snake; and *iara* is a mermaid that lives in rivers.

[2] It is interesting to note that a recent novel that achieved success among fantasy fans in Brazil was *The Banner of the Elephant and the Macaw*, inspired by Brazilian colonial history and folklore, written by Christopher Kastensmidt, a Texan who has been living in Porto Alegre since 2001.

In this sense, I am reminded of Chimamanda Ngozi Adichie's TED Talk, *The Danger of a Single Story*. The situation she describes—setting her own stories in England instead of Nigeria because that was the kind of story she used to read—is similar to the one I just reported above. There is nothing wrong with exploring different settings; what is wrong is to overlook or actively ignore our own culture because we do not value it enough.

Past and Future Challenges

Here is some data from recent research: the report *Reading Portraits in Brazil* (whose latest edition was published in 2016), one of the most thorough pieces of research on the Brazilian literary market, states that Brazilians read, on average, 4.9 books a year (and finish only half of these). The same report states that 30 percent of the population has never bought a book. Recently, another report, *Production and Sales from the Brazilian Editorial Sector*,[3] stated that literary market revenues decreased 25 percent between 2006 and 2018 (2019). A report from the World Bank Group estimates that Brazil will need 260 years to reach the same readership level as developed countries.

The data above shows that the future is bleak. Nonetheless, every creative writing initiative at PUCRS has met and exceeded expectations. Granted, it is a private university, which means most undergraduate students come from privileged backgrounds (at least privileged enough, considering 40 percent of the university students have some kind of scholarship or student loan). In our Graduate Program in Letters (which includes a creative writing concentration), however, 94 percent of students receive partial or full scholarships from the Education Ministry.[4] We can say, therefore, that there are many people interested in pursuing a creative writing degree, even though the literary market faces so many problems.

Another challenge, especially in undergraduate study, is the quality of previous education. Some students come from private schools and show ease when writing and a good reading background; some are pursuing a second degree as mature students (since no creative writing degree existed a few years ago); and some who went to public or private schools where the quality of

---

[3] My translation. In the original, *Produção e Vendas do Setor Editorial Brasileiro,* as referred in De Souza Gabriel (2019).

[4] As I'm writing this chapter, scholarships from the Education Ministry are facing severe cuts and it is not known if they will be available in the near future.

education was poor. The educational system in Brazil is uneven, to say the least, which means we have, in the same class, both students with extensive writing experience (sometimes even published authors) alongside students who face extreme difficulty when writing, but are nevertheless passionate about it.

Many Brazilians struggle with self-esteem: the feeling of not belonging, of not being good enough or being unable to reach the same level as more developed countries. Since we have no lack of literary talent, I think it this is therefore something akin to impostor syndrome. This feeling is deeply rooted, connected to our difficult past and present, and something that needs to be addressed in academic environments too: students (and teachers) need to know that what they write is not worse than what is written in North America or Europe. On the other hand, the difficulties listed above regarding educational quality and readership levels no doubt impact our literary ecosystem as a whole.

Let's go back to the example of the student who wanted to write in English. In a world where self-publishing is just one click away, where success stories of fanfiction-turned-bestseller abound, it is not surprising to find students like this, who dream of breaking away from an unwelcoming literary market. When someone tells me they prefer to write in English, I take it with a grain of salt; though I question how a young writer, perhaps not even twenty years old yet, can express themselves better in their second language. Conrad and Nabokov pulled it off, certainly, but each had years and years of practice. No doubt access to culture and literature in English is widespread and easy for those with a computer (though again it is important to note that 30 percent of Brazilians have never connected to the Internet), but writing well in Portuguese is hard enough—why then should we aim to write in English? Do students want to do this because they really are more comfortable expressing themselves in a different language, or are they just discouraged by the Brazilian literary market?[5]

This matter is addressed in part by offering a creative writing class in English—namely, an elective class I have been teaching since 2015. Interested students come not only from our other undergraduate courses, but from other departments as well (Communication Studies, Law, Medicine, Architecture, and Physics) and, over the course of a semester, they have the opportunity to practice writing fiction and poetry in English. Even though Portuguese is our native language, undergraduate and graduate students also have the option to submit their final papers, dissertations and theses in English if they so desire; a desire we are able

---

[5] I teach Creative Writing in English as an undergraduate elective class. All the other graduate and undergraduate classes, however, are in Portuguese.

to accommodate since we share faculty members with the Letters program, in which students prepare to become English teachers. This practice, however, although helpful in building the university's international profile, is not the main focus of our creative writing initiative.

Steps Toward Uniqueness

The facts and reflections above provide a general introduction to the challenges faced by Brazilian writers. Every country, developed or not, will have their own set of challenges, and my aim here is not to downplay the problems others face, only to share our particular situation. I would therefore like to propose some steps towards uniqueness: practices we can follow as a developing country that only recently welcomed creative writing into our universities, that looked abroad for inspiration and guidance, but that, from now own, needs to start thinking about what makes our creative writing uniquely our own.

One step would be to view an undergraduate degree in creative writing as a set of tools instead of a career. We have therefore tried to build a curriculum that offers more than just writing workshops and literary theory seminars: students learn to write short stories, poems, essays, plays, screenplays, and game design documents; they plan YouTube channels, experiment with programming languages and attend creative entrepreneurship courses. Our understanding is that creative writing is a toolbox, not a career, and so students need to be prepared to put those tools to good use in a variety of work situations. This is a need that we identified within our university, city, and country: a need to justify a writing degree to a society that does not yet understand all the advantages of being an expert on language and creativity. Also, while bachelor degrees in Brazil are usually four years long, our creative writing undergraduate degree falls into the category of what the Education Ministry calls "technical degrees"—a shorter university course that is five semesters-long (1,600 hours).

Another step is the creative essay: the reflective piece that accompanies the creative element of final papers (in undergraduate degrees) and dissertations and theses (in graduate studies). This assignment has the untapped potential to interface with literary theory in a unique way. It's not necessarily creative non-fiction, but something analogous, in the sense that it allows for creative experimentation while entering into a dialog with theory. This critical element is common in other creative writing programs, and, personally, I believe that it holds great potential for originality—making it a unique genre that is akin to traditional essays from literary scholars, but imbued with the DNA of creative writing.

This critical component of a creative writing degree was, at first, considered the price we had to pay to be part of the university, and some students still show resistance to writing it (*"Why can't we just write our novels? Isn't it enough?"*). The creative piece is, and indeed should be, the main focus, but we have been exploring how flexible the critical element can be, with positive results: from creative process journals to personal essays, our students have been writing critical pieces that are informative, creative, innovative, and provide a balance between theory and authorial voice. This seems to me, therefore, to be something worth exploring further. That is not to say writers writing about writing have a privileged point of view or that this kind of theoretical exploration is better than any other kind, but rather that the blend of subjectivity and objectivity that comes from this particular environment is something unique.

Possibly the most important step is to value local culture and literature; in particular, myths, legends, traditions, and folklore. Translated literature should improve our knowledge and provide us with new sources of inspiration, instead of limiting us. Literary fiction writers have understood this interconnected relationship between influence and inspiration for a while, but young genre writers need to be encouraged to explore these possibilities further. It is also important to encourage younger students, especially those fresh out of high school, to read national authors. Again, that seems to be even more important for those students who are writing genre literature. Brazilian science fiction and fantasy is not as well-known among our young writers.

A more institutional approach would be to encourage internationalization at home (I@H), something that the university as a whole needs to explore further. Expanding international knowledge and sensibilities means more than traveling abroad, and more than just offering classes in English (EMI—English as a Medium of Instruction)—though such efforts are valuable, it is also important to consider how we can expand our cultural, artistic, and academic international knowledge without the need to travel or to invite foreign scholars to our classrooms. Learning about what other universities do, in particular in terms of different curricula and practices, encourages us to compare our culture and practices with others, and this is a good thing: not in order to evaluate which practice is better, but rather to find points of dialog that will help us to reinforce and value our own experiences.

Finally, I would like to highlight the importance of fostering social outreach activities. There has been a recent shift in university evaluations by the Brazilian

Education Ministry that proposes placing a greater importance on social outreach programs. That includes volunteer work, innovative research that is shared with local communities, free clinics, and projects like the one conducted by the Graduate Program in Letters, where students read to children in the University Hospital and manage their library. Our creative writing program is constantly looking to generate positive social impact: if we offered writing workshops in poor communities, for instance, we would be spreading the love for books and writing, which would in turn contribute to a better educational future for those communities, for instance, and potentially a better literary market in the long term.

Conclusion

Brazil, like other developing countries, faces many problems in politics, education, and the economy, not to mention crime rates; that shouldn't mean, however, that all solutions need to come from abroad. As noted by Roberto Schwarz, in his essay "Ideias fora do lugar" ["Misplaced Ideas"], simply transplanting practices, cultures, and art from one place to another is problematic in many ways. In Brazil, as with other colonized countries, the "difference, comparison and distance" is part of what defines this vast field of international dialog (Schwarz 1992). In Brazilian creative writing programs, it was extremely important to look to foreign experiences as a starting point, particularly as a way to convince universities and existing Literature programs that there was a future for creative writing in our country. After the first (successful) years, however, it is now time to look to ourselves and to value our culture, practices, myths, and folklore as sources of inspiration, our literary tradition as a source of pride. The reflections in this essay are just the beginning—there is much to discuss. The healthy dialog between the national and the international holds the key to growing and developing programs which maintain a unique local identity and in this way offer the best possible outcomes for our programs, students, and literary market.

I do not know if there is a way to remain "uniquely Brazilian." So much of our culture is inspired, informed, and influenced by foreign experiences that it becomes hard to delimitate exactly where "they" end and "we" begin. At this time, however, when we look at what we have built, we feel proud: hundreds of creative writing students attending workshops, elective classes, short courses, and undergraduate and graduate programs. Just fifteen years ago, the scene was very different. Brazilian writing culture has changed, but this particular history is young, and only time will tell how "unique" we are becoming.

References

Adichie, C. N. (2009), "The danger of a single story," TED Talk. Available online: https://www.ted.com/talks/chimamanda_adichie_the_danger_of_a_single_story

De Sourza Gabriel, R. (2019), "Mercado Editorial Brasileiro encolheu 25% entre 2006 e 2018," *Jornal O Globo*. May 28. Available online: https://oglobo.globo.com/cultura/mercado-editorial-brasileiro-encolheu-25-entre-2006-2018-23699428

Failla, Z (org.). (2016), *Reading Portraits in Brazil*, 4th edition. São Paulo: Sextante. Available online: http://cbl.org.br/upload/reading-portraits-in-brazil.pdf

Graduate Program in Letters (2019), Pontifical Catholic University of Rio Grande do Sul (PUCRS). Available online: http://www.pucrs.br/humanities/graduate-program-in-letters/

McGurl, Mark (2009). "The Program Era: Postwar Fiction and the Rise of Creative Writing," Cambridge: Harvard University Press.

Schwarz, R. (1992). "Ideias fora do lugar," in "Ao Vencedor As Batatas," São Paulo: Duas Cidades.

15

Teaching Creative Writing in a Threatened Language

Rúnar Helgi Vignisson
University of Iceland

Some experts predict that the Icelandic language will vanish from the face of the earth in the twenty-first century (Rögnvaldsson 2018, Henley 2018). That would be the end of a language which has been spoken on a windswept island in the middle of the Atlantic Ocean since the settlers brought it along from Scandinavia, in some cases via the British Isles, eleven hundred years ago. For the first few centuries, Icelanders shared this language, often called Old Norse, with the people of Norway, Sweden, and Denmark, which meant for instance that Icelandic poets could impress the kings of Scandinavia with their skaldic poetry, some of which still exists. At the end of the fourteenth century, linguistic paths diverged, causing somewhat of an existential watershed. The Norwegians no longer understood Icelanders, which left the islanders, who were few and far away, as the only speakers of this tongue in the world. Some have claimed, somewhat bitterly, that this watershed was more tragic than the loss of independence to Norway in 1262. Why? Because Icelanders had only themselves to talk to—which is still the case (Árnason 2018: 46). Even though the population has grown rapidly in the past century, we still don't reach half a million, which makes Iceland one of the smallest speech communities in the world.

Scholars believe that historical writing for Norwegian kings was a kind of industry in Iceland until around 1400 (Árnason 2018: 46). The Sagas of Icelanders, prose narratives about events in Iceland and Norway in the tenth, eleventh, and twelfth centuries, make up the bulk of the literary heritage produced during that period. A lot of it has survived famine and turf houses, and it can still be read by Icelanders in the original, even though some of the vocabulary now looks quaint. Sagas have been required reading in elementary schools and high schools in Iceland to date, which means that to an extent they are the basis for literary output in the country. By the same token, they are the database of the Icelandic language.

One of the manuscripts that has survived and is still required reading is *Snorri's Edda*, sometimes called the *Prose Edda*, compiled in the thirteenth century. It contains much of what is known about Nordic mythology, but big sections of it are devoted to instructions on writing poetry. For a long time, it served as a textbook on creative writing, probably one of the first of its kind in the world. While Icelanders don't write poetry of that nature anymore, *Snorri's Edda* stands as a landmark in our literary history, laying the foundations for a creative writing program that wasn't established until the twenty-first century.

Land, People, and Language

Icelanders have long defined their identity by their language. The Nordic Prize-winning poet Snorri Hjartarson captured this in the first line of a 1949 poem: "Country, nation, language, a trinity true and one" (Friðriksson 2008: 60). The poem was written at the peak of Icelandic nationalism, only five years after the country gained full independence from Denmark. At the time, it was an accepted truism that language was the defining feature of Icelandic identity and that the essence of Icelandic culture was bound up in the language. This belief was undisputed until the turn of the century, reverberating most memorably in the rhetoric of president Vigdís Finnbogadóttir (1980–1996). Since then much water has flowed under the bridge. Nearly 20 percent of the country's inhabitants are now non-native speakers of Icelandic, the number of immigrants and international residents having skyrocketed in the twenty-first century according to Statistics Iceland. As a result, the country has become multilingual and multicultural. While Poles make up the largest ethnic group, English is the most widely used interlanguage. The boom in tourism after the 2008 financial crisis and the advent of all kinds of digital platforms in English, easily accessible to young and old, further buttresses the Anglo-Saxon language. In kindergartens, toddlers of Icelandic-speaking parents have recently been observed playing in English. Teenagers and many adults tend to throw in a lot of English words, even on national radio and television, which used to be strongholds of pure Icelandic. An abundance of loan words is considered to be a sign of a language in trouble since it means that the language is not being fully acquired by the youngest generation (Rögnvaldsson 2018). The oldest generations, which are generally not fluent in English, complain that they can't communicate in Icelandic at restaurants and stores in downtown Reykjavík anymore. No wonder that recent research questions the link between land, people, and language (Jóhannsdóttir 2010). People are now more ambivalent when it comes to requiring immigrants to learn Icelandic, some demanding that the government provide free access to language courses, while others consider language requirements heavy-handed, encroaching on people's right to use the language of their choice. There are even those who find insisting on one national language mortally nationalistic.

While I as the present director of the Creative Writing Program at the University of Iceland do not endorse the nationalistic allegation, I am aware that it is no longer self-evident to run the nation's only creative writing program in Icelandic. It entails excluding non-speakers of Icelandic which may be considered an undemocratic gesture in light of the current composition of the nation. The English Department at the University of Iceland offers the odd workshop, but to be admitted to a full-fledged creative writing program, a non-speaker of Icelandic would have to go abroad. One may argue that in an ideal world every citizen has a right to seek further education in his or her native language or at least in a lingua franca, which would force Icelandic society to adjust to the multicultural makeup of the nation. In the age of identity politics, such a demand may seem natural and fair, notwithstanding the fact that Iceland is still defined by law as a monolingual society. What is more, the laws entrust the government with ensuring that Icelanders can use their language in all fields of Icelandic life. Everyone should also be enabled to learn Icelandic (Government of Iceland legislation 2011). In recent years, the number of students studying Icelandic as a second language at the University of Iceland has actually gone up considerably while the number of Icelandic students enrolled to study Icelandic language and literature at the Icelandic Department has gone down.

That said, nurturing the Icelandic language can hardly be deemed an unworthy or suspect endeavor in its context. Every group needs a language to communicate in, to enjoy and contribute to the culture its members share, and therefore must nurture it in order for it to meet the demands of the day. There is nothing inherently wrong in that undertaking; on the contrary, it's a necessity, for otherwise any language is bound to stagnate and deteriorate. The cultivation of one language does not necessarily come at the expense of another and Icelandic students certainly learn other languages as well. Nurturing one's mother tongue is also an existential issue, for its deterioration—or even the threat of imminent extinction—robs its speakers of an instrument which is crucial to their wellbeing in a particular environment, distancing them from a lot of what is theirs and making them feel bereaved in the process, even more mortal. The question that many speakers and writers of Icelandic face now is "whether to suffer the slings of outrageous fortune, or to take arms against a sea of troubles, and by opposing end them," as Hamlet put it so famously (Shakespeare, Hamlet, Act 3, Scene 1), Hamlet, or *amlóði* [amleth], being a figure in a Nordic legend which Shakespeare made use of (Gollancz 1898: xxviii–xxix).

Running a Creative Writing Program in Icelandic

The first creative writing workshop in Iceland was offered by the Department of Icelandic at the University of Iceland in 1987. In 2002, a minor was introduced, but a full-fledged program wasn't established until 2008. A master's program was founded in 2011. In 1987, and actually also in 2011, it seemed a given that all writing in the workshop would be in Icelandic, the official language of the country. The decision wasn't challenged back then and still hasn't been seriously challenged although occasionally a student will, in vain, seek permission to hand in assignments in English. Hence, it's the only creative writing program in the world that is dedicated to writing in Icelandic. In other respects, the program is more international, being modeled on the American approach, most notably the one associated with the Iowa Writers' Workshop, which has been adapted to the Icelandic scene without colonial or imperialistic accusations being raised. Unlike Iowa, where students enroll in a fiction, poetry, or non-fiction program, we offer a program that is not divided by genres. Our students have to attend workshops in more than one literary genre, which means that they can only specialize to a limited degree. This has turned out to be a good thing, the cross-pollination enabling participants to enrich their texts in the chosen genre. The structure of the program has also helped us avoid one of the pitfalls of writing programs: churning out writers who are all cast in more or less the same mold.

The environment in which the Icelandic Creative Writing Program operates, as outlined above, tends to highlight its role in nurturing and maintaining the Icelandic language. The program is fully financed by the Icelandic government, which again is bound by the aforementioned edicts. We are also under the auspices of the Department of Icelandic and Cultural Studies, which would make it sacrilegious to teach in any other language. A decision to start teaching in English would signal a radical change of direction, one which would be likely to cause an uproar in the country, although academic courses are frequently conducted in English at Icelandic universities to accommodate exchange students. Such a departure would mean that an Icelandic mindset would be exchanged for an English one. We have already seen that happen in the music industry, where many Icelandic musicians now write their lyrics in English, which raises questions about authenticity: these lyrics often don't sound Icelandic at all. They are after all writing in a second language, as would be the case with writers. The hugely important example of Halldór Laxness, Iceland's only Nobel Prize laureate in literature to date, should be kept in mind. During a period when some of his colleagues had considerable success writing in Norwegian or Danish, he chose to stick to Icelandic, and since then most Icelandic authors have followed suit. Had Laxness received the Nobel Prize for writing in Danish, we might not have seen the thriving literary scene in the Icelandic language that we have enjoyed since the middle of the twentieth century.

The fate of the Icelandic language in North America also serves as a warning. Around 20 percent of the Icelandic nation is estimated to have emigrated to the plains of the US and Canada in the early twentieth century (Bragason 2018: 21), and most of them were nationally minded, determined to keep speaking their native tongue. They published books and newspapers in Icelandic and founded schools where their children were taught in Icelandic. A century later, there are very few speakers of Icelandic left in North America and no one uses it for daily communication. All that is left in daily usage among the descendants are a few Americanized words (Svavarsdóttir 2018: 257). The environment in which the immigrants found themselves demanded that they adopt the English tongue. Today, Icelanders are also surrounded by speakers of English, both in the real world and in cyberspace.

So, what does it mean to teach almost solely in Icelandic?[1] It means, among other things, that our students draw primarily on the Icelandic literary and cultural heritage that is inherent in the language. Language is an archive that collects the wisdom, the traditions, the sayings of its speakers. Icelandic reaches all the way back to Norway in the ninth century, so there is a great deal of immediately accessible history at hand, in fact the entire history of settlement on this rugged and somewhat inhospitable island. Many expressions in daily use are derived from the Icelandic Sagas. There is even a neighborhood in Reykjavík in which all the street names are drawn from characters in the Sagas. These characters are still among us, as are the vivid characters of Laxness's novels.

Teaching in Icelandic also means bending your tongue around long, ancient words and phrases, which can create an odd tension between past and present,

---

[1] It should be noted here that although the official language of the program is Icelandic, we do occasionally bring in English-speaking instructors to teach an intensive course over a period of a few days.

especially when modern speakers don't know the origin of idioms. It means conjugating verbs and declining nouns in every sentence, often in quite intricate ways, for every noun can have sixteen different forms. It means that you need a special keyboard in order to be able to use the letters that are unique to Icelandic, such as *á, æ, þ,* and *ð.* Technically, it means that you go the extra mile, so to speak, and that's exactly where Icelandic has fallen short. Digital support is insufficient, which is considered by the Multilingual Europe Technology Alliance to be a dangerous sign because it means that the language can't be used in all fields of daily life (Rögnvaldsson et.al. 2012).

What is more, teaching in Icelandic means that practically no one in the world understands your writing. You might as well have written in a secret code. If you want to reach a wider audience, you need to translate your work or, as is most often the case, find someone to do it, which is not always easy. In Iceland you are not likely to sell more than 15,000 copies of a book at most; in fact, you are more likely to sell fewer than 500 copies, and you may not even exceed one hundred, although we publish more books per capita than most nations. If you are going to make a living as an Icelandic writer, you had better garner some of the subsidies handed out by the government to support writing in Icelandic, which means that you have to fit the criteria the selection committees set for such subsidies, in terms of what counts as a writer in this country.

But most importantly, for a native speaker of the language, teaching in Icelandic means that you can be authentic in your writing and don't need to worry about inappropriate appropriation when dealing with things Icelandic. You have direct access to your inner person, as direct as one can have language-wise. In my opinion, based on trying to master four second languages, you can never fully represent yourself and your culture by means of a second language, one that you have to learn from scratch after you have passed the natural age of language acquisition. A first language is in your blood and bones, but when using a second language you will always be a bit removed from the reality you are trying to deal with. Here I side with the Kenyan author Ngũgĩ wa Thiong'o, who claims that "the choice of language and the use to which language is put is central to a people's definition of themselves in relation to their natural and social environment" (Thiong'o 2007: 146). I take issue with the Nigerian author Chinua Achebe, who resorted to English in order to reach a wider audience, maintaining that one of the best things the colonizers had left behind was a language that united people and nations. Of course, you can adjust a language to a new environment over time, as the first settlers of Iceland must have done, but then the long history of a native tongue is lost if it's a case of overriding a pre-existing language. A whole world is even lost. Ironically, our students are still required to read quite a bit in English, since everything they need isn't available in Icelandic translation, which means that they have to read a second language, one which most of them don't have a perfect understanding of and therefore read with an accent, so to speak. In the process, they need to appropriate what they have read in the foreign language, make it their own, as the Icelandic verb for translating signifies.[2] There, the translation process is actually beneficial and helps them avoid copying another culture without self-reflection and cognitive content.

Finding a Voice in a Second Language

All applications to the Creative Writing Program at the University of Iceland are reviewed by the admissions committee without sex, age, or nationality being disclosed. As a result, no consideration is given to the sex ratio in the program, or other ratios for that matter, although the latter category is rarely tested due to the Caucasian nature of the Icelandic population. One year we ended up with only one male student, creating an imbalance that some of the students had problems with. However, in most cases, there has been a direct correlation between the number of accepted males/females and the number of male/female applicants. Affirmative action has been considered but not adopted since it would lead to males being admitted on the basis of inferior applications. The value of equal sex ratio has in other words been deemed of less importance to the quality of the program than admitting the applicants who submitted the best portfolios. Usually, we end up with a 2:3 sex ratio in favor of the females in the program as a whole which reflects the overall ratio at the university. I for one would prefer the ratio to be more even. That way our classroom would represent the outside world to a greater extent and views of both sexes would be more likely to be put forward which could only broaden the horizon of the participants. Polyphony is desirable.

As for the admissions committee, we make sure that gender equality exists within it. It is made up of the director of the program and two members nominated by the Writers Union of Iceland. One year they are asked to nominate two women, the next a man and a woman in order to maintain equality over a two-year period. They are also asked to nominate writers who are likely to be

---

[2] The Icelandic verb for translating, *þýða*, is closely related to the word *þjóð* which means nation. With a tongue in cheek we could say that *þýða* entails nationalizing words.

knowledgeable about most literary genres between them. The members are all Icelandic since the portfolios are in Icelandic although applicants are allowed to include a few pages written in English, for there is more to creative writing than just the language. Although gender equality among the committee members is secured, they may still be affected by traditions and other social pressures. Most of these writers are recipients of annual subsidies from the Ministry of Culture and Education, which means they have been validated by the institution. And then there is their Icelandicness to grapple with.

Being Icelandic is rather unique in the world as our numbers and location suggest. It entails a special relationship with the world. For one thing we are islanders, located in the Atlantic Ocean, between Europe and America. We have had to be self-reliant to a great extent through the ages since we are so removed from others. At times this manifests itself in nationalistic discourse as well as a wariness of the foreign, even racism, latent as such leanings may be. For decades, the US Navy had a base in Iceland, and during part of that period the Icelandic government introduced severe restrictions on their mingling with Icelanders, especially with Icelandic women. This kind of distrust of the foreign still appears in various protective measures: import restrictions on meat, subtitled movies, disinclination for selling resources such as land rights to foreigners, even overly generous praise for the domestic literary output. At the same time, Icelanders are prone to an inferiority complex which sometimes takes the form of megalomania, the yearning to be a player on the big stage, something that may have contributed to the spectacular crashing of Icelandic banks in 2008 (Vignisson 2013). As contradictory as it may seem, it also rears its ugly head as a cultural cringe, often manifesting itself in succumbing to foreign influence. Many stores and restaurants now boast English names because that's considered more business-savvy than the quaint and often long Icelandic names. All these issues will be ingrained in our admissions committees and cannot be easily uprooted. We want the members to be aware of them and be critical of them; otherwise they may affect the way they handle applications from non-native speakers of Icelandic, few as they may be.

So far, we have only had one applicant who isn't a native speaker of Icelandic. She is of Polish descent and was, after some deliberation, accepted on the grounds that her texts were promising and that her command of Icelandic seemed good enough to enable her to work with it in a creative way. We also hoped that she might become one of our first immigrant writers, who have been conspicuously absent from Icelandic literature throughout its history. Where is our Amy Tan, our Jhumpa Lahiri, our Eva Hoffman? some of us have asked in recent years, bemoaning the lack of such a valuable perspective. Our Polish applicant is a first-generation immigrant who studied Icelandic as a second language at the University of Iceland. Her Icelandic isn't faultless, but she is able to write a coherent literary text despite making some grammatical mistakes. When asked what kind of writer she would like to become in Icelandic, she replied that she wanted her texts to be in perfect Icelandic, which means that she has to rely on copy editors, who are likely to affect her expression. I have drawn her attention to the Polish-Australian author Ania Walwicz, who has made a name for herself by writing in non-native English. In that manner, Walwicz has managed to convey the view of the immigrant, the other, in Australian society. Would our student like to take on a similar role? No, she wants her texts to be in perfect Icelandic.

She may have sensed the emphasis on writing pure Icelandic which still prevails in published texts despite the copious borrowed words often found in spoken Icelandic nowadays. She may not want to be *the* immigrant in Icelandic literature, fearing that what she has to offer will be devalued, not taken seriously, what with the animosity immigrants sometimes suffer in this day and age all over the world. She may not want to appear an imperfect writer or individual, writing like a child. She may want to keep her dignity by presenting herself as a fully assimilated Icelander instead of being marginalized.

Still, she cannot escape her origin and the way it has shaped her. She was born in another country and her mother tongue belongs to a language group that is non-Germanic, unlike Icelandic. Amy Tan resents being categorized as a representative of all people of Chinese descent in America. She wants to be seen as just a writer. Yet she has made her name through writing about Chinese immigrants in America. Philip Roth, who was Jewish, first found his subject matter when a friend pointed out to him he should write about Jews in America. Should our student write about Poles in Iceland? What she decides on remains to be seen, but so far, she has expressed strong desire to write about Icelandic nature, reveling in all the words about natural phenomena found in the Icelandic vocabulary (Þorsteinsson 2018). There she heads for the core of Icelandic identity, the affinity with nature. While she enjoys using these words, her view of Icelandic nature is notably different from a native Icelander's. Her eye sometimes lingers on things that the Icelander may find too commonplace to notice, making her perspective an invaluable asset.

Our Polish student has to find a voice in Icelandic that will be accepted by the literary community if she is going to get published. She doesn't want to alienate Icelandic readers, who are not used to reading L2 Icelandic. In her eye-opening book *Toward an Inclusive Creative Writing*, Janelle Adsit points out the pitfalls of such a task when the readership is uncritical and hasn't "self-examined its sexist, racist, ableist, xenophobic, and heteronormative assumptions" (Adsit 2017: 22). Although Icelanders have encountered increased diversity in the population for the past two decades or so, there has not been much serious debate on the issue, nor have there been introduced holistic measures to tackle the changing composition of the nation. Do we want to be a melting pot or a mosaic? Prejudice against immigrants is rampant in certain sectors and frequently appears undisguised in popular media. What voices will our Polish student have access to, and will the voice she settles on be approved and endorsed by the general public? If Icelandic readers really are as prejudiced as they sometimes appear, honed by insular culture for centuries, she may not have many choices when it comes to finding an acceptable voice. She may indeed be escorted to predefined categories of conception of immigrants even though immigrant writing is more or less unknown in Iceland. If she is lucky she might, however, be granted a period of grace in light of the novelty of her voice.

I have no doubt that immigrant writers such as our student can enrich and even renew Icelandic literature. By Icelandic literature I refer to literature written in Icelandic. This definition has been uncontested so far, but now we may have to ask ourselves whether literature written by Icelandic citizens who wish to write about things Icelandic in another tongue can also qualify as Icelandic literature. We may end up with two categories of Icelandic literature, i.e., literature written in Icelandic and literature written in other languages in or about Iceland. Our program, being part of the Icelandic Department, has not been willing to acquiesce such a division but may have to consider it in the near future if the center cannot hold.

How to be

There are no plans to discontinue the Creative Writing Program at the University of Iceland. There is a consensus in the literary world that it has renewed Icelandic literature, turning out a number of award-winning authors (Sverrisson 2019) and enriching literary life in general through all kinds of activities. There are no plans to discontinue speaking Icelandic either. In fact, the Icelandic government has started work on the House of the Icelandic Language which is meant to accommodate the Department of Icelandic, including the Creative Writing Program. The official line is to keep up the good work, Icelandic shall prevail. Subsidies to support Icelandic publishers have been introduced, as well as special grants for writers of children's books, all in the belief that increased production is necessary to maintain the language. Everything is full speed ahead it seems. But doubts linger in the minds of many, for Icelanders at large seem to be going in the opposite direction. Of course, languages are organic, constantly adapting to a fluid environment, but do they have to mutate into something totally different in the process? There are indications that the more foreigners speak a language, the more simplified it becomes, and the more simplified, the more likely it is to survive (Johnson 2019). Icelandic is generally considered one of the more complex languages in Europe. Will it have to compromise in order to serve Icelandic residents in the future? Would that create a rift between past and present with disastrous effects for Icelandic culture? While we digest these questions, and sometimes shrink from facing them head on, the teachers at our creative writing program stick to the belief that Icelandic reality can be rendered most authentically in the medium that is the Icelandic language. Like rangers in a national park, we stay on the watch, knowing that there is a whole world at stake.

References

Adsit J. (2017), *Toward an Inclusive Creative Writing*, London and New York: Bloomsbury Academic.

Árnason, K. (2018), "Upptök íslensks ritmáls," in A. Kristinsson and H. Þorgeirsson (eds) *Á vora tungu*, Reykjavík: Háskólaútgáfan, 23–51.

Bragason, Ú. (2018), "Menning og saga: Yfirlit um fyrri rit og rannsóknir," in B. Arnbjörnsdóttir, H. Þráinsson, Ú. Bragason (eds) *Sigurtunga: Vesturíslenskt mál og menning*, Reykjavík, Háskólaútgáfan, 21–34.

Friðriksson, E. (2008), "Language change vs. stability in conservative language communities: A case study of Icelandic," PhD diss., Faculty of Arts, University of Gothenburg, Gothenburg. Available online: https://gupea.ub.gu.se/bitstream/2077/18713/1/gupea_2077_18713_1.pdf (accessed November 12, 2019).

Gollancz, I. (1898), *Hamlet in Iceland*, London: D. Nutt. Available online: https://archive.org/details/hamletinicelandb00golluoft/page/n8 (accessed November 14, 2019).

Government of Iceland (2011), "Act respecting the status of the Icelandic language and Icelandic sign language No 61/2011." Available online: https://www.government.is/Publications/Legislation/Lex/?newsid=cd01f04d-cf9b-11e7-941f-005056bc4d74 (accessed November 14, 2019).

Henley, J., (2018), "Icelandic language battles threat of digital extinction," *The Guardian*, February 26. Available online: https://www.theguardian.com/world/2018/feb/26/icelandic-language-battles-threat-of-digital-extinction (accessed November 14, 2019).

Johnson (2019), "Why widely spoken languages have simpler grammar," *The Economist*, August 8. Available online: https://www.economist.com/books-and-arts/2019/08/08/why-widely-spoken-languages-have-simpler-grammar?fbclid=IwAR3lKA8SD2nIFc99YVLcPYEAHwbQ_9g4eDUfxMX8x6GuFERcbOYlKSHQMtU (accessed November 14, 2019).

Jóhannsdóttir, A. (2010), *"Land, þjóð og tunga – þrenning sönn og ein." Þjóðerni og sjálfsmynd á tímum hnattvæðingar.* MA Thesis, University of Iceland. Available online: https://skemman.is/handle/1946/6181 (accessed November 14, 2019).

Ministry of Education, Science and Culture (2011), "Act respecting the status of the Icelandic language and Icelandic sign language." Available online: https://www.government.is/media/menntamalaraduneyti-media/media/frettir2015/Thyding-log-um-stodu-islenskrar-tungu-og-islensks-taknmals-desember-2015.pdf (accessed November 12, 2019)

Rögnvaldsson, E. (2018), "Icelandic in social and digital upheaval: Is there reason to worry?" Lecture at Uppsala University, October 11, 2018. Available online: https://notendur.hi.is/eirikur/Uppsala.htm (accessed November 13, 2019).

Rögnvaldsson, E., Jóhannsdóttir, K., Helgadóttir, S. and Steingrímsson, S. (2012), "META-NET White Paper Series: Icelandic," Multilingual Europe Technology Alliance. Available online: http://www.meta-net.eu/whitepapers/volumes/icelandic (accessed November 14, 2019).

Shakespeare, W. (1987), *Hamlet*, New York, Signet Classic.

Statistics Iceland, "Innflytjendum heldur áfram að fjölga." Available online: https://www.hagstofa.is/utgafur/frettasafn/mannfjoldi/mannfjoldi-eftir-bakgrunni-2018/ (accessed November 14, 2019).

Svavarsdóttir, Á. (2018), "Að flytja mál milli landa: Breytilegar málaðstæður heima og heiman," in B. Arnbjörnsdóttir, H. Þráinsson, Ú. Bragason (eds) (2018) *Sigurtunga: Vesturíslenskt mál og menning*, Reykjavík, Háskólaútgáfan, 257–77.

Sverrisson, Á. (2019), "Byrjendur en ekki viðvaningar," *DV* August 12, 2019. Available online: https://www.dv.is/fokus/2019/8/12/ritdomur-um-thad-er-alltaf-eitthvad-byrjendur-en-ekki-vidvaningar/?fbclid=IwAR3HgGjlJhkBIIEEC1euw4piiNJ5uBruA3r0RPCXQJdHhwtg-TgzgwLsamc (accessed November 14, 2019).

Thiong'o, N. (2007), "The Language of African Literature," in T. Olanian and A. Quayson (eds) *African Literature – An Anthology of Criticism and Theory*, Malden: Blackwell Publishing.

Vignisson, R. (2013), "Losing Faith," *Overland*. Available online: https://overland.org.au/2013/03/losing-faith/ (accessed November 14, 2019).

Þorsteinsson, O. (2018), "Betra að tjá sig á íslensku," *Fréttablaðið* 16, November 16. Available online: https://www.pressreader.com/iceland/frettabladid/20181116/282548724304992 (accessed November 14, 2019).

Contributors

Bernardo Bueno is a professor at the Pontifical Catholic University of Rio Grande do Sul (PUCRS) in Brazil, where he also acts as Director of Undergraduate Creative Writing. His research and writing interests are Creative Writing, Digital Humanities, Fantasy, Science Fiction, and Geek Culture. He is the editor of *Scriptorium,* PUCRS University's Open-Access Journal of Creative Writing, and published the novel *Dias Lendários (Legendary Days,* 2019) and the short story collection *Minimundo* (2006).

Fan Dai is a professor in the Department of English at Sun Yat-sen University, China. Her research interests include creative writing in English as a foreign language, translation/self-translation, and discourse analysis. She publishes in both areas as well as creative works in both Chinese and English.

Dan Disney is a professor with Sogang University's Department of English. His research interests focus on contemporary poetry, translation studies, and creative production in native and non-native languages. He has published extensively on the ethics of creativity, and his most recent books include the poetry collection *either, Orpheus* (2016) and, together with Matt Hall, *New Directions in Australian Poetry* (2021).

Nora Ekström is a teacher at Open University of the University of Jyväskylä. Her research interests focus on feedback and pedagogy of creative writing. She is also interested in developing pedagogy of creative writing for children, as part of Finnish basic education in the arts. Her most recent chapter connects academic research with improving children's education in creative writing (2018).

Ross Gibson is Centenary Professor in Creative and Cultural Research at the University of Canberra.

Graeme Harper is the Dean of the Honors College and Professor at Oakland University. He is an internationally published fiction writer, scriptwriter, professor, and cultural critic, who has published more than twenty books and over 140 articles and chapters. His awards include the Australian National Book Council Award (for New Fiction) and the Premier's Award, among others, and scholarships and fellowships from the ORS, The British Academy, AHRC, BBC, and many others. He is founding Editor-in-Chief of the journal *New Writing: the International Journal for the Practice and Theory of Creative Writing*.

Sophie Iakovidou is an assistant professor at Democritus University of Thrace. She studied Modern Greek literature in Aristotle University of Thessaloniki. She has conducted postgraduate studies in Paris (MA Université Paris IV- La Sorbonne and PhD In INALCO) and in Birmingham as an associated researcher. Her main interests focus on literary theory and comparative literature, and her monograph, *G. Ioannou, le corps de l'ouevre. Psyché de l'écrivain, sociopoétique de l'oeuvre*, is in print.

Lania Knight is a senior lecturer in Creative Writing, and Course Leader for English Literature and Creative Writing at University of Gloucestershire in Cheltenham, UK. She has a PhD in English and Creative Writing from University of Missouri. Her first novel *Three Cubic Feet* (2012) was a finalist for the Lambda Literary Award in Debut Fiction. She has a second novel *Remnant* (2018) and several short stories and essays published online and in print.

Triantafyllos H. Kotopoulos is an associate professor in Creative Writing and Modern Greek Literature, the Scientific Director and Supervisor of the Joint Interdisciplinary Postgraduate Program in Creative Writing at the University of Western Macedonia in collaboration with the Aristotle University of Thessaloniki, as well as of the Joint Interdisciplinary Postgraduate Program of the Hellenic Open University. He has published texts about Mimis Souliotis (2019), Thanos Mikroutsikos (2017), Setting-Character-Plot (2011), Studies on Children's, Young Adults' and Adults' Literature (2012), Creative Writing in the Kindergarten (2013), Adjustments to the Curriculum of Greek Language in High School (2008) and four poetry collections.

Iordanis Koumasidis teaches at National Kapodistrian University of Athens and Hellenic Open University. His research interests focus on creative writing, literary theory, and philosophy. He has published four books. His most recent book is about epistemology of literary theory (forthcoming, 2021).

Bronwyn Law-Viljoen is Associate Professor and Head of the Department of Creative Writing at the University of the Witwatersrand. She is interested in the intersection of visual art and literature. Her novel, *The Printmaker*, was shortlisted for the *Sunday Times* Fiction Award, won the 2018 Oliver Schreiner Prize, and appeared in French in 2019. She is at work on her second novel, which is set in New York, Johannesburg, and the Eastern Cape.

Ling Li is currently a PhD candidate at Sun Yat-sen University in the School of Foreign Languages. Her research interests focus on the practice and pedagogy of creative writing in English as a second/foreign language in the Chinese context, bilingual creativity, and World Englishes. She is the co-author of the paper "The Academic Aspects of Creative Writing in English in the Teaching and Research in EFL" (2019).

Sam Meekings is Assistant Professor of creative writing at Northwestern University in Qatar. He is the author of *Under Fishbone Clouds* (called "a poetic evocation of the country and its people" by the *New York Times*), *The Book of Crows*, and *The Afterlives of Dr Gachet*. He has a PhD in creative writing from Lancaster University and has taught writing at NYU (Global Campus) and the University of Chichester in the UK. He researches issues of identity in grief narratives, and the practices and processes of digital storytelling.

Marshall Moore is a course leader in English, Creative Writing and Publishing at Falmouth University in the UK. He is the author of several novels and collections of short fiction, the most recent being *Inhospitable* (2018). With Xu Xi, he is the co-editor of the anthology *The Queen of Statue Square: New Short Fiction from Hong Kong*. He holds a PhD in creative writing from Aberystwyth University, and his current research focuses on the disconnects between the publishing industry and the academy, and on the mythology and lore that surround creative practice and pedagogy.

James Shea is Associate Professor in the Department of Humanities and Creative Writing at Hong Kong Baptist University. He is the author of two poetry collections, *The Lost Novel* (2014) and *Star in the Eye* (2008). He has taught at Nebraska Wesleyan University, University of Chicago, Columbia College Chicago's MFA Program in Poetry, DePaul University, and as a poet-in-residence in the Chicago public schools.

Hanna Sieja-Skrzypulec is a creative writing instructor at the Literary and Artistic Studies of the Jagiellonian University. She is a literary scholar and a scriptwriter, who also coordinates cultural and publishing projects. She wrote the first scientific dissertation on the history of creative writing in Poland and has published numerous articles in the field of writing.

Jonathan Taylor is Senior Lecturer in Creative Writing at the University of Leicester. He writes both creatively and critically. His books include the memoir *Take Me Home* (2007), the novel *Melissa* (2015), the poetry collection *Cassandra Complex* (2018) and the monograph *Laughter, Literature, Violence, 1840-1930* (2019).

Maria Taylor is Lecturer in Creative Writing at De Montfort University, Leicester, UK. She is interested in writing that focuses on the experience of dual cultural heritage. Her debut collection *Melanchrini* was shortlisted for the Michael Murphy Memorial Prize. A new collection, *After Lives* is scheduled for 2020.

Holly Thompson is an instructor at Yokohama City University in the International College of Liberal Arts. She is the author of the novel *Ash* (2001); NCTAsia Freeman Award Honor verse novel *Falling into the Dragon's Mouth* (2016); and two young adult novels in verse: *The Language Inside* (2013), and *Orchards* (2011), awarded the APALA Asian/Pacific American Award for Literature. Thompson serves as Regional Advisor of the Japan chapter of the Society of Children's Book Writers and Illustrators, visits schools worldwide, and teaches creative writing at Yokohama City University, at Grub Street Boston, and UC Berkeley (online).

Stephanie Vanderslice is Professor of Creative Writing and Director of the Arkansas Writer's MFA Workshop at the University of Central Arkansas. Her column, "The Geek's Guide to the Writing Life" appears regularly in the *Huffington Post*. Her essays and stories have been featured in the Fiction Writer's Review, American Literary Review, and many others. She has also written several books on teaching creative writing, including the recently published *The Geek's Guide to the Writing Life*: a twenty-first-century guide for aspiring writers that simultaneously shatters the most common myths of the writer's world.

Rúnar Helgi Vignisson is Associate Professor at the University of Iceland's Department of Icelandic and Cultural Studies. He oversees creative studies at the school. He is also an acclaimed writer and translator.

Phillippa Yaa de Villiers is an award-winning South African writer and performance artist who performs her work nationally and internationally. She is noted for her poetry, which has been published in collections and in many magazines and anthologies, as well as for her autobiographical one-woman show, *Original Skin*. Among her many awards are the National Arts Festival/de Buren Writing Beyond the Fringe Prize 2009, and in 2011 a South African Literary Award. She is the recipient of the 2012 Overseas Scholarship for studies in Creative Writing at Lancaster University.

Index

Ingram Content Group UK Ltd.
Milton Keynes UK
UKHW051457150623
423417UK00015B/149